Leopold

Wetland Management District

Comprehensive Conservation Plan

Table of Contents

List of Figures and Tables

Chapter 1: Introduction and Background

Introduction

The Leopold Wetland Management District (WMD), established in 1993, manages over 12,000 acres of Waterfowl Production Areas (WPAs) in 17 southeastern Wisconsin counties, covering some of the most important waterfowl areas of Wisconsin (see Figure 1). The District also administers 45 conservation easements, totaling 3,000 acres in 21 eastern Wisconsin counties. WPAs consist of wetland habitat surrounded by grassland and woodland communities. While WPAs are managed primarily for ducks and geese, they also provide habitat for a variety of other wildlife species such as non-game grassland birds, shorebirds, wading birds, mink, muskrat, wild turkey, and deer.

The Leopold Wetland Management District is named after Aldo Leopold, who is widely acknowledged as the father of wildlife conservation in America. In tribute to his philosophy, the Leopold Wetland Management District is dedicated to preserving, restoring, and enhancing wildlife habitat in Wisconsin for the benefit of present and future generations.

The U.S. Fish and Wildlife Service

The Leopold WMD is administered by the U.S. Fish and Wildlife Service (Service). The Service is the primary federal agency responsible for conserving, protecting, and enhancing the nation's fish and wildlife populations and their habitats. It oversees the enforcement of federal wildlife laws, management and protection of migratory bird populations, restoration of nationally significant fisheries, administration of the Endangered Species Act, and the restoration of wildlife habitat such as wetlands. The Service also manages the National Wildlife Refuge System.

Baraboo Wetland Management at Leopold Wetland Management District. USFWS photo.

The National Wildlife Refuge System

District lands are part of the National Wildlife Refuge System, which was founded in 1903 when President Theodore Roosevelt designated Pelican Island in Florida as a sanctuary for Brown Pelicans. Today, the System is a network of about 545 refuges and wetland management districts covering about 95 million acres of public lands and waters. Most of these lands (82 percent) are in Alaska, with approximately 16 million acres located in the lower 48 states and several island territories.

The National Wildlife Refuge System is the world's largest collection of lands specifically managed for fish and wildlife. Overall, it provides habitat for more than 5,000 species of birds, mammals, fish, amphibians, reptiles, and insects. As a result of international treaties for migratory bird conservation and other legislation, such as the Migratory

Figure 1: Location of Leopold Wetland Management District

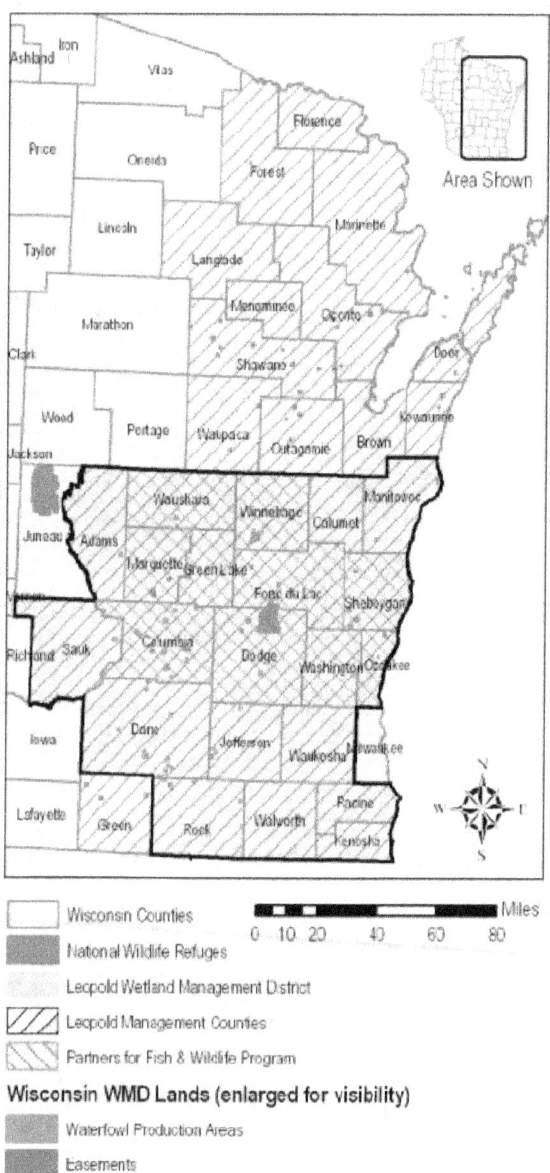

Bird Conservation Act of 1929, many refuges have been established to protect migratory waterfowl and their migratory flyways. The Horicon Refuge, for example, serves a dual purpose both as a critical nesting ground and as an important link in the Mississippi Flyway network of refuges that serve as rest stops and feeding stations for migrating ducks and geese.

Refuges also play a crucial role in preserving endangered and threatened species. Among the most notable is Aransas National Wildlife Refuge in Texas, which provides winter habitat for the highly endangered whooping crane. Likewise, the Florida Panther Refuge protects one of the nation's most endangered predators. Refuges also provide unique recreational and educational opportunities for people. When human activities are compatible with wildlife and habitat conservation, they are places where people can enjoy wildlife-dependent recreation such as hunting, fishing, wildlife observation, photography, environmental education, and environmental interpretation. Many refuges have visitor centers, wildlife trails, automobile tours, and environmental education programs. Nationwide, approximately 30 million people visited national wildlife refuges in 2004.

The National Wildlife Refuge System Improvement Act of 1997 established several important mandates aimed at making the management of national wildlife refuges more cohesive. The preparation of Comprehensive Conservation Plans (CCPs) is one of those mandates. The legislation directs the Secretary of the Interior to ensure that the mission of the National Wildlife Refuge System and purposes of the individual refuges are carried out. It also requires the Secretary to maintain the biological integrity, diversity, and environmental health of the National Wildlife Refuge System.

Revised goals for the National Wildlife Refuge System were adopted on July 26, 2006, and incorporated into Part 601, Chapter 1, of the Fish and Wildlife Service Manual (601 FW 1). The goals are:

- Conserve a diversity of fish, wildlife, and plants and their habitats, including species that are endangered or threatened with becoming endangered.
- Develop and maintain a network of habitats for migratory birds, anadromous and interjurisdictional fish, and marine mammal populations that is strategically distributed and

Blue dasher. USFWS photo.

carefully managed to meet important life history needs of these species across their ranges.

- Conserve those ecosystems, plant communities, wetlands of national or international significance, and landscapes and seascapes that are unique, rare, declining, or underrepresented in existing protection efforts.
- Provide and enhance opportunities to participate in compatible wildlife-dependent recreation (hunting, fishing, wildlife observation and photography, and environmental education and interpretation).
- Foster understanding and instill appreciation of the diversity and interconnectedness of fish, wildlife, and plants and their habitats.

District Purposes

The purposes for the District are based upon its land acquisition authorities. Lands are acquired under the authority of the Migratory Bird Hunting and Conservation Stamp Act, and since 1958, under Public Law 85-585 as "Waterfowl Production Areas." The purpose of lands acquired under the Migratory Bird Hunting Conservation Stamp Act is "...as Waterfowl Production Areas" subject to "...all the provisions of such act (the Migratory Bird Conservation Act of 1929,16 U.S.C. 715d) ...except the inviolate sanctuary provisions...," and "...for any other management purpose, for migratory birds."

District Vision

The planning team considered past vision statements and emerging issues and drafted the following vision statement as the desired future state of the District:

> Waterfowl and other migratory birds find District lands isles of refuge in a landscape of increasing residential development. Native plants and animals, amazing in their diversity, flourish on District and private lands from the efforts of many active partners. Neighbors and visitors enjoy and value District land and work to conserve the region's natural heritage.

Purpose and Need for Plan

This CCP articulates the management direction for the Leopold Wetland Management District for the next 15 years. Through goals, objectives, and strategies, this CCP describes how the District intends to fulfill its purpose and contribute to the overall mission of the National Wildlife Refuge System. Several legislative mandates within the National Wildlife Refuge System Improvement Act of 1997 have guided the development of this plan. These mandates include:

- Wildlife has first priority in the management of refuges.
- Wildlife-dependent recreation activities, namely hunting, fishing, wildlife observation, wildlife photography, environmental education and interpretation are priority public uses of refuges. We will facilitate these activities when they do not interfere with our ability to fulfill the refuges' purpose or the mission of the Refuge System.
- Other uses of the Refuge will only be allowed when determined appropriate and compatible with Refuge purposes and mission of the Refuge System.

The plan will guide the management of Leopold WMD by:

- Providing a clear statement of direction for the future management.

- Making a strong connection between District activities and conservation activities that occur in the surrounding area.
- Providing neighbors, visitors, and the general public with an understanding of the Service's land acquisition and management actions in the District.
- Ensuring District actions and programs are consistent with the mandates of the National Wildlife Refuge System.
- Ensuring that District management considers federal, state, and county plans.
- Establishing long-term continuity in District management.
- Providing a basis for the development of budget requests on the Districtís operational, maintenance, and capital improvement needs.

History and Establishment

The WMD has its roots in a 1974 interagency agreement based on U.S. Fish and Wildlife Service Director Lynn Greenwalt's authorization for federal purchase of land and waters in Wisconsin. These lands would be managed by mutual agreement between the Service and the Wisconsin Department of Natural Resources (Wisconsin DNR) under a signed Memorandum of Understanding (MOU).

Management of the WPAs was accomplished according to the MOU signed in 1974 and several addenda after that. In general, Wisconsin Department of Natural Resources personnel were responsible for on-the-ground management activities, and Service personnel were responsible for administration. Federal management authority was under the guidelines of the National Wildlife Refuge System Administration Act with the day-to-day activities spelled out in the Wisconsin Wetland Management Guidelines.

As WPA acreage increased, so did the time and commitment of management personnel. A Wisconsin DNR "Workload Analysis" in the late 1980's documented a staff shortage for management activities on the WPAs. The Wisconsin DNR Director of the Bureau of Wildlife Management and the Service's Regional Director began meeting in early 1990 to discuss transferring management of the WPAs to the Service. The date selected for the transfer was September 30, 1995.

The transition date was later moved forward when the Service received funding for District Managers and summer temporaries to work with the Wisconsin DNR in the summer and fall of 1992. The final transition and establishment of the St. Croix and the Leopold WMDs took place July 1, 1993.

The advent of the Service's Partners for Fish and Wildlife Program and conservation easement responsibilities in the late 1980s further defined the WMD's role. Private land habitat restoration projects, and protection and management of wetlands, flood plains, and other important habitats on conservation easements added greatly to the workload and habitat diversity of the District.

Legal Context

In addition to the acquisition authorities of the District, and the National Wildlife Refuge System Improvement Act of 1997, several federal laws, executive orders, and regulations govern its administration. Appendix E contains a partial list of the legal mandates that guided the preparation of this plan and those that pertain to District management.

Chapter 2: The Planning Process

Meetings and Involvement

The planning process for this CCP began in July 2006. The Wisconsin Wetland Management Districts, which include Leopold WMD and St. Croix WMD, shared a planning process that included similar timelines and key meetings held jointly. The planning was conducted jointly because the Districts face the same issues, and it makes sense to address the issues consistently and share knowledge and experience between Districts.

Initially, members of the regional planning staff and District staff identified a list of issues and concerns that were associated with the management of the Districts. These preliminary issues and concerns were based on staff knowledge of the area and contacts with citizens in the community.

District staff and Service planners then asked District neighbors, organizations, local government units, and interested citizens to share their thoughts at open houses and through written comments. In September 2006, three open houses were held in New Richmond, Portage, and Waukau, Wisconsin. The meetings were advertised through news briefs in local papers. Total attendance for the three open houses was 30. Three written comments were received by the St. Croix District during the 30-day comment period.

In January 2007 a biological review of the Districts' biological programs provided technical comments and recommendations. In addition to personnel from U.S. Fish and Wildlife Service national wildlife refuges and District personnel, the review team consisted of a panel of experts and partners from the U.S. Geological Survey, the North American Waterfowl Management Plan Science Support Team, and the Wisconsin Department of Natural Resources. The review team considered the programs of both Districts.

Leopold WMD staff identified management issues and concerns as part of the planning process. USFWS photo.

A visitor services review was independently conducted for each District. The visitor services review of Leopold WMD was held March 29-31, 2006, and helped clarify visitor services issues and identified potential actions to consider in formulating alternatives. The visitor services review team included regional and refuge visitor services specialists, a planner from the Service's Regional Office in Minneapolis, and District staff.

Publication of Draft CCP

A Draft Comprehensive Conservation Plan and Environmental Assessment was released to the public on July 25, 2008. The availability of the document was announced in the Federal Register and through an update mailing to all parties on the planning mailing list. A press release was sent to media outlets throughout the District, as well. The draft document as either a compact disc or hard copy was sent to 75 persons or organizations with special interests in the District. In addition, the draft document was distributed to approximately 50 persons or organizations that had requested all documents produced by the Region's Conservation Planning

Division. The document was also available as an Adobe pdf file on the Region's planning website. A public open house was held on August 13, 2008, at a community room in the town of Portage to receive any comments on the draft document. Two representatives of the Wisconsin Department of Natural Resources and a newspaper reporter attended. A 30-day comment period closed on August 25, 2008. Comments received and responses to them are included in an appendix to this document

Issues

Issues play an important role in planning. Issues focus the planning effort on the most important topics and provide a base for considering alternative approaches to management and evaluating the consequences of managing under these alternative approaches. The issues and concerns expressed during the first phase of planning have been organized under the following headings.

Habitat Management

Background: Managing habitat is at the heart of providing for wildlife. The presence of high quality habitat is a necessary, but not sufficient, condition for abundant wildlife use. For example, a WPA may contain very high quality habitat for puddle ducks, but they may not occur on the WPA at the usual time because of poor conditions on wintering grounds or extreme weather during migration. When the forces external to the WPA weaken, however, the habitat base is there to provide for the ducks. On the other hand, low quality habitat will cause wildlife to be absent or less abundant. If a WPA has inadequate habitat, ducks will be absent or occur at very low levels, regardless of the timing or duration of other factors such as weather or conditions on wintering grounds. Recognizing that external factors may limit wildlife use on a WPA, it is reasonable to focus on the things that we can control and provide habitat conditions that offer the greatest potential for the species of concern to us (Schroeder et al. 1998).

Main Concerns:

1. The WMD has identified management strategies that would improve habitat conditions, but the strategies can not be applied as needed. The needs exceed the existing capability of staff hours and budgets. The result is that habitat conditions offer less than their potential for species of concern.

Habitat management, Leopold WMD. USFWS photo.

2. Invasive species are a particular challenge within habitat management as they degrade native habitats and reduce biological diversity. Control techniques for invasive species place further demands on the staff and budget of a WMD, and effective control techniques have not been identified for all invasive species.

3. To be most effective, habitat management should be based on good data and sound science. Basic biological information is required to understand the habitat needs of species of concern. Biological data is also needed to evaluate the effectiveness of management strategies within an adaptive management framework. Faced with pressing day-to-day demands, WMD staff find it difficult to allocate the time and resources to develop and discover the desirable biological information. Activities to answer this concern would include literature searches, expert technical workshops, and on-the-ground studies.

4. Management actions sometimes draw negative reaction from neighbors to WPAs. For example, a neighbor may complain about the appearance of a blackened field and the smoke that was generated during a prescribed burn. Or, a citizen may complain about the cutting of

trees as part of a prairie restoration. There is concern that this negative reaction will lead to opposition to the management activity and an inability to apply the desired treatment. If we are not able to apply particular strategies at the appropriate time, habitat on the WPA will change and there will be less benefit to wildlife.

5. Habitat management, control of invasive species, biological monitoring, and community outreach require staff and funding for programs, facilities, and equipment. Plans and planning need to articulate these needs and ensure they are represented in databases and other documents used in budget decision-making.

Vesper Sparrow nest. USFWS photo.

Habitat Loss and Fragmentation

Background: The loss and degradation of habitat has been identified as an important factor in the decline of many species worldwide and at many scales. Development is considered the most lasting form of habitat loss, since the presence of pavement and buildings hinders the return to natural conditions. Development can result in habitat fragmentation where remaining patches of habitat not only support less wildlife, but also may isolate populations vulnerable to a lack of genetic diversity and in an increased "edge" effect, which may increase the effect of predators and nest parasitism (U.S. Fish and Wildlife Service 2002). Wisconsin, along with other Midwest states, is forecast to have continued housing growth in rural areas through 2030 (Radeloff et al. 2006). In its Wildlife Action Plan, the Wisconsin DNR identified habitat loss and fragmentation as a major issue faced by land managers (Wisconsin Department of Natural Resources 2005). The Wisconsin WMD counties are experiencing and are expected to continue to experience housing development and its accompanying effects over the next 25 years.

Main Concerns:

1. Development is occurring around some existing waterfowl production areas. The development may be reducing the value of the WPAs to wildlife – the effect is not known with certainty. If the value of the WPA for wildlife is reduced, we need to think of how, or if, we should continue to manage the land.

2. The effect of habitat loss and fragmentation is best dealt with at a broad landscape level in which several entities (federal, state, local, non-governmental organizations, private landowners) have responsibilities. There is an opportunity for improved coordination among responsible entities.

3. How the forecasted development in the WMDs should affect land acquisition decisions is not clear. The criteria for land acquisition used in landscapes dominated by agriculture or other conservation lands may not be appropriate in counties with forecasted high levels of development.

Land Acquisition

Background: Managers of a WMD, in addition to managing existing WPAs, are responsible for identifying tracts that would be worthwhile to acquire for inclusion in the WMD. The primary goal of the acquisition program is to acquire a complex of wetlands and uplands that provide habitat in which waterfowl can successfully reproduce. Identifying lands for purchase as waterfowl production habitat requires weighing a number of biological factors related to breeding waterfowl within an often rapidly changing social and economic context – all the while keeping an eye on cost and efficiency.

Main Concerns:

1. Expanding housing development and changing land use in the Wisconsin WMDs offers particular challenges to the land acquisition program. The challenges are both direct and

indirect. Directly, development causes the loss of opportunities through conversion of land to uses that would be difficult to reclaim or restore. And, areas near development are less desirable as waterfowl production habitat. Indirectly, the demand for development is causing a rapid rise in property values with the result that less habitat can be purchased with the funds available.

2. With the current and forecasted continued development, there is a concern that the possible loss of habitat will cause more acquisitions to emphasize the opportunity considerations ("buy while we can") in comparison to the biological considerations and value to waterfowl.

3. How to proceed with land acquisition for the WMDs has increased uncertainty given the above concerns and the lack of biological information on waterfowl production in areas of residential development. The criteria that guide acquisition in western Minnesota, the Dakotas, and Montana are likely not applicable to Wisconsin without modification.

Visitor Services

Background: The National Wildlife Refuge System Improvement Act of 1997 established six priority uses (hunting, fishing, wildlife observation, photography, environmental education, interpretation) for the Refuge System, which includes waterfowl production areas. The Service is to facilitate these uses when compatible with the purpose of the WPA and the mission of the Refuge System. WPAs differ from national wildlife refuges in that they are open to hunting, fishing, and trapping by specific regulation and open to the other wildlife-dependent activities by notification in general brochures available at the District office. New and existing WPAs are thus "open until closed" in contrast to national wildlife refuges, which are "closed until opened." Hunting has long been associated with WPAs. The other wildlife-dependent activities are increasingly being encouraged by developing interpretive signs, kiosks, and wildlife trails. Identification signs and small parking areas are usually placed at each WPA to facilitate its use by the public.

Main Concerns:

1. Some visitor facilities are sub-standard. Higher quality experiences and greater satisfaction among visitors may be possible with improved visitor facilities.

2. Unauthorized uses (horseback riding, ATVs, dogs off leash, for example) occur on WPAs. The uses lead to habitat degradation and disturbance to wildlife that ultimately reduce wildlife numbers and health. Better habitat conditions and less wildlife disturbance would result from a reduction in unauthorized uses.

3. The public sometimes requests use of WPAs for other than the six priority uses. In order for the public to understand our purpose and mission and its relation to public uses, the compatibility analyses should be consistent within Wisconsin and, ideally, within the Region.

Service Identity

Background: People often approach and interact with staff of the WMD as if they work for the Wisconsin Department of Natural Resources and administer state areas. Because the missions of the two agencies are different, the misperception can lead to misunderstanding. When WMD employees interact with people directly, the misperception can be cleared up through conversation. Over the last several years the Service has acted to develop an improved "corporate identity" through unified standards for publications, uniforms, signs, and vehicles. The experiences of Wisconsin WMD personnel suggest that much work still remains in developing the Service identity.

Main Concern:

1. If people do not understand the purpose and mission of the WPAs and the Service, they are not likely to understand our management. The lack of understanding may lead to a lack of support, and, ultimately, to indifference or opposition to our management. If the public had a clear perception of the Service, the public would be able to differentiate between the federal and state missions and understand the actions of the WMD staff. With that understanding the public would make more informed decisions about fish and wildlife issues in general and, particularly relevant to a WPA management, more informed reactions to on-the-ground management activities.

Wilderness Review

As part of the CCP process, lands within the District were reviewed for wilderness suitability. No lands were considered suitable for Congressional designation as wilderness as defined by the Wilderness Act of 1964. The District does not contain 5,000 contiguous acres of roadless, natural lands. Nor does the District possess any units of sufficient size to make their preservation practicable as wilderness. District lands and waters have been substantially altered by humans, especially by agriculture. Extensive modification of natural habitats and manipulation of natural processes has occurred. Adopting a "hands-off" approach to management of District lands would not facilitate the restoration of a pristine or pre-settlement condition, which is the goal of wilderness designation.

Chapter 3: The District Environment and Management

Introduction

Wetland Management District

The Leopold WMD covers 34 counties in eastern Wisconsin (Figures 11 to 27 beginning on page 48). This includes 21 counties approved for waterfowl production area acquisition, a 10-county Partners for Fish and Wildlife private lands district, and a 34-county Wetland Management District, involving management and enforcement of U.S. Department of Agriculture's Farm Service Agency Conservation Easements (CEs). Currently, there are 53 fee-titled WPAs and 45 CEs.

Monarch butterfly. USFWS photo.

Geographic/Ecosystem Setting

Historic Vegetation

The nature and distribution of vegetation types in Wisconsin are described by Curtis, in his 1959 book Vegetation of Wisconsin. The southern forests covered the southern half and western third of the state. Dominant species were primarily oak on the drier sites; sugar maple, basswood, slippery elm, red oak and ironwood on the mesic sites; and silver maple and American elm dominating the lowland sites. In pre-settlement times these forests covered approximately 5.2 million acres with another 7.3 million acres of what is considered oak savanna also falling into this category (Figure 2). In this region the closed woodlands and oak savannas provided no distinct boundaries but blended together. Scattered throughout the southern forest type were areas of true tall grass prairie. These prairies covered just over 2 million acres and were most dominant in the southwest corner of the state, becoming smaller and more scattered as one moved northeast. Forests dominated the northern half of Wisconsin. These northern forests supported jack, red, and white pine with red maple and red oak on the dry sites. The more mesic stands of the northern forests were dominated by sugar maple but hemlock and/or beech may have been co-dominant. Finally, the northern lowland (swamp) forests of Wisconsin are split into the tamarack-black spruce bog forests, the white cedar-balsam fir conifer swamps, and the black ash-yellow birch-hemlock hardwood swamps.

Land Use/Cover

Of the approximately 9.5 million acres of prairie and oak savanna that Wisconsin hosted just 150 short years ago, only one-half of 1 percent (less than 10,000 acres) of the prairies and less than one-tenth of 1 percent (less than 1,000 acres) of the savanna remains. Farming, urban sprawl, fire suppression, and other developments continue to threaten the few acres of prairie and savanna that remain. A quote that appears in Curtis's book provides a view of what we have lost in the last 150 years. This quote

Figure 2: Presettlement Landcover, Leopold Wetland Management District

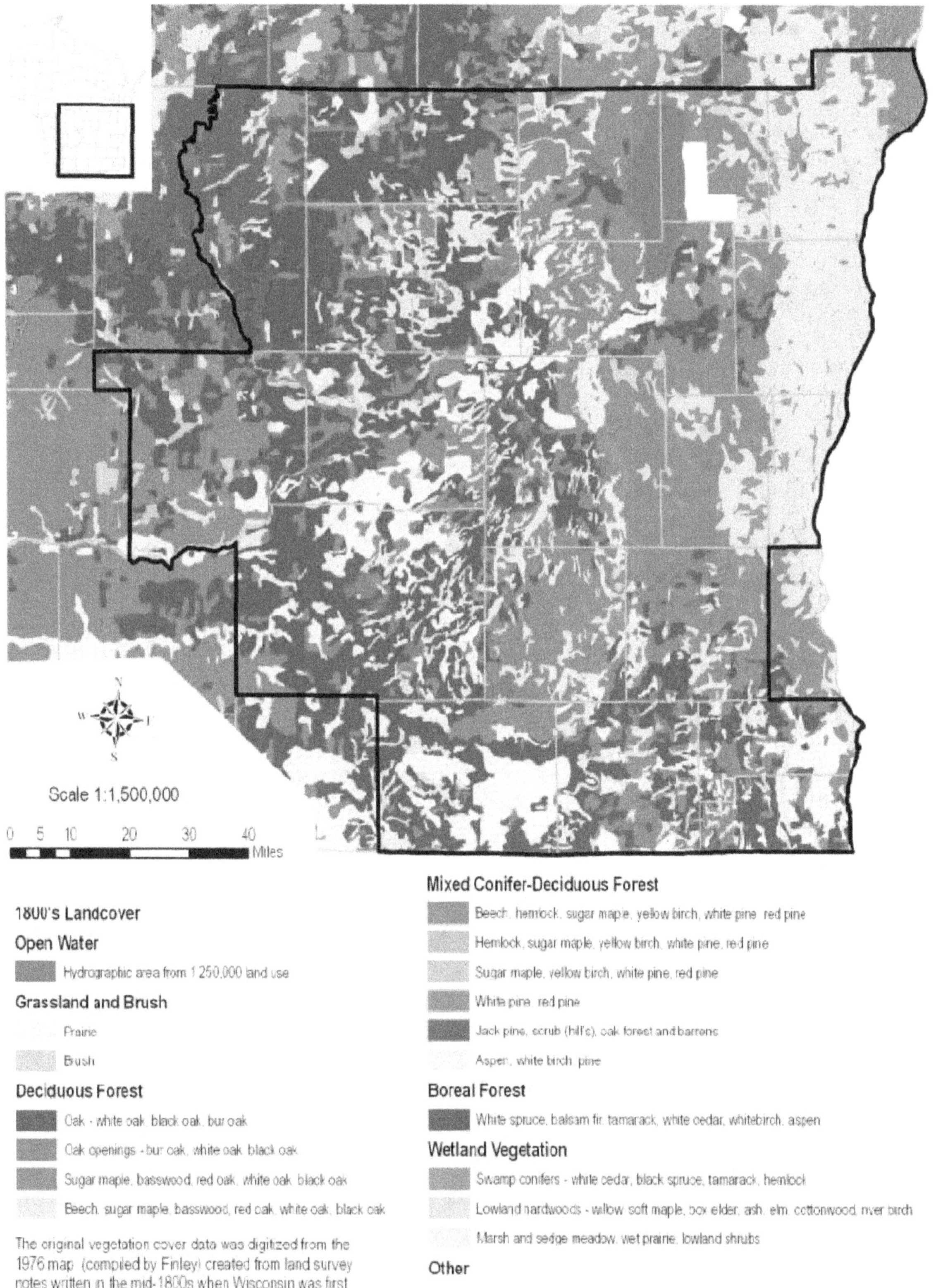

The original vegetation cover data was digitized from the 1976 map (compiled by Finley) created from land survey notes written in the mid-1800s when Wisconsin was first surveyed.

is through the eyes of a Lieutenant D. Ruggles (1835) in writing about the prairies around Fort Winnebago in Columbia County:

> "In some instances, the prairies are found stretching for miles around, without a tree or shrub, so level as scarcely to present a single undulation; in others, those called the "rolling prairies", appears in undulation upon undulation, as far as the eye can reach presenting a view of peculiar sublimity, especially to the beholder for the first time. It seems when in verdure, a real troubled ocean, wave upon wave, rolls before you, ever varying, ever swelling; even the breezes play around to heighten the illusion; so that here at near two thousand miles from the ocean, we have a fac-simile of sublimity, which no miniature imitation can approach."

This is an interesting quote since the prairie Lt. Ruggles was speaking of was known as the Arlington Prairie. This prairie covered portions of Dane and Columbia Counties and included the property that is now called Schoenberg Marsh WPA. It is fitting then, that this WPA is also where the District has re-established local Wisconsin genotype native grasses and forbs for harvest and further seeding.

Shoveler Sink WPA in northern Dane County also lies within this "rolling prairie" and contains a unique geological feature as indicated in its name. Wisconsin geologists believe the sinkhole and the surrounding sandstone bluff on the WPA are natural features formed at the close of the Pleistocene era. In theory the site was initially a spring or groundwater discharge feature. Over time, as the hydraulic head in the bedrock aquifer system lessened, the system reversed itself and surface water now flows into the "sink."

The northern forests, much like the southern forests and prairies, have been altered through logging, farming, fire prevention, and urbanization. Because of this, few stands of "virgin" timber exist outside of those protected by conservation organizations, some Forest Service and State Forest areas, lands within the Wisconsin DNR State Natural Areas program.

Each of these communities are represented within the boundaries of the Leopold WMD, from the prairies and oak savannas of Green, Rock, Dane and Columbia Counties to the tamarack-cedar swamps of Forest and Florence Counties and all variations in between. Each community provides opportunities and challenges for restoration, protection, and management, which helps the District do its part to further the Service mission of conserving, protecting, and enhancing fish, wildlife, and plants and their habitats for the continuing benefit of the American people.

In 2002 about 60 percent of the land area in the District was in farms (Table 1). On a statewide basis, about 45 percent of Wisconsin land is farmland. The counties with the highest proportion of farm land in the District are Calumet, Columbia, Dodge, Fond du Lac, and Rock with more 70 percent of their lands in farms. The counties with the least proportion of farm land are Adams, where about 44 percent of the county is in forest, and Waukesha, where about 12 percent of the county is urban land cover. Both of these counties have less than 30 percent of their land in farms. Within the District, 174,584 acres of land were enrolled in Conservation Reserve or Wetlands Reserve Programs in 2002. This represents 3.7 percent of the farm land or 2.3 percent of the total land area of the District.

A land cover map was completed for Wisconsin in 1999. The map was created though automated computer interpretation of satellite images. The work was completed by the partnership WISCLAND. The land cover for the District and nearby areas is depicted in Figure 3 on page 14. Percent land cover for each county are shown in Table 1.

Migratory Bird Conservation Initiatives

Several migratory bird conservation plans have been published over the last decade that can be used to help guide management decisions for the Districts. Bird conservation planning efforts have evolved from a largely local, site-based orientation to a more regional, even inter-continental, landscape-oriented perspective. Several transnational migratory bird conservation initiatives have emerged to help guide the planning and implementation process. The regional plans relevant to Leopold WMD are:

- The Upper Mississippi River/Great Lakes Joint Venture Implementation Plan of the North American Waterfowl Management Plan
- The Partners in Flight Boreal Hardwood Transition [land] Bird Conservation Plan
- The Upper Mississippi Valley/Great Lakes Regional Shorebird Conservation Plan

Table 1: Land Cover in the Leopold Wetland Management District

County	Urban	Agricultural	Grassland	Forest	Water	Wetland	Barren	Shrubland
Adams	0.3%	19.3%	16.3%	44.6%	6.2%	11.0%	0.9%	1.4%
Calumet	1.3%	63.9%	1.4%	3.2%	19.3%	9.4%	1.4%	0.0%
Columbia	1.2%	50.9%	12.4%	17.7%	2.8%	13.9%	1.0%	0.1%
Dane	5.5%	54.6%	13.2%	15.8%	3.1%	6.3%	1.6%	0.0%
Dodge	1.5%	62.3%	9.8%	3.9%	3.9%	16.9%	1.7%	0.0%
Fond du Lac	2.0%	62.2%	10.5%	4.6%	5.5%	13.5%	1.7%	0.1%
Green Lake	1.2%	45.5%	11.8%	11.9%	7.2%	21.5%	0.7%	0.1%
Jefferson	1.8%	57.7%	11.6%	7.5%	4.5%	15.4%	1.3%	0.0%
Kenosha	6.8%	52.5%	11.8%	11.2%	3.1%	9.3%	3.8%	1.5%
Manitowoc	2.2%	73.1%	3.3%	6.5%	0.3%	13.3%	1.2%	0.0%
Marquette	0.5%	27.6%	17.1%	30.0%	2.6%	21.9%	0.2%	0.2%
Ozaukee	6.9%	49.2%	19.3%	9.1%	1.6%	10.6%	1.1%	2.2%
Racine	7.6%	53.9%	11.5%	12.1%	2.9%	6.9%	3.8%	1.3%
Rock	4.0%	72.0%	10.4%	8.5%	1.0%	3.9%	0.3%	0.0%
Sauk	1.5%	40.7%	13.9%	35.9%	1.2%	5.8%	1.0%	0.0%
Sheboygan	3.6%	57.6%	10.4%	11.4%	0.9%	12.0%	1.5%	1.5%
Walworth	2.6%	59.0%	10.1%	12.4%	3.8%	7.6%	4.0%	0.5%
Washington	3.4%	49.1%	16.6%	11.6%	1.4%	15.3%	1.9%	0.7%
Waukesha	11.9%	29.4%	24.3%	13.3%	4.6%	13.9%	1.6%	1.0%
Waushara	0.3%	34.6%	20.2%	27.4%	2.0%	13.9%	1.5%	0.0%
Winnebago	5.4%	50.9%	3.8%	3.4%	24.1%	11.0%	1.3%	0.0%
Wisconsin	1.6%	30.8%	10.7%	37.5%	3.4%	14.1%	1.1%	0.9%

- The Upper Mississippi Valley/Great Lakes Regional Waterbird Conservation Plan

All four conservation plans will be integrated under the umbrella of the North American Bird Conservation Initiative (NABCI) in the Prairie Hardwood Transition Bird Conservation Region (BCR 23, see Figure 4 on page 15). Each of the bird conservation initiatives has a process for designating priority species, modeled to a large extent on the Partners in Flight method of computing scores based on independent assessments of global relative abundance, breeding and wintering distribution, vulnerability to threats, area importance, and population trend. These scores are often used by agencies in developing lists of priority bird species. The Service based its 2001 list of Non-game Birds of Conservation Concern primarily on the Partners in Flight, shorebird, and waterbird status assessment scores.

Wildlife Species of Management Concern

As described in the Biological Integriy, Diversity, and Environmental Health policy (601 FW 3), the goal of habitat management on units of the National Wildlife Refuge System is to ensure the long-term maintenance and, where possible, restoration of healthy populations of native fish, wildlife, plants, and their habitats. Resources of concern include species, species groups, and/or communities that support District purposes as well as Service trust resource responsibilities (including threatened and endangered species and migratory birds). Resources of concern are also native species and

Figure 3: Current Landcover, Leopold Wetland Management District

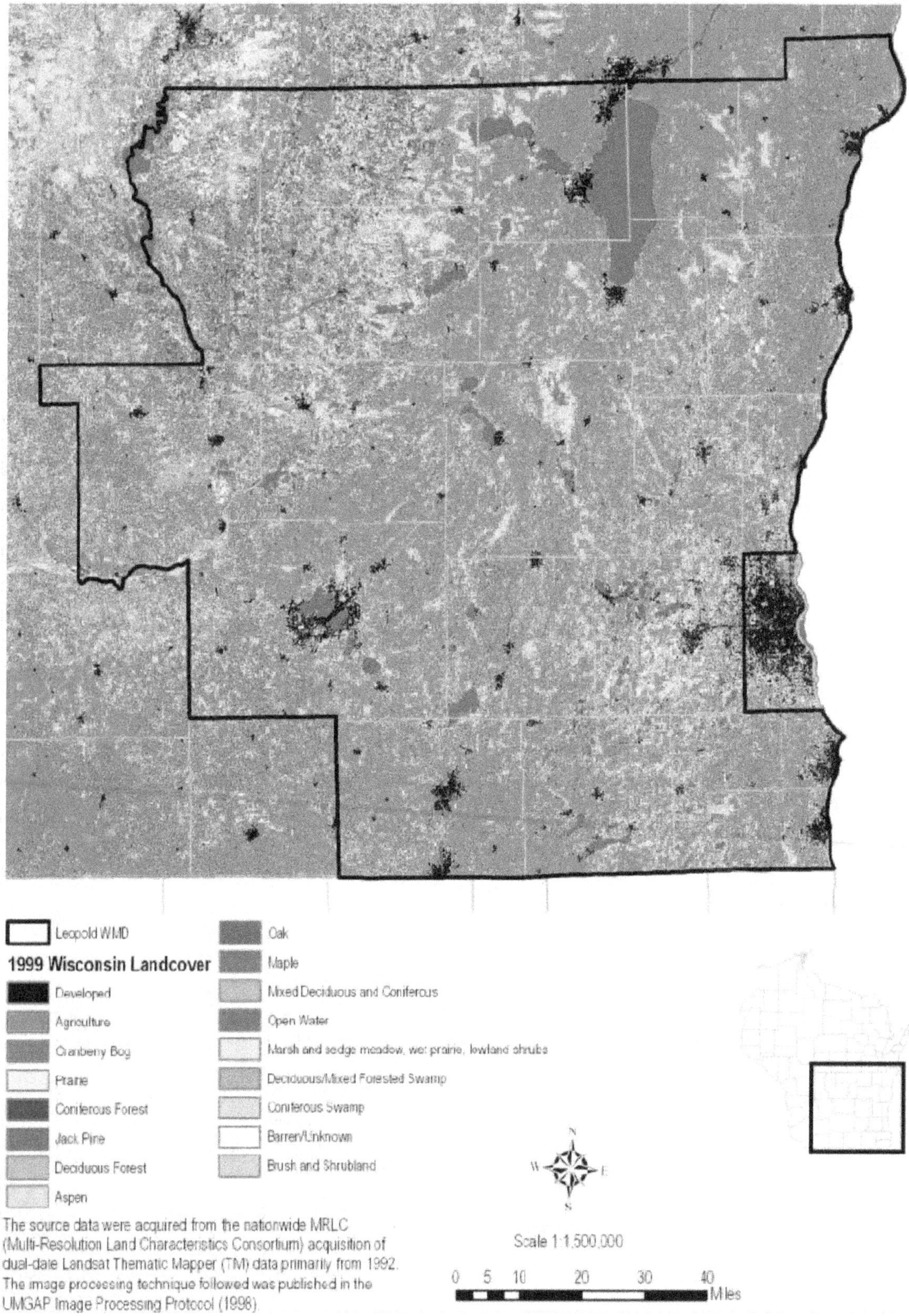

The source data were acquired from the nationwide MRLC (Multi-Resolution Land Characteristics Consortium) acquisition of dual-date Landsat Thematic Mapper (TM) data primarily from 1992. The image processing technique followed was published in the UMGAP Image Processing Protocol (1998).

Figure 4: Bird Conservation Region, Leopold Wetland Management District

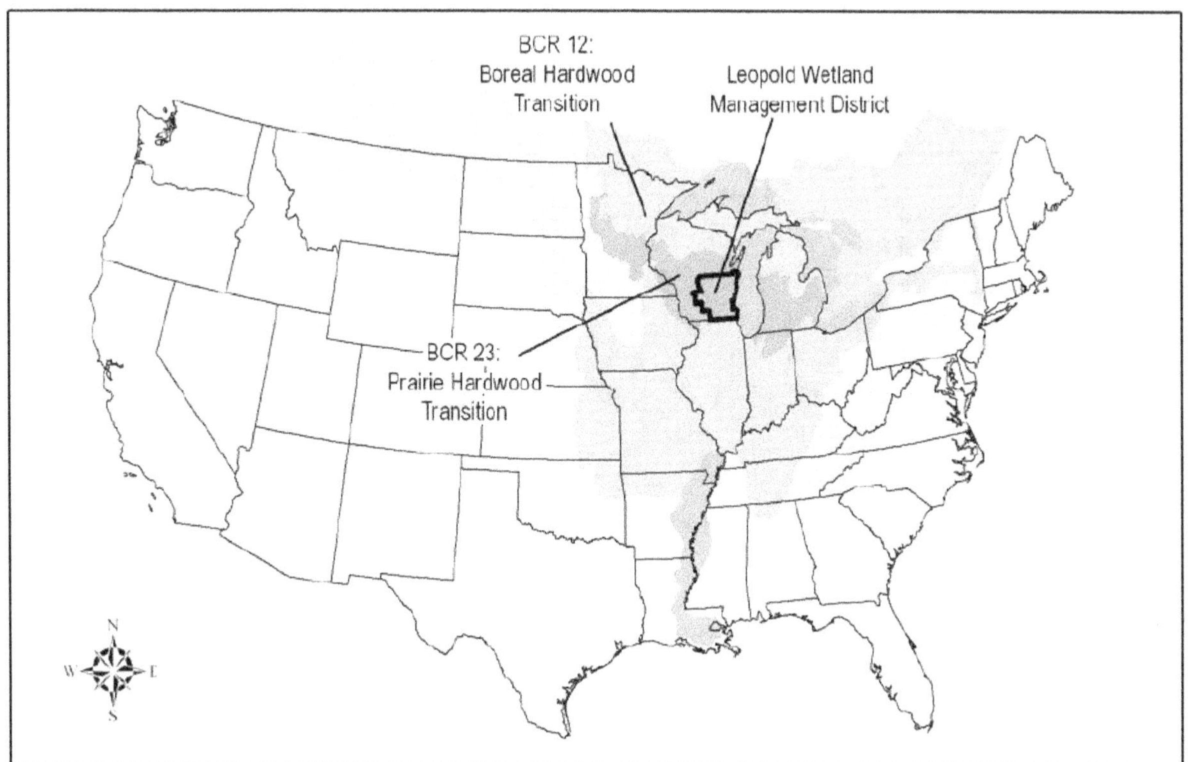

natural, functional communities such as those found under historic conditions that are to be maintained and, where appropriate, restored on a refuge (601 FW 3.10B[1]. Resources of concern take into account the conservation needs identified within international, national, regional, or ecosystem goals/plans; state fish and wildlife conservaton plans; recovery plans for threatened and endangered species; regional fisheries management plans; and previously approved resource management plans.

Appendix D summarizes information on the status and current habitat use of important wildlife species found on lands administered by the District. Individual species, or species groups, were chosen because they are listed as Regional Resource Conservation Priorities or State-listed threatened or endangered species. Other species are listed due to their importance for economic or recreational reasons, because the District or its partners monitor or survey them, or for their status as an overabundant or invasive species.

Other Conservation and Recreation Lands in the Area

Other U.S. Fish and Wildlife Service land within the District include Horicon National Wildlife Refuge (more than 21,000 acres) and Fox River National Wildlife Refuge (about 1,000 acres). Necedah National Wildlife Refuge, which is more than 43,000 acres in size, is located a few miles west of Adams County, which is in the northwest part of the District.

The Wisconsin Department of Natural Resources manages over 307,000 acres of conservation and recreation lands within the District (Figure 5). The DNR lands include 58 State Wildlife Areas with a total acreage close to 144,000 acres. The largest Wildlife Area is more than 12,000 acres. The DNR manages more than 18,000 acres of natural areas, 22,000 acres of parks and trails, and nearly 29,000 acres of other wildlife habitat within the District. Most of the lands managed for wildlife and some other state lands are open to wildlife-dependent recreation.

Figure 5: Conservation Lands Adjacent to the Leopold Wetland Management District

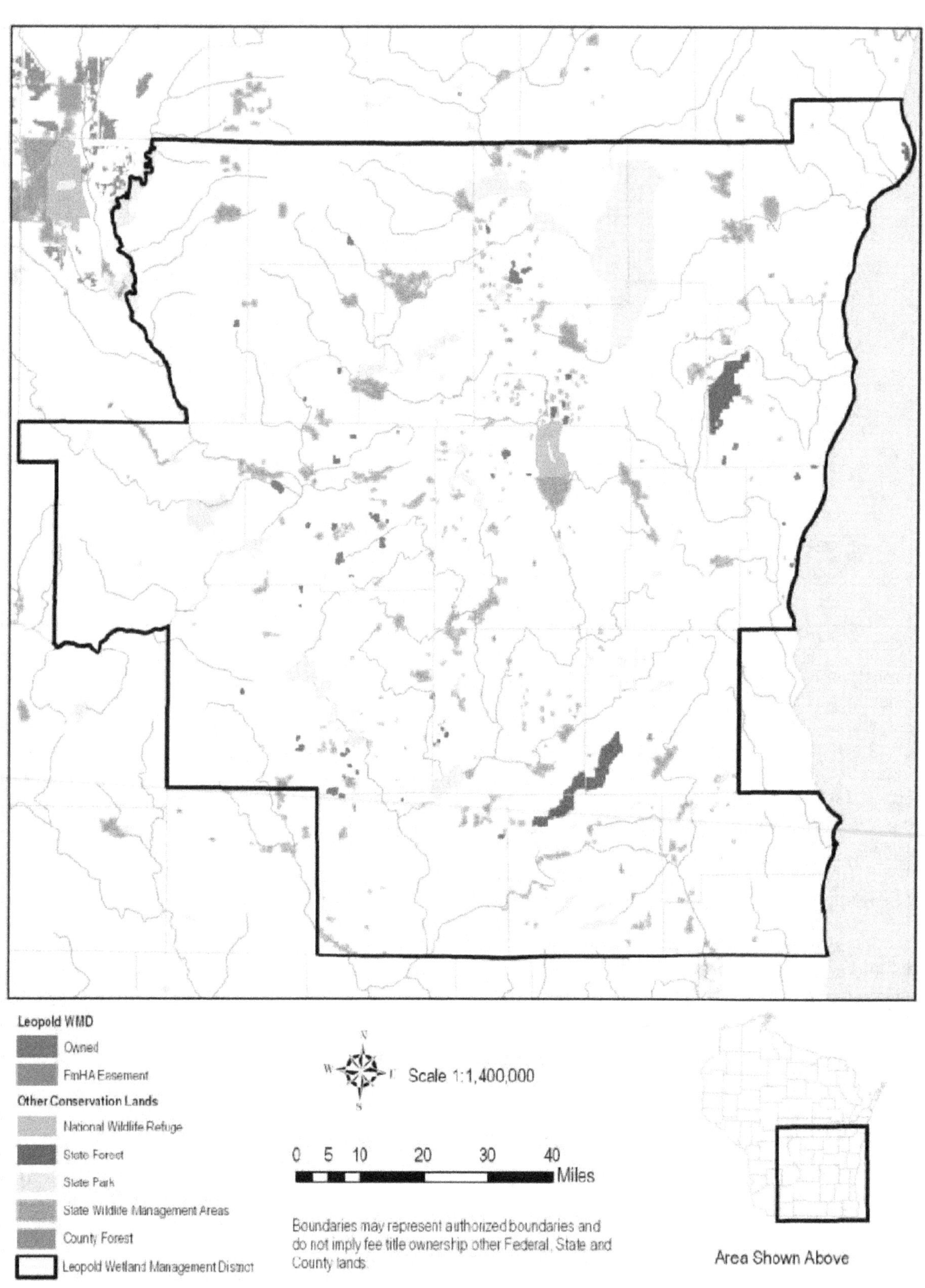

Wisconsin Strategy for Wildlife Species of Greatest Conservation Need

Using Wisconsin's State Wildlife Action Plan (WWAP), the State of Wisconsin has analyzed state animal species, identified those most in need of attention because they are declining or are dependent on habitat or places that are declining, and suggested conservation measures to ensure the survival of these species. The document describing their analysis and findings is filled with information that helps identify conservation needs. For each Ecological Landscape of Wisconsin (Figure 6), it provides information on the overarching needs and opportunities in the landscape as well as lists of the natural communities that are major and important management opportunities. It also lists those Species of Greatest Conservation Need with high, moderate, or low degrees of probability of occurring in the landscape. The State's analysis provides a good basis for coordination of District activities with the State and other conservation organizations.

Socioeconomic Setting

Just as the environmental characteristics vary across the District, so do the socioeconomic characteristics (Table 2 on page 19). Milwaukee influences the southeastern portion of the District. The counties of Racine, Washington, and Waukesha in the southeast have the highest median household income and the highest median housing value in the District. Most of the District has a low minority population, much like the State of Wisconsin. The exception is the relatively higher Hispanic population in the three southeastern counties of Kenosha, Racine, and Walworth. Counties with a high urban population include the counties Kenosha, Racine, Waukesha near Milwaukee and the counties of Dane (Madison), Rock (Janesville and Beloit), and Winnebago (Oshkosh). The counties with the highest percentage of college educated people in the District are Dane, Ozaukee, and Waukesha. In comparison to the rest of the District and the State of Wisconsin, Adams, Marquette, and Waushara Counties in the northwestern part of the District have a higher median age, essentially no urban population, and well below median household income and housing value.

The population of the District is expected to grow about 1 percent per year over the next 20 years (Table 3 on page 20). The counties projected to grow at the highest average annual rate are Calumet, Dane, Kenosha, Sauk, Walworth, and Washington. The District is projected to increase in population about 374,000 from 2005 to 2025. For additional detailed descriptions of the characteristics and projections for the counties and their implications for recreation see the regional demographic profiles prepared by the Applied Population Lab and Wisconsin Department of Natural Resources for the Wisconsin SCORP 2005-2010 planning process.

Potential District Visitors

We used block group data from the 2000 census to estimate how many people lived near WPAs. For the WPAs managed by the District, we learned that about 302,000 people lived within 5 miles of a WPA in 2000; 968,000 within 10 miles; and 1,549,000 within 15 miles.

In order to refine our understanding and estimate the potential market for visitors to the WPAs, we looked at 1998 consumer behavior data for an area within an approximate 15-mile distance from WPAs. The data were organized by zip code areas, which made the buffers around the WPAs irregular and not equidistant at all boundary points. We thought the distance was a good approximation for a reasonable drive to a WPA for an outing.

The consumer behavior data used in the analysis is derived from Mediamark Research Inc. data. The company collects and analyzes data on consumer demographics, product and brand usage, and exposure to all forms of advertising media. The consumer behavior data were projected by Tetrad Computer Applications Inc. to new populations using Mosaic data. Mosaic is a methodology that classifies neighborhoods into segments based on their demographic and socioeconomic composition. The basic assumption in the analysis is that people in demographically similar neighborhoods will tend to have similar consumption, ownership, and lifestyle preferences. Because of the assumptions made in the analysis, the data should be considered as relative indicators of potential, not actual participation.

We looked at potential participants in birdwatching, photography, freshwater fishing, hunting, and hiking. The consumer behavior data apply to persons more than 18 years old. For the area that we

Figure 6: Wisconsin Ecological Landscapes

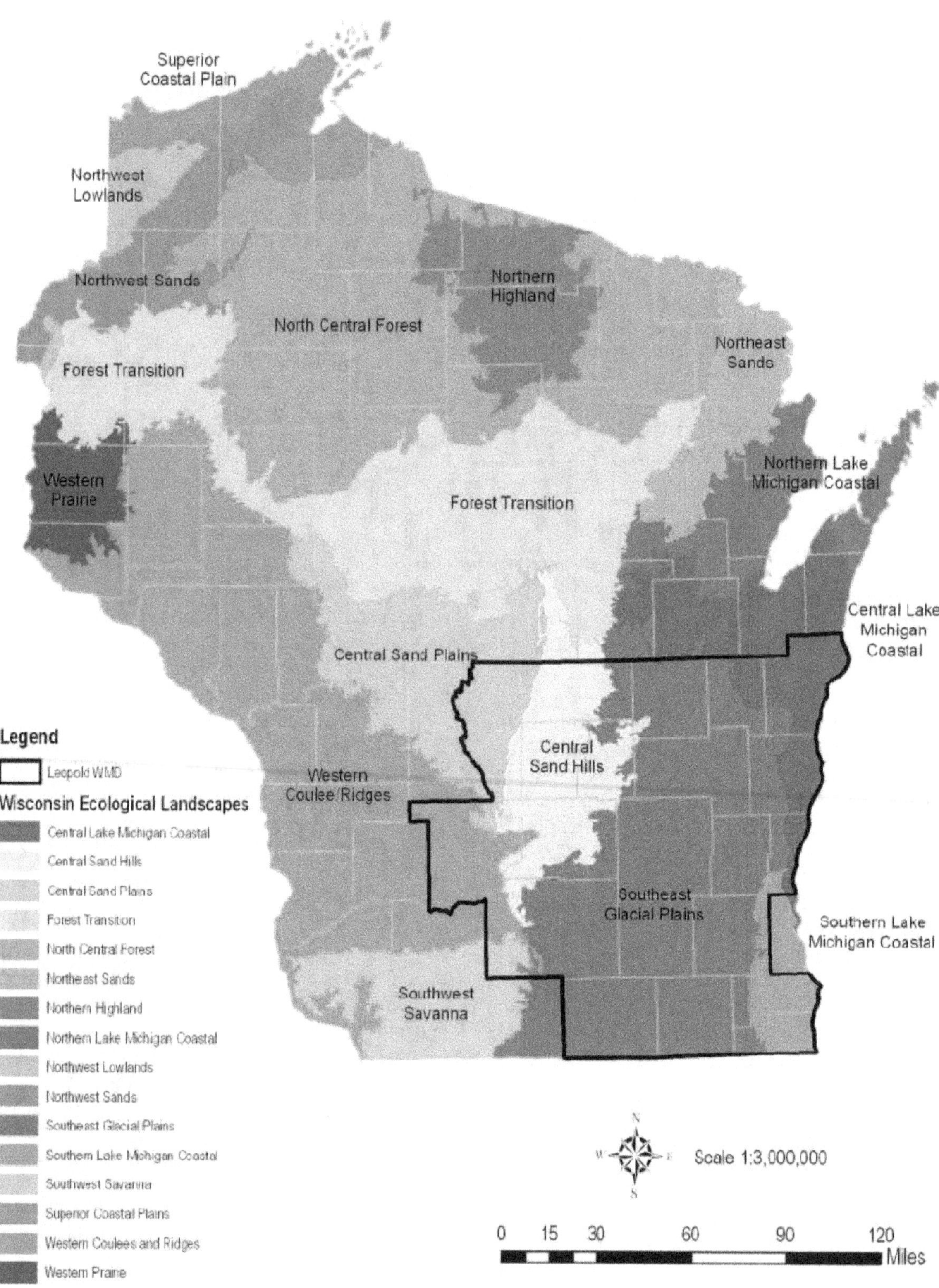

Table 2: Socioeconomic Data, Counties Within the Leopold Wetland Management District[1]

County	Total Population	Percent Urban	Median Age	Percent Female	College[2] Educated	Percent Hispanic	Percent American Indian	Percent Asian	Percent Black	Median HH Income	Median Housing Value[3]
Adams County	19,920	0.0	44.5	49.3	10	1.4	0.6	0.3	0.3	$33,408	$83,600
Calumet County	40,631	60.3	35.2	50	21	1.1	0.3	1.5	0.3	$52,569	$109,300
Columbia County	52,468	36.8	38.0	49.6	17	1.6	n/a	0.3	0.9	$45,064	$115,000
Dane County	426,526	84.5	33.2	50.5	41	3.4	n/a	3.5	4.0	$49,223	$146,900
Dodge County	85,897	47.8	37.0	47.7	13	2.5	n/a	0.3	2.5	$45,190	$105,800
Fond du Lac County	97,296	62.1	36.9	51	17	2.0	0.4	0.9	0.9	$45,578	$101,000
Green Lake County	19,105	25.1	40.9	51	14	2.1	02	0.3	02	$39,462	$90,100
Jefferson County	74,021	57.8	36.6	50.4	17	4.1	n/a	0.4	0.3	$46,901	$123,800
Kenosha County	149,577	88.6	34.8	50.4	19	7.2	n/a	0.9	5.1	$46,970	$120,900
Manitowoc County	82,887	60.9	38.3	50.5	15	1.6	0.4	2.0	n/a	$43,286	$90,900
Marquette County	14,555	0.0	40.9	n/a	10	n/a	n/a	n/a	n/a	$35,746	$87,000
Ozaukee County	82,317	74.6	38.9	50.7	39	1.3	n/a	1.1	0.9	$62,745	$177,300
Racine County	188,831	87.0	36.1	50.5	20	7.9	n/a	0.7	10.5	$48,059	$111,000
Rock County	152,307	78.2	35.9	50.8	17	3.9	n/a	0.8	4.6	$45,517	$98,200
Sauk County	55,225	50.1	37.3	50.6	18	1.7	n/a	0.3	0.3	$41,941	$107,500
Sheboygan County	112,646	70.8	36.8	49.8	18	3.4	n/a	3.3	1.1	$46,237	$106,800
Walworth County	93,759	64.0	35.1	50.3	22	6.5	n/a	0.7	0.8	$46,274	$128,400
Washington County	117,493	65.2	36.6	50.1	22	1.3	n/a	0.6	0.4	$57,033	$155,000
Waukesha County	360,767	87.8	38.1	50.8	34	2.6	n/a	1.5	0.7	$62,839	$170,400
Waushara County	23,154	0.3	42.1	50	12	3.7	0.%	0.3	0.3	$37,000	$85,100
Winnebago County	156,763	84.2	35.4	50	23	2.0	0.5	1.8	1.1	$44,445	$97,700
Leopold WMD											
State of Wisconsin		68.3%	36.0	50.6%	22	3.6	0.8	1.6	5.6	$43,791	$112,200

1. *Source: Census 2000 as reported in Wisconsin SCORP*
2. *Percent college educated calculated for persons age 25 and older.*
3. *Housing value is calculated for owner occupied housing units.*

Table 3: Wisconsin Department of Administration Official Population Projections June 2003

County	Historical			Projections					Average Annual Percent Increases	
	1980	1990	2000	2005	2010	2015	2020	2025	2005-2020	2005-2025
Adams	13,457	15,682	19,920	20,796	21,528	21,969	22,137	22,440	0.64	0.53
Calumet	30,867	34,291	40,631	44,182	47,398	50,381	53,473	56,336	2.10	1.83
Columbia	43,222	45,088	52,468	54,434	56,366	58,135	59,753	61,669	0.98	0.89
Dane	323,545	367,085	426,526	455,927	480,573	503,017	527,534	554,848	1.57	1.45
Dodge	75,064	76,559	85,897	88,192	90,565	92,842	94,882	96,828	0.76	0.65
Fond du Lac	88,964	90,083	97,296	100,163	103,031	105,777	108,494	110,748	0.83	0.70
Green Lake	18,370	18,651	19,105	19,321	19,666	19,913	20,064	20,032	0.38	0.25
Jefferson	66,152	67,783	75,767	79,030	82,161	85,178	88,302	91,464	1.17	1.05
Kenosha	123,137	128,181	149,577	157,935	165,678	173,624	181,693	190,145	1.50	1.36
Manitowoc	82,918	80,421	82,893	84,574	86,307	88,055	89,860	90,821	0.63	0.49
Marquette	11,672	12,321	14,555	15,052	15,579	16,035	16,293	16,583	0.82	0.68
Ozaukee	66,981	72,831	82,317	85,047	87,238	89,692	92,496	95,417	0.88	0.81
Racine	173,132	175,034	188,831	193,189	197,662	202,404	206,989	211,326	0.71	0.63
Rock	139,420	139,510	152,307	156,691	160,911	165,354	169,648	174,018	0.83	0.74
Sauk	43,469	46,975	55,225	58,121	60,930	63,520	65,821	68,208	1.32	1.16
Sheboygan	100,935	103,877	112,656	116,070	119,411	122,921	126,540	130,018	0.90	0.80
Walworth	71,507	75,000	92,013	96,182	100,634	106,588	111,237	113,506	1.57	1.20
Washington	84,848	95,328	117,496	123,570	129,085	134,255	139,214	145,314	1.27	1.17
Waukesha	280,203	304,715	360,767	374,891	386,460	397,922	409,570	424,472	0.93	0.88
Waushara	18,526	19,385	23,066	25,675	26,548	27,228	27,726	28,136	0.80	0.64
Winnebago	131,772	140,320	156,763	162,076	166,717	171,369	176,614	182,767	0.90	0.85
Leopold WMD	1,988,161	2,109,120	2,406,076	2,511,118	2,604,448	2,696,179	2,788,340	2,885,096	1.10	0.99

included in our analysis, the estimated maximum participants for each activity are: birdwatching (66,398), photography (97,790), hunting (61,263), freshwater fishing (115,837), and hiking (82,874). We interpret the estimates to represent the core audience for repeated trips to a WPA.

Climate and Climate Change Impacts

The District's climate is continental with cold winters and warm summers. Leopold Wetland Management District is large, and the long-term temperature averages vary from one end of the District to another. Lake Michigan moderates the temperatures in the eastern portion of the District. The average annual precipitation is higher in the southern part of the District than in the central and northern part. The normal temperatures and annual precipitation averages for the period 1971-2000 for a region that includes Columbia, Dane, Dodge, Green, Jefferson, and Rock Counties present an adequate indication of the climate of the District. The region has an average annual temperature of 45.9 degrees Fahrenheit. July is the warmest month with an average temperature of 71.3 degrees Fahrenheit. The coldest month is January with an average temperature of 16.8 degrees Fahrenheit. Annual precipitation is 34.11 inches. The average monthly precipitation exceeds 3 inches for April, May, and September. The average monthly precipitation exceeds 4 inches for June, July, and August. (Source: Wisconsin Agricultural Statistics Service, Wisconsin 2004 Agricultural Statistics, at www.nass.usda.gov/wi/rlsetoc.htm.)

The U.S. Department of the Interior issued an order in January 2001 requiring federal agencies, under its direction, that have land management responsibilities to consider potential climate change impacts as part of long range planning endeavors.

The increase of carbon dioxide within the earth's atmosphere has been linked to the gradual rise in surface temperature commonly referred to as global warming. In relation to comprehensive conservation planning for wetland management districts, carbon sequestration constitutes the primary climate-related impact to be considered in planning. The U.S. Department of Energy's *"Carbon Sequestration Research and Development"* defines carbon sequestration as "...the capture and secure storage of carbon that would otherwise be emitted to or remain in the atmosphere."

Muskrat. USFWS photo.

Vegetated land is a tremendous factor in carbon sequestration. Terrestrial biomes of all sorts – grasslands, forests, wetlands, tundra, and desert – are effective both in preventing carbon emission and acting as a biological "scrubber" of atmospheric carbon dioxide. The Department of Energy report's conclusions noted that ecosystem protection is important to carbon sequestration and may reduce or prevent loss of carbon currently stored in the terrestrial biosphere.

Conserving natural habitat for wildlife is the heart of any long-range plan for national wildlife refuges and wetland management districts. The actions proposed in this CCP would conserve or restore land and habitat, and would thus retain existing carbon sequestration on the District. This in turn contributes positively to efforts to mitigate human-induced global climate change.

One Service activity in particular – prescribed burning – releases carbon dioxide directly to the atmosphere from the biomass consumed during combustion. However, there is actually no net loss of carbon, since new vegetation quickly germinates and sprouts to replace the burned-up biomass and sequesters or assimilates an approximately equal amount of carbon as was lost to the air (Boutton et al. 2006).

Several impacts of climate change have been identified that may need to be considered and addressed in the future:

- Habitat available for cold water fish such as trout and salmon in lakes and streams could be reduced.
- Forests may change, with some tree species shifting their range northward or dying out, and other trees moving in to take their place.
- Ducks and other waterfowl could lose breeding habitat due to stronger and more frequent droughts.
- Changes in the timing of migration and nesting could put some birds out of sync with the life cycles of their prey species.
- Animal and insect species historically found farther south may colonize new areas to the north as winter climatic conditions moderate.

The managers and resource specialists on the District need to be aware of the possibility of change due to global warming. When feasible, documenting long-term vegetation, species, and hydrologic changes should become a part of research and monitoring programs on the District. Adjustments in management direction may be necessary over the course of time to adapt to a changing climate.

The following is an excerpt from the 2000 report, *Climate Change Impacts on the United States: The Potential Consequences of Climate Variability and Change*, produced by the National Assessment Synthesis Team, an advisory committee chartered under the Federal Advisory Committee Act to help the US Global Change Research Program fulfill its mandate under the Global Change Research Act of 1990. These excerpts are from the section of the report focused upon the eight-state Midwest region.

Observed Climate Trends

Over the 20th century, the northern portion of the Midwest, including the upper Great Lakes, has warmed by almost 4 degrees Fahrenheit (2 degrees Celsius), while the southern portion, along the Ohio River valley, has cooled by about 1 degree Fahrenheit (0.5 degree Celsius). Annual precipitation has increased, with many of the changes quite substantial, including as much as 10 to 20 percent increases over the 20th century. Much of the precipitation has resulted from an increased rise in the number of days with heavy and very heavy precipitation events. There have been moderate to very large increases in the number of days with excessive moisture in the eastern portion of the basin.

Scenarios of Future Climate

During the 21st century, models project that temperatures will increase throughout the Midwest, and at a greater rate than has been observed in the 20th century. Even over the northern portion of the region, where warming has been the largest, an accelerated warming trend is projected for the 21st century, with temperatures increasing by 5 to 10 degrees Fahrenheit (3 to 6 degrees Celsius). The average minimum temperature is likely to increase as much as 1 to 2 degrees Fahrenheit (0.5 to 1 degree Celsius) more than the maximum temperature. Precipitation is likely to continue its upward trend, at a slightly accelerated rate; 10 to 30 percent increases are projected across much of the region. Despite the increases in precipitation, increases in temperature and other meteorological factors are likely to lead to a substantial increase in evaporation, causing a soil moisture deficit, reduction in lake and river levels, and more drought-like conditions in much of the region. In addition, increases in the proportion of precipitation coming from heavy and extreme precipitation are very likely.

Midwest Key Issues

Reduction in Lake and River Levels

Water levels, supply, quality, and water-based transportation and recreation are all climate-sensitive issues affecting the region. Despite the projected increase in precipitation, increased evaporation due to higher summer air temperatures

American badger. USFWS photo.

is likely to lead to reduced levels in the Great Lakes. Of 12 models used to assess this question, 11 suggest significant decreases in lake levels while one suggests a small increase. The total range of the 11 models' projections is less than a 1-foot increase to more than a 5-foot decrease. A 5-foot (1.5-meter) reduction would lead to a 20 to 40 percent reduction in outflow to the St. Lawrence Seaway. Lower lake levels cause reduced hydropower generation downstream, with reductions of up to 15 percent by 2050. An increase in demand for water across the region at the same time as net flows decrease is of particular concern. There is a possibility of increased national and international tension related to increased pressure for water diversions from the Great Lakes as demands for water increase. For smaller lakes and rivers, reduced flows are likely to cause water quality issues to become more acute. In addition, the projected increase in very heavy precipitation events will likely lead to increased flash flooding and worsen agricultural and other nonpoint source pollution as more frequent heavy rains wash pollutants into rivers and lakes. Lower water levels are likely to make water-based transportation more difficult with increases in the costs of navigation of 5 to 40 percent. Some of this increase will likely be offset as reduced ice cover extends the navigation season. Shoreline damage due to high lake levels is likely to decrease 40 to 80 percent due to reduced water levels.

Adaptations: A reduction in lake and river levels would require adaptations such as re-engineering of ship docks and locks for transportation and recreation. If flows decrease while demand increases, international commissions focusing on Great Lakes water issues are likely to become even more important in the future. Improved forecasts and warnings of extreme precipitation events could help reduce some related impacts.

Agricultural Shifts

Agriculture is of vital importance to this region, the nation, and the world. It has exhibited a capacity to adapt to moderate differences in growing season climate, and it is likely that agriculture would be able to continue to adapt. With an increase in the length of the growing season, double cropping, the practice of planting a second crop after the first is harvested, is likely to become more prevalent. The carbon dioxide fertilization effect is likely to enhance plant growth and contribute to generally higher yields. The largest increases are projected to occur in the northern areas of the region, where crop yields are currently temperature limited. However, yields are not likely to increase in all parts of the region. For example, in the southern portions of Indiana and Illinois, corn yields are likely to decline, with 10-20 percent decreases projected in some locations. Consumers are likely to pay lower prices due to generally increased yields, while most producers are likely to suffer reduced profits due to declining prices. Increased use of pesticides and herbicides are very likely to be required and to present new challenges.

Adaptations: Plant breeding programs can use skilled climate predictions to aid in breeding new varieties for the new growing conditions. Farmers can then choose varieties that are better attuned to the expected climate. It is likely that plant breeders will need to use all the tools of plant breeding, including genetic engineering, in adapting to climate change. Changing planting and harvest dates and planting densities, and using integrated pest management, conservation tillage, and new farm technologies are additional options. There is also the potential for shifting or expanding the area where certain crops are grown if climate conditions become more favorable. Weather conditions during the growing season are the primary factor in year-to-year differences in corn and soybean yields. Droughts and floods result in large yield reductions; severe droughts, like the drought of 1988, cause yield reductions of over 30%. Reliable seasonal forecasts are likely to help farmers adjust their practices from year to year to respond to such events.

Changes in Semi-natural and Natural Ecosystems

The Upper Midwest has a unique combination of soil and climate that allows for abundant coniferous tree growth. Higher temperatures and increased evaporation will likely reduce boreal forest acreage, and make current forestlands more susceptible to pests and diseases. It is likely that the southern transition zone of the boreal forest will be susceptible to expansion of temperate forests, which in turn will have to compete with other land use pressures. However, warmer weather coupled with beneficial effects of increased carbon dioxide is likely to lead to an increase in tree growth rates on marginal forestlands that are currently temperature-limited. Most climate models indicate that higher air temperatures will cause greater evaporation and hence reduced soil moisture, a situation conducive to forest fires. As the 21st century progresses, there will be an increased likelihood of greater environmental stress on both deciduous and coniferous trees, making them susceptible to disease and pest infestation, likely resulting in increased tree mortality.

As water temperatures in lakes increase, major changes in freshwater ecosystems will very likely occur, such as a shift from cold water fish species, such as trout, to warmer water species, such as bass and catfish. Warmer water is also likely to create an environment more susceptible to invasions by non-native species. Runoff of excess nutrients (such as nitrogen and phosphorus from fertilizer) into lakes and rivers is likely to increase due to the increase in heavy precipitation events. This, coupled with warmer lake temperatures, is likely to stimulate the growth of algae, depleting the water of oxygen to the detriment of other living things. Declining lake levels are likely to cause large impacts to the current distribution of shoreline wetlands. There is some chance that some of these wetlands could gradually migrate, but in areas where their migration is limited by the topography, they would disappear. Changes in bird populations and other native wildlife have already been linked to increasing temperatures and more changes are likely in the future. Wildlife populations are particularly susceptible to climate extremes due to the effects of drought on their food sources.

Geology and Soils

A majority of the District is quite similar to the glaciated prairie region of western Minnesota. This similarity is recognized with the inclusion of these glaciated prairie areas in Category 2, Prairie and Pothole Parklands, in the Service's revised Waterfowl Habitat Acquisition Plan. The counties that lie within the Leopold WMD boundaries owe much of their ecology to the glacial history of Wisconsin (see Figure 7). Glaciers most recently flowed into Wisconsin about 25,000 years ago and reached their greatest extent, covering approximately two-thirds of the state, some 14,000 to 16,000 years ago. The retreat of the ice front was interrupted a number of times by re-advances, the last one touched northwestern Wisconsin about 10,000 years ago. The advancing ice was channeled into the lowlands now occupied by Lakes Superior and Michigan, Green Bay, and the Fox River, and was impeded by the uplands of the Bayfield, Keweenaw and Door Peninsulas. The ice thus split into six major lobes as it flowed southward across the state. The Green Bay Lobe, which had few obstructions in its path, penetrated as far south as present-day Janesville in Rock County.

Ruddy Duck. USFWS photo.

Soil types have characteristic properties that determine their potential and limitations for specific land uses. Knowledge of soils can contribute to managing the District's wildlife habitat programs. The Soil Survey Geographic Database is the most detailed level of soil mapping done by the Natural Resources Conservation Service (NRCS). This database was completed for Wisconsin in 2006. At the level of the waterfowl production area, soil data can be used to identify the potential natural vegetation.

Water and Hydrology

Hydrologic features vary across the ecological landscapes of the District, although the past draining of wetlands is consistent throughout the District. According to the Wisconsin DNR, watershed and groundwater pollution vary considerably across the District (see Figure 8 on page 26). From a practical perspective, the relevance of hydrology to the establishment and management of a WPA is best analyzed and discussed at a local scale.

Figure 7: Ice Age Deposits of Wisconsin

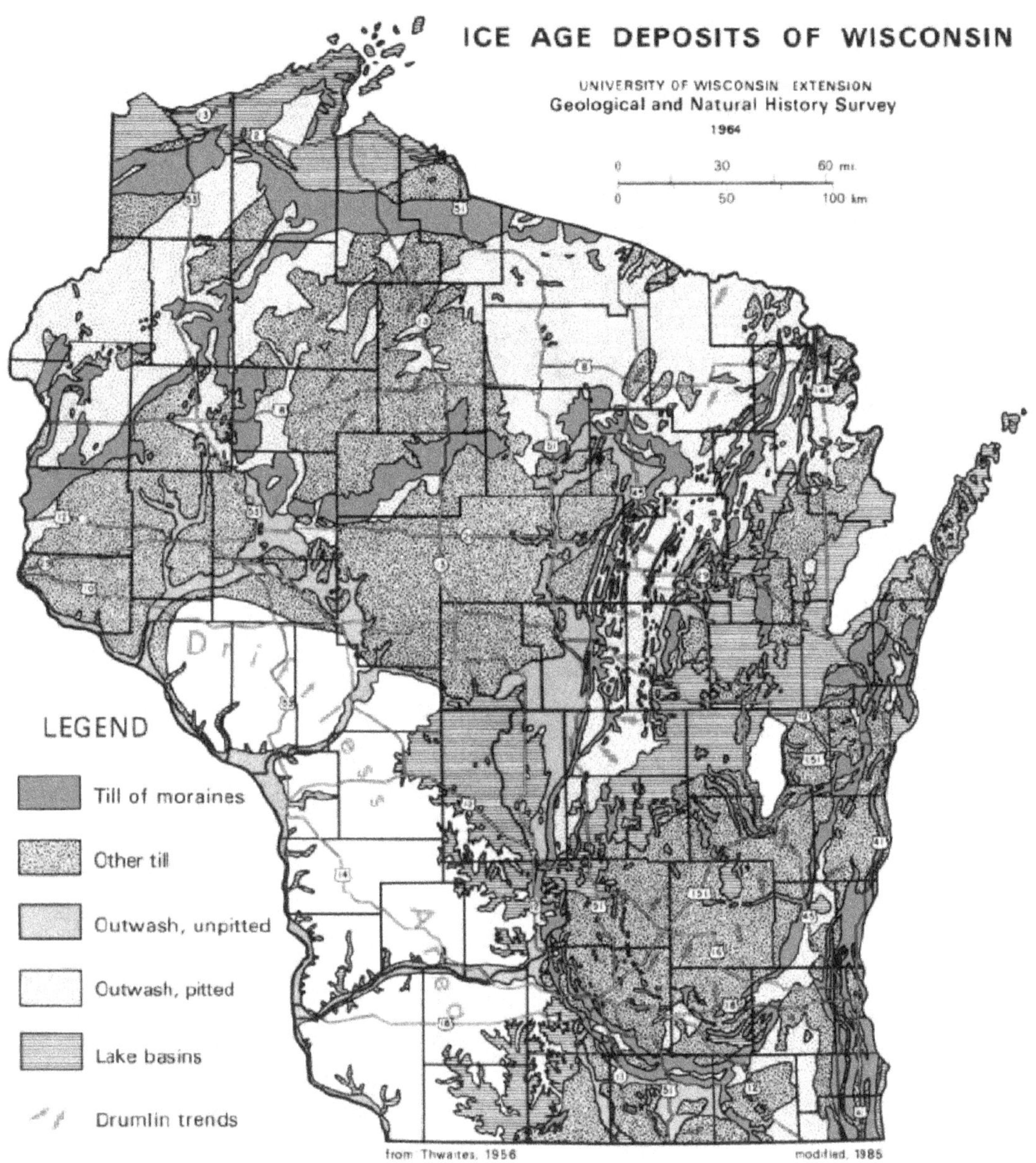

District Resources

Wetlands

Wetlands are lands where saturation with water is the dominant factor determining the nature of soil development and the types of plant and animal communities living in the soil and on its surface (Cowardin et al. 1979). It is estimated that the contiguous United States contained 221 million acres of wetlands just 200 years ago (Dahl 1990). By the mid-1970s, only 46 percent of the original acreage remained (Tiner 1984). Wetlands now cover about 5 percent of the landscape of the lower 48 states.

Wetlands are important to both migratory and resident wildlife. They serve as breeding and nesting habitat for migratory birds and as wintering habitat for many species of resident wildlife.

Figure 8: Wisconsin Groundwater Contamination Susceptitiblity Model

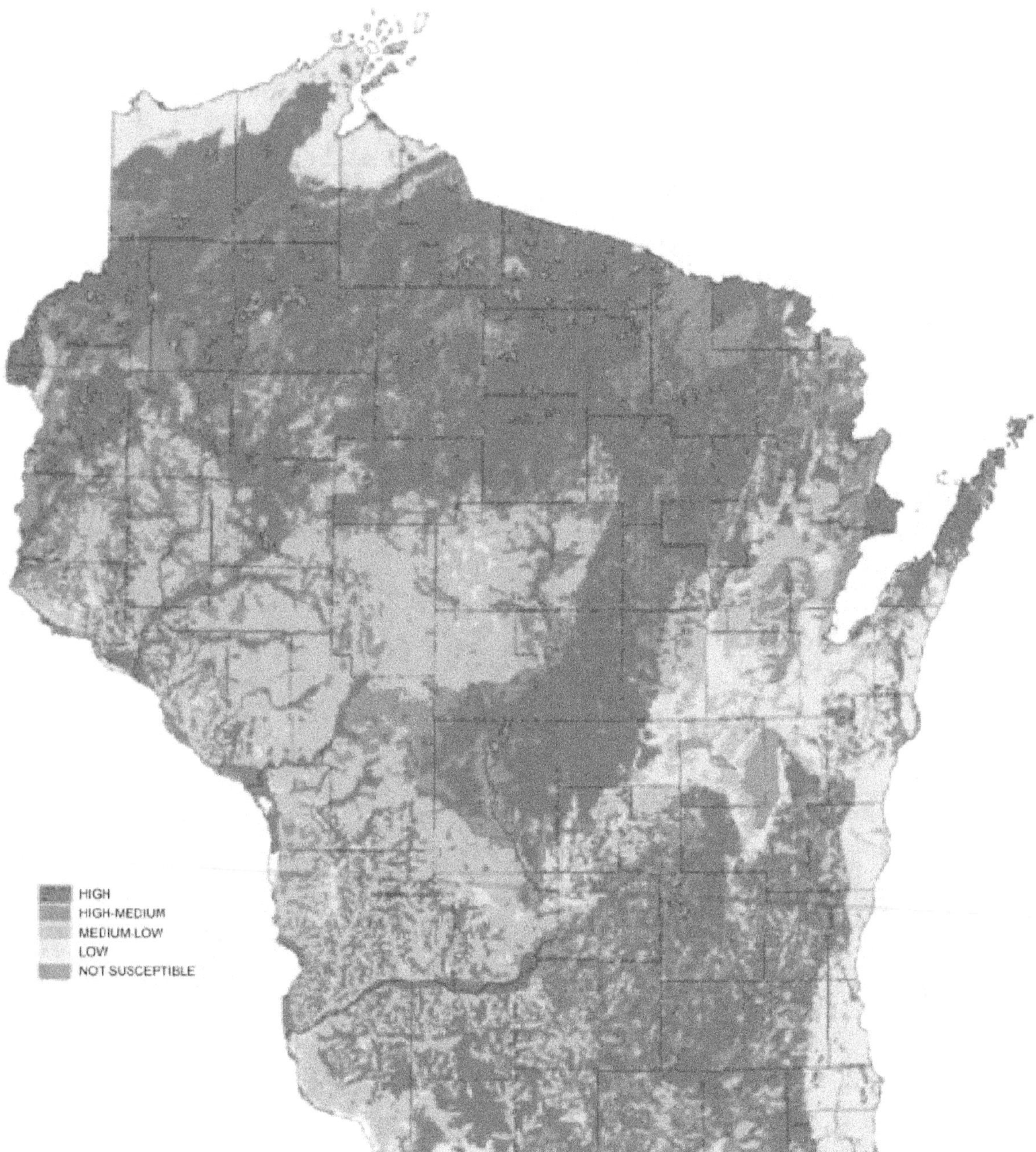

Humans also benefit from wetlands as these habitats improve water quality and quantity, reduce flooding effects, and provide areas for recreation.

Wetlands are classified using a number of attributes including vegetation, water regimes (the length of time water occupies a specific area), and water chemistry. District wetlands are classified using the following water regime descriptions (Cowardin et al. 1979):

- Temporarily flooded-surface water is present for brief periods during the growing season. The water table usually lies below the soil surface most of the season, so plants that grow in both uplands and wetlands are characteristic.
- Seasonally flooded-surface water is present for extended periods especially early in the growing season, but is absent by the end of the season in most years. When surface water is absent, the water table is often near the surface.
- Semipermanently flooded-surface water persists throughout the growing season in most years. When surface water is absent, the water table is usually at or very near the land surface.
- Permanently flooded-water covers the land throughout the year in nearly all years. Vegetation is composed of obligate hydrophytes, such as cattails.

The District has focused on saving and restoring small wetlands. Wetland diversity is important because wetlands change continuously; a single wetland can not be maximally productive all the time. Waterfowl use different types of wetlands at different times during the breeding season. Laying hens may forage in ephemeral, temporary, and seasonal wetlands early in the season and shift to semi-permanent and permanent wetlands after the brood is hatched. Marsh birds need a variety of wetlands in close proximity so they can shift from one wetland to another as the wetlands cycle through different phases. Wetland complexes include a variety of basins, some shallow and some deep, in close proximity. Diverse wetland complexes are rare today because most shallow ephemeral, temporary, and seasonal basins have been drained.

Freshwater wetlands like those in the District are among the most productive in the world (Weller 1982). The dynamic water cycle creates a rich environment for many waterfowl and other marsh birds. Cycling water accelerates decomposition of marsh vegetation, resulting in a natural fertilizer. When the basins recharge in the spring, the water becomes a soup of nutrients and supports a diverse and healthy population of aquatic invertebrates, which feed reproducing waterfowl and marsh birds throughout the spring and summer. In the larger basins, the vegetation changes from densely closed cattail or bullrush to completely open over a period

Table 4: Wetland Acres by Type, Leopold Wetland Management District

Wetland Feature	Cowardin Classification	Acres
River	R	14.3
Stock Pond	PUBF	5.6
Wetland Type I	Seasonally-flooded basin (PEMA)	12.7
Wetland Type II	Inland fresh meadow (PEMB)	1,732.2
Wetland Type III	Inland shallow fresh marsh (PEMC)	1,765.1
Wetland Type IV	Inland deep fresh marsh (PEMC)	990.1
Wetland Type V	Inland open fresh marsh (PEMH)	25.4
Wetland Type VI	Shrub swamp (PSSA)	359.3
Wetland TypeVII	Wooded swamp (PFOB)	360.3
	Total Wetland Acres	5,265.1

of years. In the process of transition, the cover vegetation moves through a phase, known as hemi-marsh, when clumps of emergent vegetation are interspersed with open water (Weller 1982). In this phase, the structure of the vegetation itself creates habitat and stimulates the production of aquatic invertebrates. The marsh, in this phase, hosts the maximum number of marsh birds. Unfortunately, the phase is only temporary and most wetlands cycle out of it in 1 to 3 years.

Wetlands within the District occur in a diverse distribution of sizes, types, locations, and associations. Table 4 displays the amount of wetland acres by type within the District. This data is likely skewed against Type I wetlands because of their ephemeral nature. Additionally many Type VI wetlands have converted from Type II sedge meadows as a result of drainage and the exclusion of fire.

Plant Communities

Plant Communities Associated With Wetlands

Wetlands throughout the District provide both resting cover and food resources for migratory birds. Substantial emergent and submergent aquatic vegetation occurs in freshwater wetlands. Sago pondweed, coontail, and duckweed occur in the deeper, more permanently flooded zones, while cattail, bulrush, burreed, and smartweed grow in shallow areas that may go dry during some periods.

Most palustrine basins exhibit concentric zones of vegetation that are dominated by different plant species (Kantrud et al. 1989). The terms commonly used in reference to these zones are, in decreasing order of water permanency are: deep marsh, shallow marsh, and wet meadow. The water regime in a deep marsh zone is usually semipermanent. Dominant plants include cattail, bulrush, submergent or floating plants, and submergent vascular plants, but this zone also may be devoid of vegetation if bottom sediments are unconsolidated. Shallow marsh zones are usually dominated by emergent grasses, sedges, and some forbs, but submergent or floating vascular plants also may occur. Wet meadow zones also are typically dominated by grasses, rushes, and sedges, whereas submergent or floating plants are absent.

Becker WPA in Columbia County, part of Leopold WMD. USFWS photo.

A variety of wildlife species, from ducks to rails to songbirds, use this community. Common breeding bird species include: Mallard, Blue-wing Teal, Wood Duck, Canada Geese, Sora Rail, Virginia Rail, Sandhill Crane, American Bittern, Least Bittern, Red-winged Blackbird, Yellow-headed Blackbird, Marsh Wren.

Species present during the fall migration include: Scaup, Ring-necked Duck, Widgeon, Tundra Swan, Greater Yellowlegs, Lesser Yellowlegs, Solitary Sandpiper, Pectoral Sandpiper, Least Sandpiper, Semipalmated Sandpipers.

Herptile species such as Blanchard's cricket frog, Blanding's turtle, Butler's garter snake, pickerel frog, and four-toed salamander are a few of the species of concern in Wisconsin associated with the various wetland types. Several mammal species of concern, primarily bat species such as eastern red, hoary, silver-haired, and northern long-eared bats are highly associated with District wetlands.

Plant Communities Associated With Uplands

Upland vegetation is essential to provide nesting habitat for migratory and resident bird species. Upland habitats also provide necessary habitat requirements for resident wildlife throughout the year. The District currently uses a variety of management techniques to maintain and enhance upland habitat conditions including prescribed fire, native grass seeding, tree cutting, and invasive species management.

Grasslands

Past habitat management emphasized the establishment of warm-season native grasses to provide dense nesting cover for waterfowl. Several areas on the District were planted to monotypic stands of switchgrass. These fields initially provided good cover for nesting birds; however, they lacked species composition and structural diversity. The District has begun restoring grasslands to a relatively diverse mixture of native grasses and forbs. The native grass restoration process generally involves seeding directly into or onto croplands that have come out of production as a result of WPA acquisition or cropping idle/cool-season grass fields for 3 or

Table 5: Grassland Features, Leopold Wetland Management District

Grassland Feature	Min. Acres	Max. Acres	Ave. Acres	Total Acres
Grass Introduced	0.048	49.057	5.1237	809.6
Grass Native Prairie	0.382	11.562	2.9821	47.7
Grass Seeded Cool	1.771	53.243	13.5318	622.5
Grass Seeded Warm	0.394	95.462	16.4	3,394.8
		Total Grassland Acreage		4,874.5

more years to eliminate exotic cool-season grass seeds and rhizomes, control Canada thistle and other invasive plants, and prepare a seed bed for planting native grass seed.

Some uplands in the District were historically comprised of cool-and warm-season grasses characteristic of the tall-grass prairie. Vegetation composition at local levels was determined by numerous interrelated factors, including elevation, topography, climate, soil characteristics, herbivory, and fire. Species typical of the historical mixed-grass prairie include big bluestem, little bluestem, Indian grass, porcupine grass, prairie dropseed, and switchgrass, prairie docks, lead plant, heath and smooth asters, sand coreopsis, prairie sunflower, flowering spurge, beebalm, prairie coneflower, and spiderwort.

The District has been planting native grasses and forbs as former croplands are converted to more favorable wildlife habitat. The District has approximately 4,900 acres of grassland in block sizes that range from less than 1 acre to just over 230 acres (Table 5).

Bird species that benefit from the District's grasslands include Bobolink, Dickcissel, Eastern and Western Meadowlark, Northern Harrier, Henslow's Sparrow, Upland Sandpiper, and Sedge Wren. Reptiles and amphibians of concern in Wisconsin including boreal chorus frog, Butler's garter snake, eastern massasauga rattlesnake, bull snake, Blanding's turtle, ornate box turtle, and western slender glass lizard are highly associated with the various grassland community types. Least shrew, prairie vole, badger, and western harvest mouse are just a few mammal species of conservation concern in Wisconsin which are commonly associated with grasslands.

Shrub-Scrub

This community is often found in bands around the margins of wetlands, lakes, floodplains, and glacial lakebeds. Historically shrub wetlands occurred throughout southern Wisconsin and were an integral part of prairie/savanna landscapes. Drainage for the conversion to cropland or marsh hay production likely had a negative impact on the total acreage. However, the elimination of fire from the landscape permitted the succession of many acres from sedge meadow/wet prairie type communities to shrub/scrub habitats.

Shrub/scrub communities in the District are primarily limited shrub wetland or shrub carr wetlands. Dominant plant species include red osier and silky dogwood, meadowsweet and various willows. Canada bluejoint and reed canarygrass are common grass species.

Some of the bird species of concern in Wisconsin that benefit from this community type are American Woodcock, Bell's Vireo, Willow Flycatcher, and Black-billed Cuckoo. Shrub/scrub wetlands also provide preferred habitat for several reptiles and amphibians of concern in the state including Butler's garter snake, eastern massasauga rattlesnake, four-toed salamander, queen snake, western ribbon snake, and wood turtle.

Forests

Forest communities most often associated with District WPAs are southern dry and dry-mesic woodlands dominated by oaks with basswood, sugar and red maples, shagbark hickory, and black cherry. An understory shrub layer of brambles (*Rubus spp.*), gray dogwood and hazelnut are often associated with these forest types. Most of these are small farmland woodlots, and remnants of larger woodland ecosystems. Oak savanna with less than 50 percent canopy coverage of oak species (burr, white, and black) and a herbaceous layer similar to that of the prairies, and oak woodlands, considered an intermediary between the oak savanna and oak forest, were historically significant components of the forest community types that existed throughout much of southern Wisconsin. Fire suppression and conversion to agriculture have all but eliminated these forest types from the landscape. Sugar maple is the dominant species on mesic forest sites with basswood and, near Lake Michigan, beech potentially co-dominant. Another common forest type that occurs is the floodplain forest community. These are forested wetlands along the floodplains of large rivers and may include silver maple, river birch, green and black ash, hackberry, swamp white oak, and cottonwood. Wood nettle, stinging nettle, sedges (*Carex grayii, C. lupulina, C. hystericina, and C. tuckermanii*), native grasses (*Cinna arundinacea, Elymus villosus, and Leersia virginica*), ostrich fern and green-headed coneflower are important understory herbs, and lianas such as Virginia creepers, grapes, Canada moonseed, and poison-ivy are often common.

Several bird species of concern are highly associated with these forested community types including Red-headed Woodpecker, Whip-poor-will, Wood Thrush, Acadian Flycatcher, and Cerulean Warbler. Ornate box turtle, black rat snake, and wood turtle are examples of herptile species of concern that are also considered highly associated with these forests. Bat species such the eastern red, hoary, silver-haired, and northern long-eared along with the woodland vole and the northern flying squirrel, are highly associated with District woodlands.

Shrubs and Trees in Fencerows

Some WPAs contain old fencerows that are remnants from previous land owners. The fencerows contain shrubs and trees that are beneficial for some wildlife and are, generally, a detriment to grassland bird species. Fencelines in areas of intensive agriculture may provide important habitat, travel corridors, and refugia for some species. However, in grassland ecosystems, these same features function as linear woody edges and are sources for invasive species, provide predator roosts and travel corridors, attract nest predators and parasites, and decrease the value of associated grasslands. As a result, attempts are generally made to remove remnant treelines/fencelines separating grassland fields.

Becker Savanna, part of Leopold WMD. USFWS photo.

Fish and Wildlife Communities

The variety of vegetative communities on the District provides habitat for both wetland and upland associated wildlife, such as ducks, herons, songbirds, deer, and turkey. The District also hosts furbearers, marsh birds, raptors, and a variety of woodland mammals, in addition to amphibians and reptiles. The majority of wetlands are too shallow to be fish habitat.

Birds

The District encompasses a broad range of habitats over a large geographic area. A bird species list of WPAs along the Southern Lake Michigan Coastal area would likely contain a number species not found on lands in the Southeastern Glacial Plains. As a result the District has not completed a definitive bird species list. The Wisconsin Society for Ornithology (WSO) Annotated Checklist for the state includes 426 valid species found in Wisconsin over the past 160 years. From this list the WSO has developed a field checklist of 345 species of regular to casual occurrence. The Horicon Marsh Bird Club has developed an even more refined checklist of 249 species (Appendix C). Because of the similarity in habitats and management this has been adopted as the checklist for District WPAs. A few of the most commonly identified species are listed in Table 6.

Three properties managed by the District, Robbins Shorebird WPA, Uihlein WPA, and Vienna WPA, are not only productive waterfowl areas but are also considered some of the best shorebird viewing areas in the state.

Table 6: Most Common Bird Species, Leopold WMD [1]

Pied-billed Grebe	Eastern Kingbird	**Western Meadowlark**
American Bittern	Red-eyed Vireo	Brewers Blackbird
Great Blue Heron	Blue Jay	Common Grackle
Green Heron	American Crow	Brown-headed Cowbird
Canada Goose	Tree Swallow	American Goldfinch
Wood Duck	Barn Swallow	House Sparrow
Mallard	Black-capped Chickadee	**Blue-winged Teal**
White-breasted Nuthatch	**Northern Harrier**	Sedge Wren
Red-tailed Hawk	Marsh Wren	American Kestrel
Eastern Bluebird	Ring-necked Pheasant	American Robin
Wild Turkey	Gray Catbird	Virginia Rail
Tennessee Warbler	Sora	Nashville Warbler
American Coot	Yellow Warbler	Sandhill Crane
Magnolia Warbler	Killdeer	Yellow-rumped Warbler
Greater Yellowlegs	Black-throated Green Warbler	Lesser Yellowlegs
Palm Warbler	Wilson's Snipe	Black-and-white Warbler
American Woodcock	American Tree Sparrow	Ring-billed Gull
Savannah Sparrow	Herring Gull	Fox Sparrow
Mourning Dove	Song Sparrow	Great Horned Owl
Swamp Sparrow	Barred Owl	White-throated Sparrow
Belted Kingfisher	Dark-eyed Junco	Downy Woodpecker
Northern Cardinal	Hairy Woodpecker	Rose-breasted Grosbeak
Northern Flicker	**Dickcissel**	Eastern Wood-Pewee
Bobolink	Least Flycatcher	Red-winged Blackbird
Eastern Phoebe	**Eastern Meadowlark**	

1. Species in bold are listed as USFWS Region 3 Species of Concern

The Robbins Shorebird WPA, named for renowned Wisconsin ornithologist Sam Robbins, is in an area regarded as one of Wisconsin's best inland shorebird viewing areas. Known to Wisconsin birders as the "AW Ponds" this area supports over 20 migrating shorebird species including all plovers, Red Knot, White-rumped Sandpiper, Baird's Sandpiper, Stilt Sandpiper, Western Sandpiper, Buff-breasted Sandpiper, Ruff, Dowitcher and godwits, and Wilson's and Red-necked Phalaropes.

Uihlein WPA in Winnebago County is another locally significant shorebird location (4,000-20,000 birds annually). Species such as Greater Yellowlegs, Lesser Yellowlegs, Solitary Sandpiper, Dunlin, Short-billed Dowitcher, Wilson's snipe, American Woodcock, and Wilson's Phalarope commonly stop over at this site.

Vienna WPA in northern Dane County lies in an area commonly referred as the "Highway V Ponds Area." While this area is considered a minor site (500-4,000 birds annually) the proximity to Madison makes the area a prime birding destination.

Mammals

The District has not completed extensive mammal inventories on the WPAs. A checklist of mammals in Wisconsin can be found in Appendix C. A brief list of species likely to occur on WPAs, although they have not all been confirmed, is shown in Table 7.

Amphibians and Reptiles

The District has not completed extensive herptile inventories on the WPAs. A checklist of amphibians and reptiles of Wisconsin can be found in Appendix C. A brief list of species likely to occur on WPAs, although they have not all been confirmed, is shown in Table 8.

Invertebrates

No formalized invertebrate sampling has been conducted on the WPAs. Freshwater invertebrates are important waterfowl food, but no studies have been done to determine the species present.

Threatened and Endangered Species

The District coordinates Eastern prairie fringed orchid management and monitoring activities on the Uihlein WPA. The success of this project is primarily due to the efforts of the Partners for Plants volunteers (a subgroup of the Garden Club of America), Wisconsin Department of Agriculture, Trade, and Consumer Protection, and the U.S. Fish & Wildlife Service Green Bay Ecological Services. This 10-year project has monitored the plant population on the WPA and its relationship to habitat management and water conditions.

Wilcox WPA in Waushara County hosts a population of Karner blue butterfly as a result of a lupine planting established as a seed source. The District is in consultation with Ecological Resources office in Green Bay to mitigate potential issues, per the Karner blue butterfly Wisconsin Habitat Conservation Plan, with take as a result of habitat management and seed harvest activities.

In recent years, reintroduced Whooping Cranes have been identified on Anderson WPA in Columbia County and Uihlein WPA in Winnebago County. The birds have been using the wetlands on these properties for roosting and feeding and no nesting activity has taken place on these properties as of yet.

Prairie fringed orchid. USFWS photo.

Several Wisconsin state listed species and species of concern either have the potential to be found on, or are documented as using, WPAs throughout the District. A list of state species of concern, threatened and endangered species can be found in Appendix D.

Threats to Resources

Invasive Species

Three categories of undesirable species (invasive, exotic, and noxious) are found within the District. Invasive species are those that cause or are likely to cause economic or environmental harm or harm to human health. Executive Order 13112 requires the District to monitor, prevent, and control the presence of invasive species. Exotic species are species that are not native to a particular ecosystem. Service policy directs the District to try to maintain habitats free of exotic species. Noxious weeds are designated by the U.S. Department of Agriculture or the Wisconsin Department of Agriculture as spe-

Table 7: Mammal Species Likely to Occur on Leopold WMD

Virginia Opossum	Long-tailed Weasel	Woodland Vole
Northern Short-tailed Shrew	Mink	White-footed Mouse
Masked Shrew	Badger	Deer Mouse
Pigmy Shrew	Stripped Skunk	Muskrat
Eastern Mole	Least Chipmunk	S. Bog Lemming
Star-nosed Mole	Eastern Chipmunk	House Mouse
Big Brown Bat	Woodchuck	Brown Rat
Little Brown Bat	Franklin's Ground Squirrel	White-tailed Deer
Keen's Myotis	Thirteen-lined Ground Squirrel	Eastern Cottontail
Red Bat	Eastern Gray Squirrel	Hoary Bat
Eastern Fox Squirrel	Silver-haired Bat	Red Squirrel
Coyote	Southern Flying Squirrel	Red Fox
American Beaver	Gray Fox	Southern Red-backed Vole
Raccoon	Prairie Vole	Northern River Otter
Meadow Vole		

Table 8: Amphibian and Reptile Species Likely to Occur on Leopold WMD

Central Newt	Common Snapping Turtle	Blue-spotted Salamander
Common Musk Turtle	Spotted Salamander	Blanding's Turtle
Tiger Salamander	Western Painted Turtle	Mudpuppy
Midland Painted Turtle	Eastern American Toad	Eastern Spiny Softshell Turtle
Chorus Frog	Eastern Hognose Snake	Spring Peeper
Smooth Green Snake	Cope's Gray Treefrog	Western Fox Snake
Gray Treefrog	Eastern Milk Snake	Bull Frog
Common Garter Snake	Green Frog	DeKay's Brown Snake
Northern Leopard Frog	Northern Red-bellied Snake	Wood Frog
Northern Water Snake		

cies which, when established, are destructive, competitive or difficult to control. Canada thistle and field bindweed (creeping Jenny), and leafy spurge are introduced species classified as noxious weeds in Wisconsin. Purple loosestrife and multiflora rose are introduced species classified as nuisance weeds.

Invasive, exotic and noxious weed species are relatively abundant within the District. These species are quite diverse and are found in most District habitats, although some are typically found in agricultural fields or lakes and ponds. Currently, most District control efforts focus on Canada thistle (*Cirsium averense*), spotted knapweed (*Centaurea mac-*

ulosa), purple loosestrife (*Lythrum salicaria*), black locust (*Robinia pseudoacacia*), and box elder (*Acer negundo*). The principal invasive and exotic plant species within the District are non-native buckthorns, honeysuckles, black locust, multiflora rose, garlic mustard, spotted knapweed, Canada thistle, crown vetch, teasels, leafy spurge, birds-foot trefoil, purple loosestrife, sweet clovers, wild parsnip, Japanese knotweed, reed canary grass, phragmities, and hybrid cattail. Exotic and invasive plant species pose one of the greatest threats to the maintenance and restoration of the diverse habitats found on WPAs. They threaten biological diversity by causing population declines of native species and by altering key ecosystem processes like hydrology, nitrogen fixation, and fire regimes. Left unchecked, these plants have come to dominate areas on some WPAs and reduced the value of the land as wildlife habitat. There is a bountiful seed source of many of these exotic/invasive species on the lands surrounding the WPAs, thus in order to be effective in our management plans, we must bring together a complex set of interests including private landowner, commercial, and public agencies.

Purple loosestrife. USFWS photo.

Drainage and Pesticides

Waterfowl Production Areas are often islands in a sea of intensive agriculture. Natural drainage patterns have been altered throughout the landscape, increasing the frequency, intensity, and duration of water flowing into many units. Siltation, nutrient loading, and contamination from point and non-point sources of pollution are a serious problem on many WPAs. Waterfowl Production Areas are also threatened by farming, trespass, dumping, wildfires, and pesticide applications on adjacent agricultural land. A study in Ontario examined the effects of habitat and agricultural practices on birds breeding on farmland and determined that the most important variable decreasing total bird species abundance was pesticide use (Freemark and Csizy 1993).

Recent changes in agriculture have accelerated the impact of pesticides on surrounding land. Genetically altered Round-up ready corn and soybeans have expanded the window of opportunity for pesticide applications and promises to kill everything green on fields except the genetically altered crops. Another altered crop, Bt. Corn, contains a genetically engineered insecticide.

Research has shown that insecticides commonly used for sunflowers, soybeans and corn can kill wildlife directly and indirectly (e.g. by decreasing the amount of food available to ducks). For example, ducks feed on grain much of the year but in the spring they shift to aquatic invertebrates (insect larvae, amphipods, snails, etc.) and depend on this food source for reproduction and survival. Even when pesticide applications are done carefully and wetlands are avoided, the chemicals can drift into wetlands in measurable amounts and kill aquatic invertebrates (Tome et al. 1991 and Grue et al. 1986).

Insecticides have a direct effect by killing aquatic invertebrates, but herbicides may have an indirect effect on food available to waterfowl. The Service conducted a study of the impact of agricultural chemicals on selected wetlands in four Wetland Management Districts (Ensor and Smith, 1994). Herbicides from surrounding agricultural land enter wetlands and disrupt the functional interaction between vegetation structure and aquatic invertebrate life. The changing dynamic reduces food available to breeding waterfowl.

Seasonal and semi-permanent wetlands (the majority of WPA wetlands) are the most exposed to agricultural chemicals. These wetlands are small and interspersed with croplands, which increases the probability of pesticides from over-spray and aerial drift. Most herbicides and insecticides are applied to crops in the spring and early summer, coincident with maximum runoff and waterfowl breeding. Ensor and Smith (1994) write:

"A result of our survey... indicates that prairie pothole wetlands may involve interactions of multiple herbicides (and potentially insecticides) comprising chemical "soups" unique to individual wetlands."

This study showed that "typical agricultural use" of pesticides on surrounding land had a significant impact in reducing the biological quality of WPA wetlands.

Rural Development

Rural development may threaten District lands in counties with growing populations. Lands adjoining WPAs are often seen as highly desirable rural building lots that are purchased as small hobby farms or rural home sites. This can result in the WPA being "ringed" by homes, with a series of negative impacts on the WPA. In addition to the fragmentation of habitat, such development may limit the use of prescribed fire; increase trespass on District lands by neighbors using ATVs, horses, or vehicles; increase harassment of wildlife from cats and dogs; increase use of District land by neighbors for illegal uses such as dumping, gardening, and equipment storage; and can place hunters and neighbors at odds over concerns about safety during the hunting seasons. Large-scale rural development may also bring threats from noise and storm water runoff.

Administrative Facilities

The Service is responsible for maintaining the District headquarters building and maintenance buildings. The headquarters is located on the Baraboo River WPA about 2 miles west of Portage. The headquarters building consists primarily of office space for the District, Fire, and Private Lands Programs. In addition to District staff, the Headquarters also houses a Zone Fire Management Officer and a Wildland Urban Interface Coordinator who are supervised from the Regional Office and have multi-state responsibilities for fire management. The building is a modified residential house which has 2,100 square feet and was built in the mid-1900s. There is also a 3,000-square-foot heated storage building, 3,000-square-foot storage shed, and a 900-square-foot seed storage and processing building.

The District also maintains storage facilities at the Uihlein and Schwengel WPAs.

Cultural Resources and Historic Preservation

Cultural resources are important parts of the Nation's heritage. The Service is committed to protecting valuable evidence of human interactions with each other and the landscape. Protection is accomplished in conjunction with the Service's mandate to protect fish, wildlife, and plant resources. Responding to the requirement in the National Wildlife Refuge System Improvement Act of 1997 that comprehensive conservation plans include "the archaeological and cultural values of the planning unit," the Service contracted for an archeological and historic resources study of the Leopold and St. Croix Wetland Management Districts. The St. Croix WMD is located in northwestern Wisconsin, and the report combines the information for both Districts. The study report was submitted in 2003.

Egan-Bruhy (2003) reports:

"Wisconsin has a rich and complex history of 11,500 years of change. Through time, populations adapted to the unique and changing environmental setting of the region. The archeological and historical records reflect alterations in the economy, belief systems, social organization, cultural composition, and lifeways of the people of what is now the state of Wisconsin."

"The archeological data ... provides information regarding the probability of identifying prehistoric sites in association with specific environmental attributes. An association between site location and types of water bodies, soils, and elevations was established for several of the prehistoric time periods. The analysis also indicates that there is a relatively high probability of encountering historic archaeological sites ... particularly proximate to transportation routes and along section lines....".

The Leopold and Saint Croix WMDs cover 30 counties in Wisconsin. Consequently they are likely to contain archeological sites from all of the cultural periods found in Wisconsin: PaleoIndian, Archaic, Woodland, Mississippian, Oneota, and Western (French, British, and United States) cultures. (See Chapter 3 of the Egan-Bruhy report for a more complete discussion of cultural resources on the Districts.) In addition, Indian tribes may identify sacred sites and traditional cultural properties on WPAs, and the Districts may acquire buildings and other structures of historical importance. However, as of 2006, the Service has no record of extant sacred sites, traditional cultural properties, and historic buildings and structures on any WPA.

Just 118 acres of District land have been subjected to an archeological survey. From those surveys and other sources, 89 cultural resources sites are reported on the Districts. The potential, therefore, is high for finding many more cultural resources sites.

A review of the National and/or State Registers of Historic Places by Egan-Bruhy (2003) showed the 17 counties of the District contained 54 historic/architectural properties. The places include houses, millsites, farmsteads, bridges, and churches among other properties. There are 20 National Historic Landmark properties within the District, and one property – Aldo Leopold Shack and Farm – that is proposed for designation. At this time no sites on waterfowl production areas have been nominated or placed on the National Register of Historic Places, although all sites are considered eligible until determined not eligible through the Section 106 process.

The following listed Indian tribes have been recognized by the Federal government or self-identified by the tribe as having a potential concern for traditional cultural resources, sacred sites, and cultural hunting and gathering areas in Wisconsin.

- Bad River Band of the Lake Superior Tribe of Chippewa Indians of the Bad River Reservation, Wisconsin
- Bois Forte Band (Nett Lake) of the Minnesota Chippewa Tribe, Minnesota
- Citizen Potawatomi Nation, Oklahoma
- Flandreau Santee Sioux Tribe of South Dakota
- Fond du Lac Band of the Minnesota Chippewa Tribe, Minnesota
- Forest County Potawatomi Community, Wisconsin
- Grand Portage Band of the Minnesota Chippewa Tribe, Minnesota
- Hannahville Indian Community, Michigan
- Ho-Chunk Nation of Wisconsin
- Iowa Tribe of Kansas
- Keweenaw Bay Indian Community, Michigan
- Lac Courte Oreilles Band of Lake Superior Chippewa Indians of Wisconsin
- Lac du Flambeau Band of Lake Superior Chippewa Indians of the Lac du Flambeau Reservation of Wisconsin
- Lac Vieux Desert Band of Lake Superior Chippewa Indians, Michigan
- Leech Lake Band of the Minnesota Chippewa Tribe, Minnesota
- Lower Sioux Indian Community in the State of Minnesota
- Menominee Indian Tribe of Wisconsin
- Mille Lacs Band of the Minnesota Chippewa Tribe, Minnesota
- Minnesota Chippewa Tribe, Minnesota
- Nottawaseppi Huron Band
- Oneida Tribe of Indians of Wisconsin
- Peoria Indian Tribe
- Pokagon Band of Potawatomi
- Prairie Band of Potawatomi Nation, Kansas
- Prairie Island Indian Community in the State of Minnesota
- Red Cliff Band of Lake Superior Chippewa Indians of Wisconsin
- Sac & Fox Nation of Missouri in Kansas and Nebraska
- Sac & Fox Nation, Oklahoma
- Sac & Fox Tribe of the Mississippi in Iowa
- Santee Sioux Nation, Nebraska
- Sisseton-Wahpeton Oyate of the Lake Traverse Reservation, South Dakota
- Sokaogon Chippewa Community, Wisconsin
- Spirit Lake Tribe, North Dakota
- St. Croix Chippewa Indians of Wisconsin
- Stockbridge Munsee Community, Wisconsin
- Upper Sioux Community, Minnesota
- White Earth Band of Minnesota Chippewa Tribe, Minnesota
- Winnebago Tribe of Nebraska

Although Indian tribes are generally understood to have concerns about traditional cultural properties, other groups such as church congregations, civic groups, and county historical societies could have similar concerns.

Museums and Repositories

The Districts have museum property. Archeological collections are not stored on-site, but 526 artifacts from four collections are stored in non-Federal repositories. Artifacts are owned by the Federal Government and can be recalled by the RHPO at any time. The Districts have no other types of museum property such as artwork, historical objects or documents (including photographs), nor natural resources collections. They have no scope of collections statement.

Cultural resources are important parts of the Nation's heritage. The Service is committed to protecting valuable evidence of human interactions with each other and the landscape. Protection is accomplished in conjunction with the Service's mandate to protect fish, wildlife, and plant resources.

Visitor Services

The Refuge Improvement Act established six priority uses of the Refuge System, which includes the WPAs in the District. These priority uses all depend on the presence of or the expected presence of wildlife, and are thus called wildlife-dependent uses. These uses are hunting, fishing, wildlife observation, photography, environmental education, and interpretation. Although Congress clearly expects managers to facilitate these priority uses, they must be compatible with the purpose for which the WPA was established and the mission of the Refuge System. Compatibility Determinations for the priority uses and numerous other uses in compliance with the Refuge Improvement Act and national compatibility policy and regulations are included as Appendix F of this CCP.

Waterfowl production areas differ from national wildlife refuges in that they are open to hunting, fishing, and trapping by specific regulation, and open to the other wildlife-dependent activities by notification in general brochures available at the District office. New and existing WPAs are thus "open until closed" versus national wildlife refuges, which are "closed until opened." Within the Leopold WMD, the Blue-wing WPA in Ozaukee County and Wilcox WPA in Waushara County are closed to hunting. These WPAs are closed to hunting either because there are concerns for the safety of nearby neighbors or because it was a condition of sale stipulated by previous owner.

Environmental education at Leopold WMD. USFWS photo.

Hunters and hunting have a long and linked history with WPAs. When Congress amended the Migratory Bird Hunting and Conservation Stamp Tax Act (Duck Stamp Act) in 1958, it authorized the acquisition of wetlands and uplands as WPAs and waived the usual "inviolate sanctuary" provisions for new migratory bird units. Thus, WPAs were intended to be open to waterfowl hunting, in part because waterfowl hunters, through the purchase of Duck Stamps and support for price increases of the stamp, played a major role in acquisition of these areas.

Other District Uses

Wildlife observation, photography, interpretation, and environmental education are encouraged on WPAs and are increasing in popularity with the public. In general, WPAs lack adequate fishing to support sport fishing. In addition to the wildlife-dependent recreational uses, the District occasionally receives requests for various non-wildlife-dependent uses such as dog trials, horseback riding, plant collecting, berry picking, and special events. Also, various economic uses such as haying, grazing, and timber harvest are used as habitat management tools and involve the issuance of special use permits.

The manager must often make decisions about other "uses" including requests for rights-of-way for new or expanded roads, utilities, pipelines, and communications equipment. Generally the District receives a few requests each year for these "uses," although the quantity has been increasing.

Current Management

Habitat Management

Wetland Management

The intention of the District is to restore and manage wetlands on the WPAs. As the District purchases new WPAs or round-outs to existing WPAs, restoring or enhancing wetlands often provides a challenge to securing the necessary funding to complete the work in a timely manner. The District has frequently utilized grant funds from the North American Wetland Conservation Act or donations from conservation organizations to accomplish much of the work on these projects. In addition to wetland restorations on new tracts, restorations are also completed on existing lands whenever possible. Some restoration opportunities are limited due to potential impacts on adjacent properties. This is frequently true when drainage ditches are involved.

Once wetlands are restored, management activities include maintenance of levees and water control structures, water level manipulation through natural flow and pumping, prescribed fire, and control of exotic and invasive plants. In general, the wetlands are managed to mimic natural processes and cycles.

Grasslands

As lands are acquired, uplands are restored with native prairie plantings using Wisconsin ecotype grasses and forbs. Prior to European settlement, fire influenced the structure and function of prairie and savannah in the area that is now the District. Fire was less of a factor in open forests, and even less in closed forests. Now, the natural process of fire has been replaced by fire management that includes suppression and prescribed burning. Fire is essential for proper management of native, warm-season grasses and associated forbs. Prescribed fire stimulates growth of the grasses, increases seed germination and growth of forbs, retards encroachment of woody vegetation, and reduces the fuel load. Tallgrass prairie has been established on several WPAs. Fire will play a significant role in maintaining this habitat type, which benefits grassland bird species. The District's fire program benefits from the expertise of two Regional Office employees that are housed at the District headquarters. A Fire Management Officer and a Wildland Urban Interface Coordinator are readily available for advice and consultation. Other grassland management activities may include conversion of non-native cool-season grassland to native warm-season grasses and forbs, haying, mowing, grazing, and tree and brush removal.

Forests

Most forest management consists of cutting invasive or exotic trees to restore the WPA to grassland or oak savanna. During oak savanna restoration, the native burr and white oaks are not removed. The removal of the understory vegetation and the frequent use of prescribed fire is used to stimulate the growth of the native prairie grasses and forbs. Long-term management of these areas includes periodic prescribed fire combined with occasional mechanical removal of unwanted trees and brush.

Small woodlots also occur on several WPAs, however timber stand improvements have not been conducted.

Cropland

Most cropland acres are retired and converted to native grasslands upon acquisition. Under certain circumstances the previous landowner may be allowed up to 3 years land use under Land Use Reservation (LUR) conditions stipulated in the purchase contract. It is usually specified that the final

A prescribed burn in progress at Leopold WMD. USFWS photo.

Ring-necked Pheasant. USFWS photo.

crop will be soybeans to provide a smooth seedbed and facilitate planting to native grasslands. Cooperative Farming Agreements (CFA) are often utilized in instances when it is desired to convert established cool-season field (usually retired hay or pasture land) to native plantings or when an older, often monotypic switchgrass or non-Wisconsin ecotype grass varieties, have degraded to the point that they need re-seeding. Often the Cooperative Farmer is required to conduct post-planting management of the native grassland (i.e. mowing) for 2 years as compensation to the Service for the harvestable crops.

The District usually has between 100 and 200 acres farmed under LUR or CFA in any given year.

Management of Resident Species

Federal trust species are generally those that cross state and international boundaries or are afforded national protection through various laws and treaties, such as the Migratory Bird Treaty Act and the Endangered Species Act. The well-being of waterfowl populations is a classic Federal trust responsibility and the main purpose for the creation of the Small Wetland Acquisition Program in the 1960s. This does not mean that resident species such as white-tailed deer and pheasants found on WPAs should not receive management attention. Rather it is the degree of management focus, based on the knowledge that management for trust resources like waterfowl will usually benefit the myriad of resident wildlife that share the prairie-wetland landscape.

Local and regional residents, however, may often favor the management for those species like white-tailed deer and pheasant that provide consumptive recreation opportunities. Thus, managers are often faced with requests for food plots, tree and shrub plantings, or direct stockings of game species that may have a negative effect on the primary purpose of waterfowl production and the broader goals of restoring native plant communities. The key is to seek the proper balance between practices focused on trust species and those that can accommodate the public's desire for resident wildlife management. The District currently does not manage for resident wildlife.

Habitat Management: Partners for Fish and Wildlife Program

The Partners for Fish and Wildlife Program is very important for the Leopold Wetland Management District since significant wetland, prairie and oak savanna habitat has been restored in partnership with many conservation organizations and the Wisconsin DNR. Through this program, the Service assists local landowners with restoration of a variety of habitat on their property. Projects in the past several years have included wetland, prairie grassland, oak savanna and riparian restoration projects. Projects range in size from small half-acre basins to 50-acre prairie and oak savanna restoration projects. The District private lands biologists also assist landowners with other agency programs, such as USDA agricultural programs, that provide habitat restoration funding.

Land Acquisition

Funds for land acquisition come from the Migratory Bird Conservation Fund (MBCF) account. The primary source of funds for this account come from the revenue from the sale of the Migratory Bird Hunting and Conservation Stamp, commonly known as the Federal Duck Stamp. The MBCF monies are allocated yearly for the purchase of wetlands that will become waterfowl production areas or national wildlife refuges.

The Leopold WMD is distinguished from most other wetland management districts in a number of ways:

- The District is located on the edge of the prairie rather than in the middle of it.

- The District is adjacent to the metropolitan areas of Madison and Milwaukee.
- In addition to wetland drainage, wetland degradation and loss of upland habitat caused by rural residential development is a significant threat.
- Land values for WPAs are commensurate with metropolitan/suburban land values for development.
- Development around WPAs is accelerating rapidly. A rural residential property owner feels secure that the WPA out his back door will never be sold for development. Therefore, lands adjacent to WPAs are very desirable for rural residential development.

Because of the elements listed above, an acquisition strategy has been developed for the Leopold WMD. The District has identified four focus areas (Figure 9) for priority acquisition based on current management ownership, high waterfowl production potential, and land protection by other conservation agencies/organizations. One area, Fairfield Marsh, has exceptional potential for wetland restoration. These focus project areas are:

- Uihlein WPA, Winnebago County
- Fairfield Marsh WPA, Columbia and Sauk Counties.
- Oakfield Township, Fond du Lac County
- Leeds Township, Columbia County

Additionally, a model based on current land cover, pre-settlement vegetation, and the predicted Mallard distribution model for the Great Lakes developed by Ducks Unlimited is used to identify priority acquisition areas. In the future it would be useful to include average land values and rates of urban development into the model.

Acquisition funding will always be in short supply. Funding levels have been static, which combined with increasing land values, results in fewer acres acquired. Because of land values, acquisition dollars in Wisconsin do not go as far as in the Prairie Pothole Region. And, biologically, the larger the tract of land the healthier the wildlife populations. Therefore, our acquisitions are prioritized as follows:

- Round-outs of existing WPAs.
- New WPAs over 120 acres.
- Wildlife corridors connecting WPAs/State wildlife areas.

Monitoring and Studies

A number of surveys, censuses, studies, and investigations are conducted on the District that help to monitor the status of its wildlife and plant populations. The surveys provide information for management and support state and national conservation efforts. The following paragraphs describe monitoring programs that have been completed or are presently under way and may continue to support management regimes, land acquisition strategies, or research. New studies, investigations and monitoring projects will be evaluated based on priority species and funding and may be conducted by third parties, volunteers, or staff.

Waterfowl Surveys

Waterfowl Breeding Pair Survey

The District has established two zones, east and west, which serve to focus management and biological activities. Although informal surveys have been conducted by District staff in the past, formal pair surveys began in 2005. Surveys were conducted from May 15 to May 31 on a random sample of 20 percent of Type III and Type IV wetlands in the western portion of the District.

Waterfowl Brood Survey

Similar to the Waterfowl Pair Counts noted previously, the District has completed informal brood surveys on and off throughout the years but until 2005 nothing formal had been established. In 2005 the same sample of wetlands used in the pair surveys were sampled between June 21 and July 7 for brood use. Again, the same wetlands used in the Pair Counts in 2007 will be sampled for broods.

Nesting Tunnel/Wood Duck Box Production

The District maintains 27 Delta type Mallard nesting tunnels on nine WPAs and seven Wood Duck boxes on Baraboo River WPA. In general nest success from the nesting tunnels is very high although use remains variable. Some recent research indicates that use can best be increased by locating nesting tunnels in areas that already have sufficient adjacent nesting cover.

Figure 9: Focus Areas, Leopold Wetland Management District

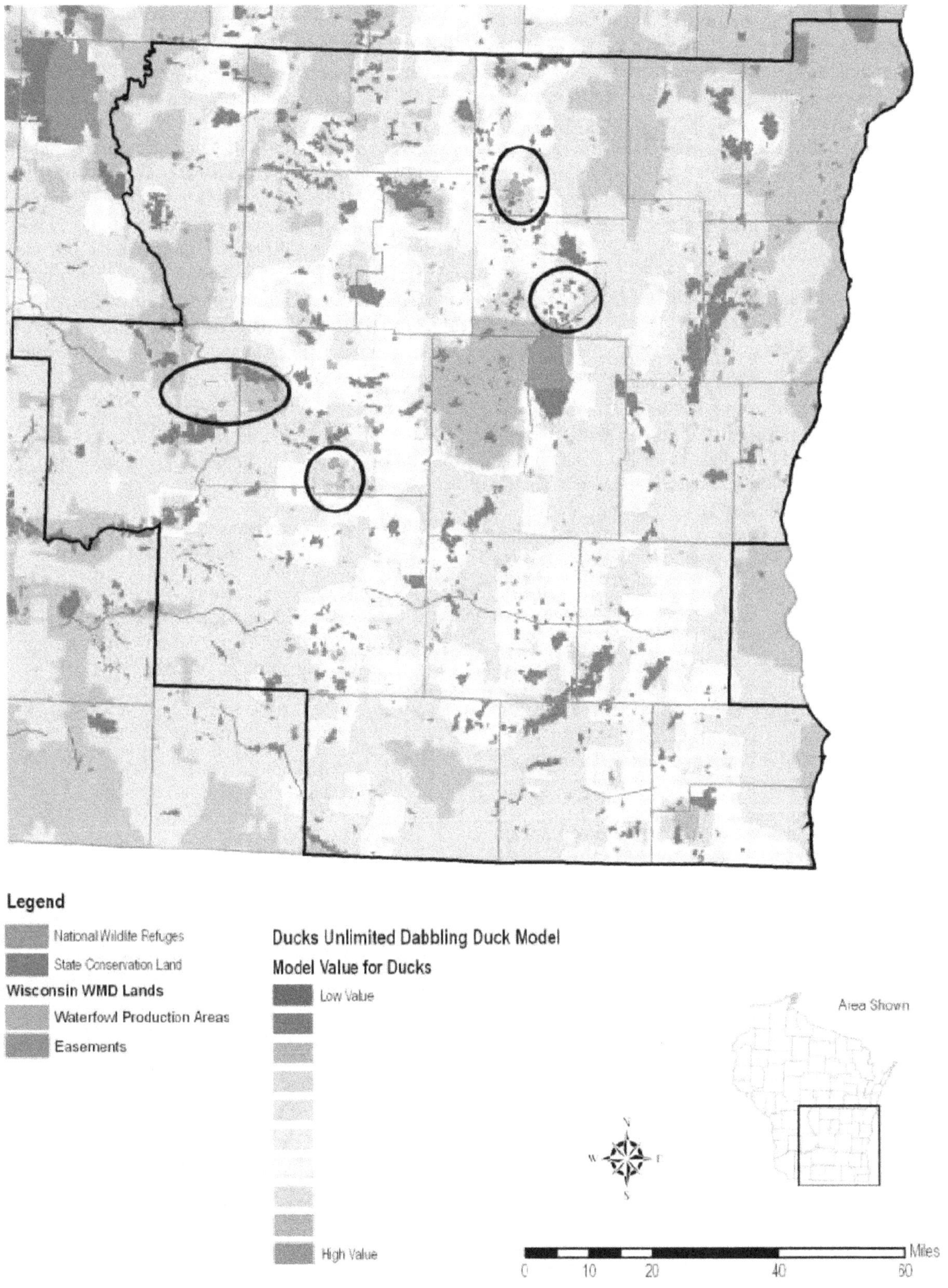

Legend

National Wildlife Refuges
State Conservation Land

Wisconsin WMD Lands

Waterfowl Production Areas
Easements

Ducks Unlimited Dabbling Duck Model

Model Value for Ducks

Low Value
High Value

Area Shown

0 10 20 40 60 Miles

Great Lakes Mallard Study

Conducted by Ducks Unlimited, this study began in 2001 and ran through 2003. The goal was to identify factors limiting the production of Mallards in the Great Lakes region. Research resulted in the development of a Mallard distribution model for the Great Lakes similar to the thunderstorm maps developed for the Prairie Pothole Region and the development of the Great Lakes Habitat Evaluation Network (HEN), which can be used as a tool to identify important areas for waterfowl breeding and the type of conservation action needed in those areas.

Evaluation of Duck Production on Private Lands in Wisconsin

Initiated in 2000 by the Wisconsin DNR, this study is directed at estimating productivity of ducks on the private landscape of southern Wisconsin. Research focuses on Mallards and Blue-winged Teal, the two most abundant breeding duck species in Wisconsin. The objectives are to directly estimate productivity of ducks on the private landscape of southern Wisconsin where wetlands and grasslands have been restored and develop planning tools for management in our state. Specifically:

1. Estimate duck recruitment parameters (habitat preferences for feeding, nesting, and brood rearing, nest success among landcover types, brood and duckling survival, and adult hen survival during the breeding season) to determine if production is adequate to maintain populations.
2. Compare duck recruitment parameters within strata of grassland and wetland abundance to evaluate the importance of habitat restoration to duck production.
3. Develop regression models to estimate the landscape potential for duck breeding pairs from wetland areas in Wisconsin.
4. Develop a map of duck management potential from duck-wetland regressions for state planning.
5. Adapt the Mallard Model to Wisconsin with data collected locally to guide management.

Conservation Planning Tools for spring migration in the Upper Mississippi River/ Great Lakes Region: understanding habitat and nutrient requirements of spring staging waterfowl and shorebirds

This cooperative study involves Ducks Unlimited, Southern Illinois University, and Ohio State University. The objectives of this study are to determine the amount and types of wetland habitat that are required to support the nutritional needs of spring migrant birds in Illinois, Wisconsin, Michigan, Indiana, and Ohio. This research will require an understanding of the current landscape condition, availability of food resources from existing wetlands, and spatial and temporal habitat use patterns during spring migration. To establish habitat objectives, planning will be focused on four key questions:

- How much habitat is needed to support desired waterfowl populations?
- What types of habitats are needed to meet these objectives?
- Where in the Upper Mississippi/Great Lakes watersheds are these habitats needed?
- Are the types, amounts, and locations of habitats needed to support spring-migrating waterfowl sufficient to meet the needs of spring-migrating shorebirds?

Horicon NWR. USFWS photo.

Bobolink. USFWS photo.

By doing so, we will ensure that habitat conservation efforts will provide maximum benefits to waterfowl, shorebirds, wetland dependent passerines, and other wetland dependent wildlife.

The results of this project will provide a planning tool that will allow more accurate and cost-effective determination of habitat priorities for the Upper Mississippi and Great Lakes watersheds. By considering first the extent to which an area is meeting its foraging habitat objectives, second the location of the area in relation to future development or other pressures, and third the amount of unprotected habitat in the area, appropriate wetland conservation and enhancement strategies can be developed.

Non-Game Bird Studies

Breeding Bird Point Counts

Breeding Bird Point Counts on WPAs throughout the District were surveyed from 1995 to 1997 through contract with money provided by Migratory Birds. We attempted to conduct surveys again in 2003 and 2004 however lack of ability to compensate volunteers for travel expenses to and from sites limited the survey to Shoveler Sink WPA in Dane County and Schoenberg Marsh and Rowe WPAs in Columbia County. Point count locations that fit within protocols are relatively easy to establish utilizing GIS and every WPA with large enough blocks of grassland cover has points assigned. To date none of the data has been evaluated.

Marsh Bird Call Back Survey

This survey has been completed once using protocols and compact disk of calls developed by Dr. Courtney Conway. The survey was conducted on Uihlein WPA prior to prolonged drawdown as part of a cattail management study.

Importance of Wet Meadows for Grassland Birds in the Upper Midwest

This study was conducted by Dr. Eileen Kirsch out of the USGS Upper Midwest Environmental Sciences Center in La Crosse from 1999 to 2002. The study was designed to provide information on the effects of habitat management, diversity of vegetation within grasslands, grassland size, and landscape features of the surrounding area on bird abundance and diversity in wet meadows. The study was conducted on several WPAs within the western portion of the District as well as other areas of Wisconsin, Minnesota, and Iowa.

Evaluation of Marsh Bird Demographic Response to Wetland Restoration in the Upper Midwest

Research is being conducted by Dr. John B. Dunning and Ms. Kathleen Coates, Department of Forestry and Natural Resources at Purdue University, starting in 2006 and is currently ongoing. The objectives of this project are to:

1. Compare marsh bird reproductive success at natural and restored wetlands using the Swamp Sparrow as a representative species.
2. Evaluate how wetland attributes influence reproductive success and nest predation rates and compare these relationships between natural and restored wetlands.
3. Determine whether each wetland functions as demographic source or sink.

Anderson, Baraboo River, Manthey, Schoenberg, and, and Vangen WPAs in Columbia County are included in this study.

Wetland/Water Quality Studies

Baraboo River WPA Water Quality Study

Establishment or enhancement of wetlands is often an effective means of reducing water-borne nutrient concentrations. However, little is known about the efficacy of floodplain wetland in removing riverine nutrients. University of Wisconsin Department of Limnology students measured soil nitrogen concentrations and rates of nitrogen removal from soils and water over the past three years. Their goal was to improve our understanding of floodplain nutrient cycling, and to understand how the floodplain responds to restoration activities. They collected soil samples in different zones of the floodplain (defined by their connection to the river) during the 2 years prior to restoration activities, and also have information on these same characteristics for 2 years post-restoration. By comparing post-restoration nitrogen removal in the floodplain after restoration, we hope to be able to evaluate the restoration benefits in terms of nutrient reduction.

Cattail Management Study

This is a joint USGS/FWS study designed to investigate the possible control of cattail in managed wetlands on refuges and wetland management districts in Regions 5 and 3. The study involves the prolonged drawdown of units combined with prescribed burns conducted on separate units in the summer (late June/early July) when carbohydrate reserves are lowest and dormant season (fall) burns prior to frozen ground conditions. The biggest issues to date have been the difficulty in achieving sufficient drying of the units in order to burn at least a portion of the peat layer, and when those conditions were achieved a reluctance to burn due to drought conditions and resultant extreme fire behavior.

Threatened and Endangered Species Monitoring

Eastern Prairie Fringed Orchid Monitoring

Since 1997 the District has conducted Eastern prairie fringed orchid management and monitoring activities on the Uihlein WPA with the Partner for Plants (PFP) volunteers (a subgroup of the Garden Club of America) and Wisconsin Department of Agriculture, Trade, and Consumer Protection (DATCP). Since management and monitoring actions have been in place the Eastern prairie fringed orchid population on this property has increased from the three individuals located in 1996 to a high of 568 in 2004, but has declined in recent years due to dry conditions.

Karner Blue Butterfly Monitoring

There is currently a documented population of Karner blue butterflies on Wilcox WPA occupying a site where 2 acres of lupine and other native species were established with the objective of providing a seed source. Surveys are conducted annually using the monitoring protocols outlined in the Karner Blue Butterfly Habitat Conservation Plan.

Prescribed Fire Monitoring

Prescribed Fire Monitoring Plan

Prescribed fire is the main tool used by the District for management of the grassland habitats. However, stringent monitoring of the behavior and effects of prescribed fire, beyond occasional photo points, has not been implemented. A Draft Fire Effects Monitoring Protocol has been developed around the breeding bird point count locations for monitoring changes in habitat and grassland bird use due to fire.

Visitor Services

The District facilitates wildlife-dependent recreational uses by distributing information and maps of the WPAs and developing wildlife trails, interpretive signs, and kiosks. The number of people visiting the District is estimated from the number of cars employees see in WPA parking lots as they go about their duties.

Hunting

Hunting is allowed on Waterfowl Production Areas within state, federal, and District regulations. Baiting is not allowed, and non-toxic shot must be used for small game. The only WPAs closed to hunting are Blue-wing WPA in Ozaukee County and Wilcox WPA in Waushara County.

Thirty-eight parking lots are provided on 24 WPAs in the District. County maps indicating WPA locations are provided on the Districts web page. The majority of hunters on WPAs are pursuing waterfowl, Wild Turkey, and deer.

The District receives one or two requests a year for special use permits for accessible hunting opportunities.

Fishing

Fishing consistent with state regulations is allowed on all WPAs. Only a limited number of WPAs have wetlands, streams, or rivers capable of supporting fish. Parking lots that can be used for fishing access are available on some WPAs.

Interpretation, Wildlife Observation, and Photography

District staff provide several interpretive programs each year to groups and conservation organizations. There are limited specific facilities on WPAs for wildlife observation or photography.

Environmental Education

District staff respond to the occasional request for environmental education programs for school groups. The District does not have a visitor services specialist and therefore does not provide structured curriculum based environmental education.

Non-wildlife-dependent Recreation.

The District receives several requests from snowmobile clubs to establish and use trails on WPAs. This has been determined to be a non-appropriate use and therefore not allowed; however, cross-country skiing is permitted as a means of winter access for wildlife observation and photography.

Pest Management

Various herbaceous and woody pest plants are found on District lands. Of primary concern are Canada thistle, spotted knapweed, purple loosestrife, box elder, black locust, and buckthorn.

Chemical, biological, and mechanical methods are employed in an integrated approach to control unwanted plant growth. Chemicals and mowing are used to control Canada thistle. *Galerucella* beetles are used to discourage purple loosestrife, which has increased on several WPAs. Small populations of spotted knapweed (*Centaurea maculosa*) have been found on many WPAs. In most cases the spotted knapweed was found in the parking lots or invading from roadside ditches where highway department mowing activities perpetuate and further its spread. More recently this pest plant has invaded into established grassland fields. Plants are hand pulled prior to seed set. Chemical control is also being evaluated on several small areas. Brush and tree species are controlled to restore oak savanna, improve woodlands, maintain grasslands, and remove wooded fence lines between grassland fields. Mechanical and/or chemical control is used to control brush and trees.

Archaeological and Cultural Resources

Cultural resources management in the Service is the responsibility of the Regional Director and is not delegated for the Section 106 process when historic properties could be affected by Service activities, for issuing archeological permits, and for Indian tribal involvement. The Regional Historic Preservation Officer (RHPO) advises the Regional Director about procedures, compliance, and implementation of cultural resources laws. The District Manager assists the RHPO by informing the RHPO about Service undertakings, by protecting archeological sites and historic properties on Service managed and administered lands, by monitoring archeological investigations by contractors and permittees, and by reporting violations.

Farm Service Agency Conservation Easements

When the Farm Service Agency (FSA), formerly the Farmers Home Administration (FmHA), acquires property through default of loans, it is required to protect wetland and floodplain resources on the property prior to resale to the public. The Service has assisted the FSA in identifying important wetland and floodplain resources on these properties. Once those resources have been identified, FSA may protect the areas through a perpetual conservation easement and transfer

White-tailed deer. USFWS photo.

management responsibility to the Service. The authority and direction comes from the Consolidated Farm and Rural Development Act (7 U.S.C. 1981 and 1985, as amended); Executive Order 11990 providing for the protection of wetlands; and Executive Order 11988 providing for the management of floodplain resources. The Service administers the easements as part of the National Wildlife Refuge System.

The District manages 45 conservation easements totaling approximately 3,000 acres located within the Wildlife Management District, a 34-county area in eastern and central Wisconsin (see Figure 10). Most of conservation easements are visited each year for boundary sign condition, trespass violations, and various other infractions. Letters are generally sent to the easement landowners notifying them of the upcoming visit and to inquire about concerns or changes in ownership. Oftentimes on-site meetings with the landowner are held to discuss and rectify findings of the annual easement check, or to address their questions and concerns regarding the easement.

Existing Partnerships

The District has partnerships with local, state, and national organizations. These partnerships benefit the District in many ways, including fostering good community relations and enhancing habitats and wildlife populations. Examples of partnerships include the following:

- *The Fairfield Marsh: A Conservation Partnership* is a Service initiative working with a community based group of local, state, and federal governments, special interest groups and landowners who call themselves FACT (Farming and Conservation Together).
- The District works closely with partners in several NAWCA grant areas: South Central Wisconsin Prairie Pothole Initiative, Southeast Coastal Wisconsin Initiative, Rush Lake/Lake Winnebago System Initiative, and the Glacial Habitat Restoration Area Initiative.
- District staff have been involved in a restoration project on Rush Lake in Winnebago County. This project uses funding through the Upper Fox River Natural Resource Damage Assessment (NRDA) and NAWCA program dollars to replace a water control structure on the outlet of the lake to facilitate better water management to improve habitat conditions for historic wetland vegetation (hard and softstem bulrushes), control carp, and manage lead shot issues.
- A seed nursery has been established in cooperation with the Madison Chapter of the Audubon Society, Madison Private Lands Office, and the Wisconsin DNR for growing and harvesting local ecotype native grass and forb seeds.
- The Partners for Fish and Wildlife Program is in partnership with the Wisconsin DNR and other partners for cost share on private lands wetland and grassland restoration projects within the District.
- The Service partnered on a cooperative restoration project with Ducks Unlimited providing funding, design, construction oversight, and contract management; NRDA which provided funding; and Wisconsin DNR as the permitting agency, to complete rehabilitation of dikes and water control structures on Uihlein WPA in Winnebago County. The District has also partnered with NRCS, Ducks Unlimited, Wisconsin DOT, Wisconsin Waterfowl Association, Wisconsin DNR, USGS, and others to restore a 200-plus acre wetland in the floodplain on the Baraboo River WPA in Columbia County.
- The District and Waterfowl USA have formed a close partnership over the years. The Northwest Indiana Chapter has provided funding for habitat restoration efforts on Oakfield WPA in Fond du Lac County and the Southern Wisconsin Chapter provided funding for land acquisition on Lund WPA in Rock County.
- District fire staff have partnered with Wisconsin tribal entities, Wisconsin DNR, the U.S. Forest Service, and the National Park Service to coordinate fire management functions.

Figure 10: Conservation Easements Managed by Leopold Wetland Management District

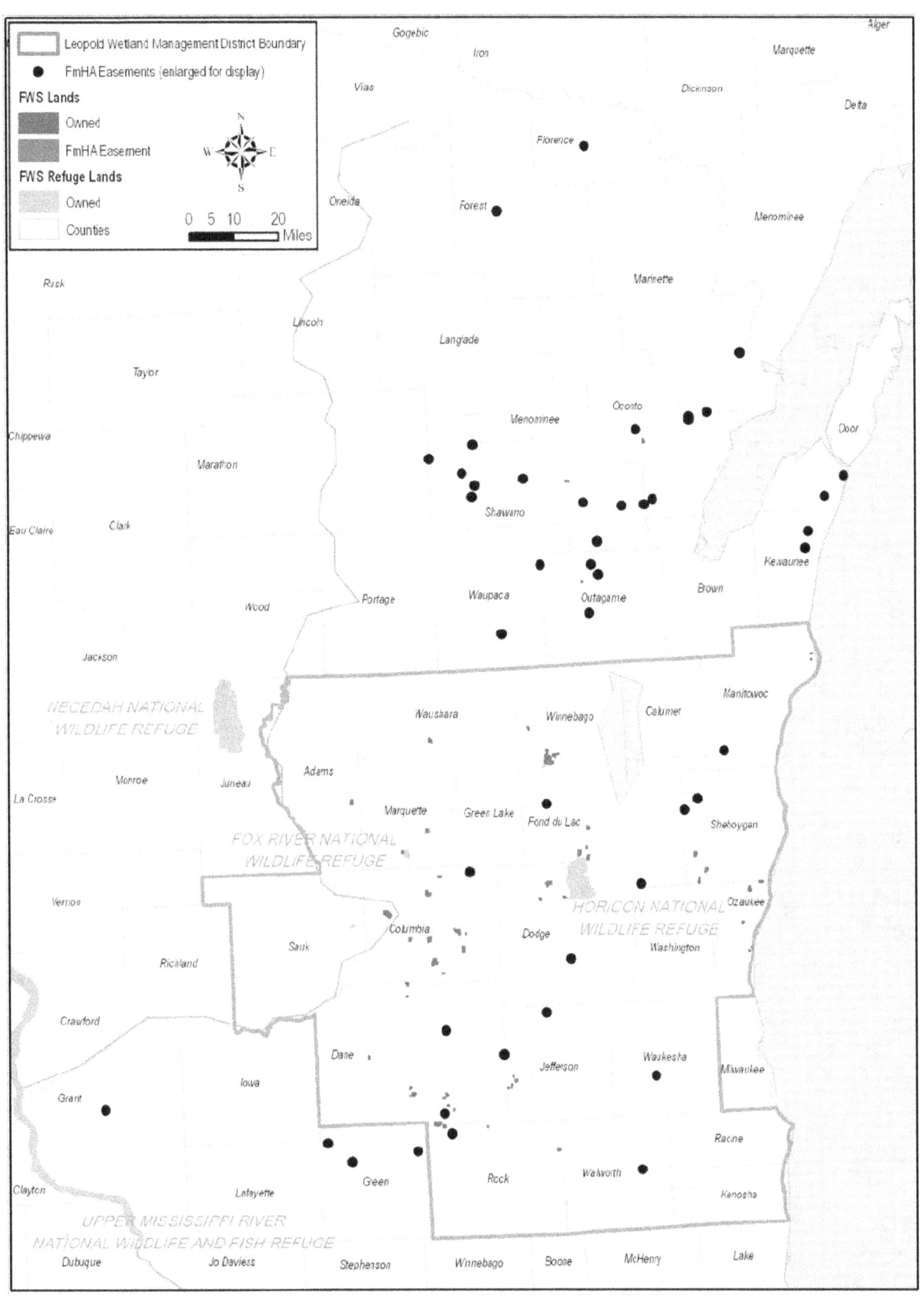

Figure 11: Index to Leopold WMD County Maps

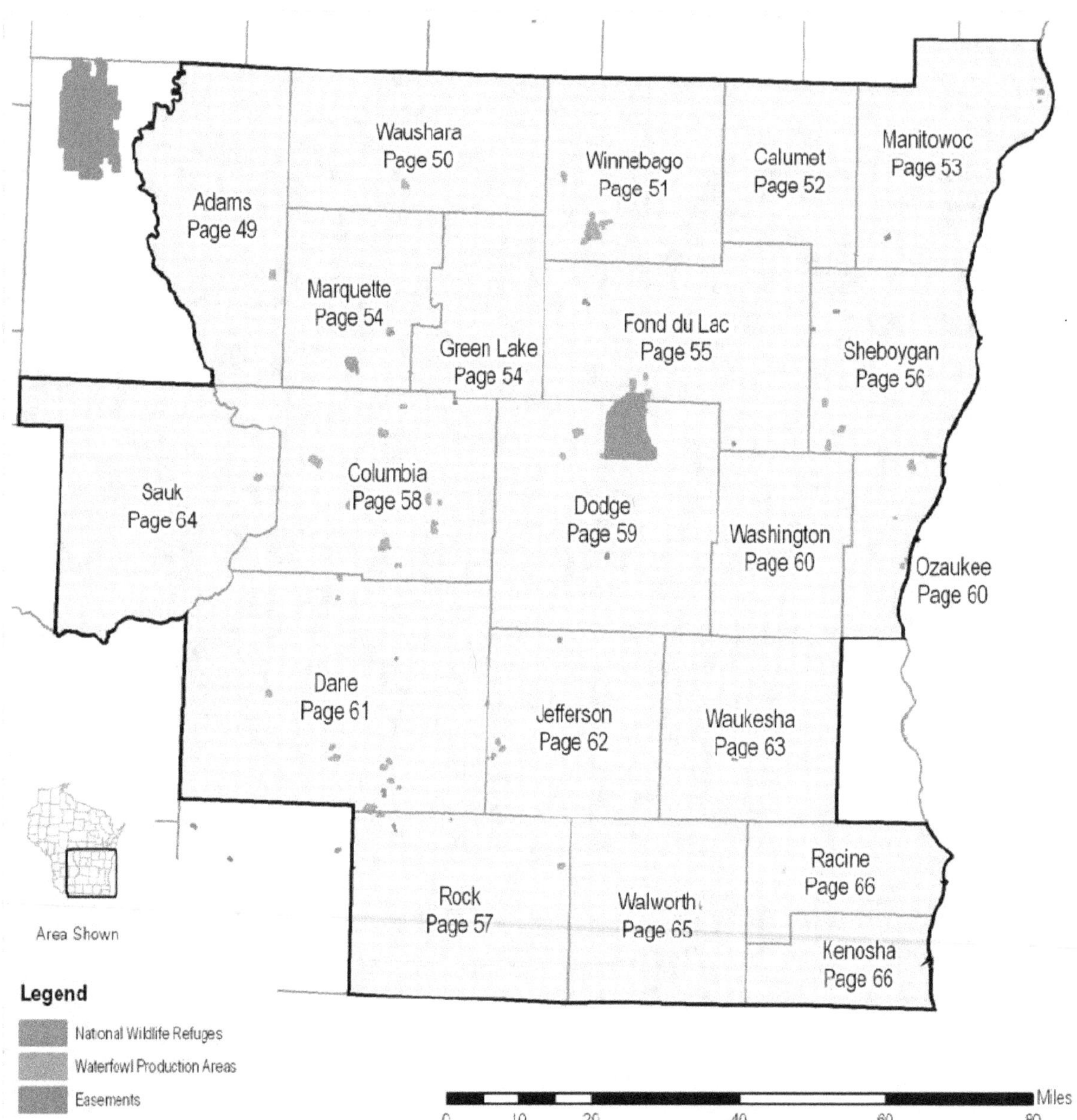

Figure 12: Adams County, Leopold Wetland Management District

Wood
Portage
Waushara
Adams
Juneau
Marquette
Sauk
Columbia
NECEDAH NATIONAL WILDLIFE REFUGE
New Chester WPA

Leopold Wetland Management District Boundary
Waterfowl Production Area
FmHA Easement
National Wildlife Refuge
Wisconsin DNR Wildlife Management Areas
Counties
Limited Access
Highway
Major Road
Local Road
Minor Road

Scale 1:440,000

0 1 2 4 6 8 Miles

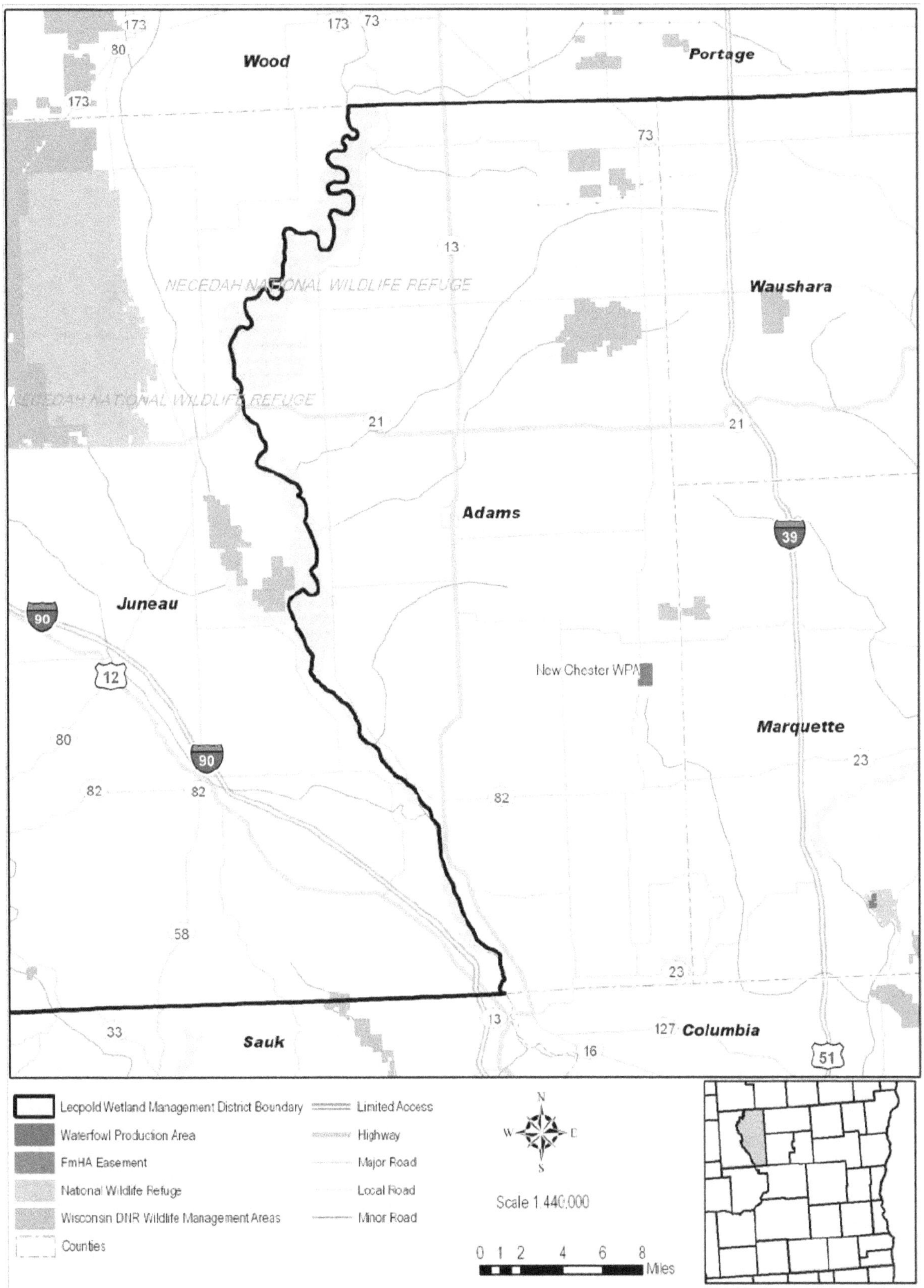

Figure 13: Waushara County, Leopold Wetland Management District

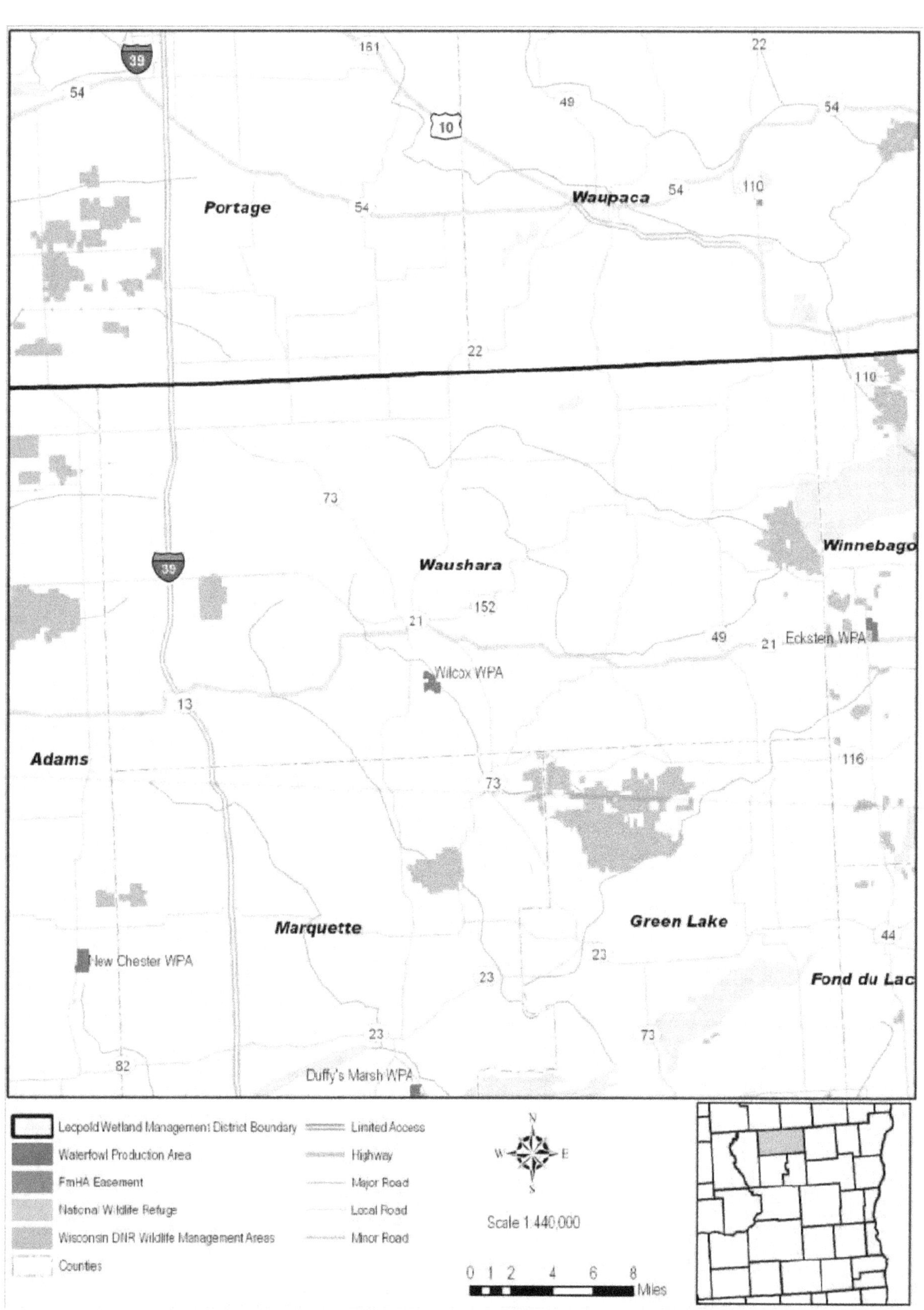

Figure 14: Winnebago County, Leopold Wetland Management District

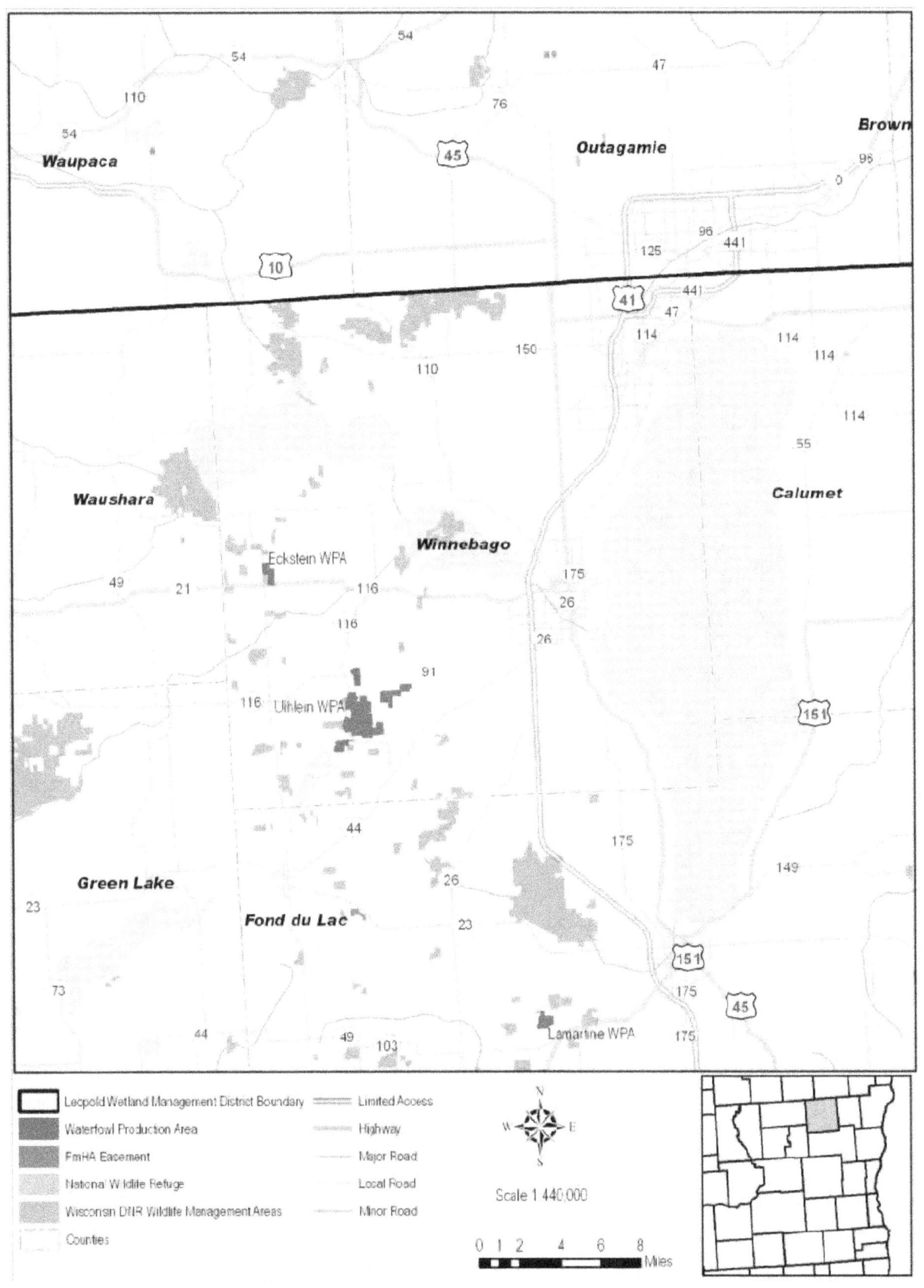

Figure 15: Calumet County, Leopold Wetland Management District

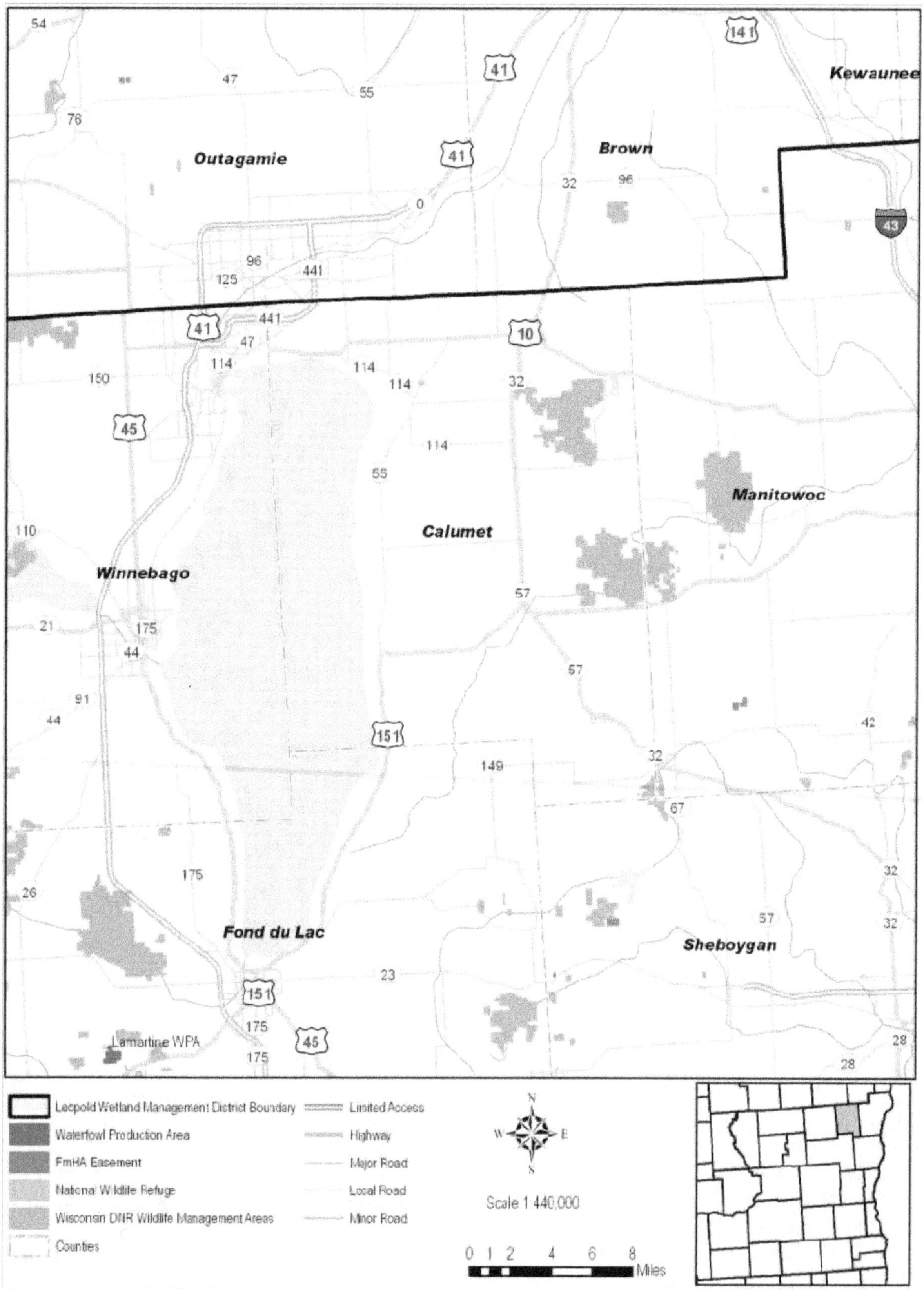
Outagamie
Brown
Kewaunee
Manitowoc
Calumet
Winnebago
Fond du Lac
Sheboygan
Lamartine WPA
Leopold Wetland Management District Boundary
Waterfowl Production Area
FmHA Easement
National Wildlife Refuge
Wisconsin DNR Wildlife Management Areas
Counties
Limited Access
Highway
Major Road
Local Road
Minor Road
N
W
E
S
Scale 1:440,000
0 1 2 4 6 8
Miles

Figure 16: Manitowoc County, Leopold Wetland Management District

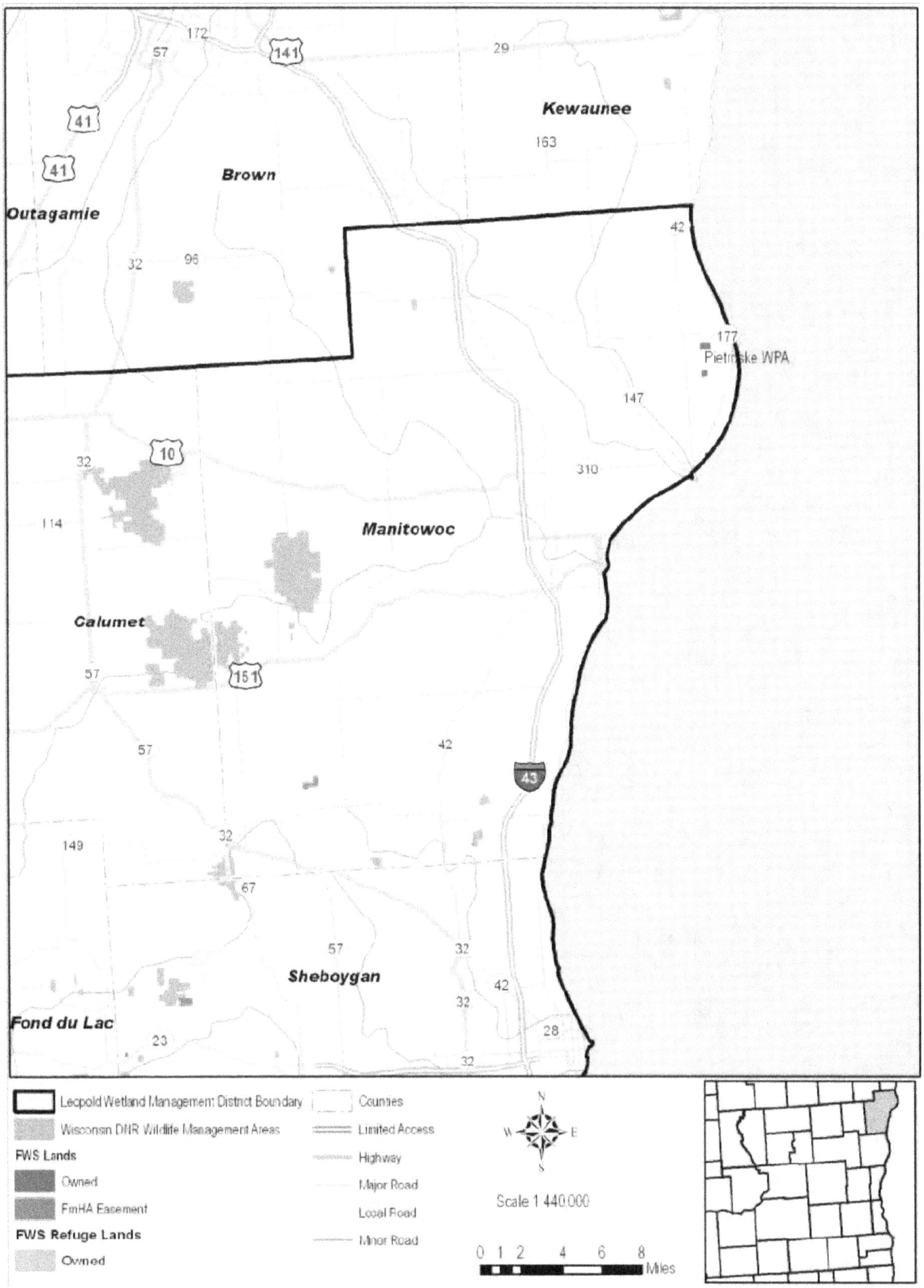

Figure 17: Marquette and Green Lake Counties, Leopold Wetland Management District

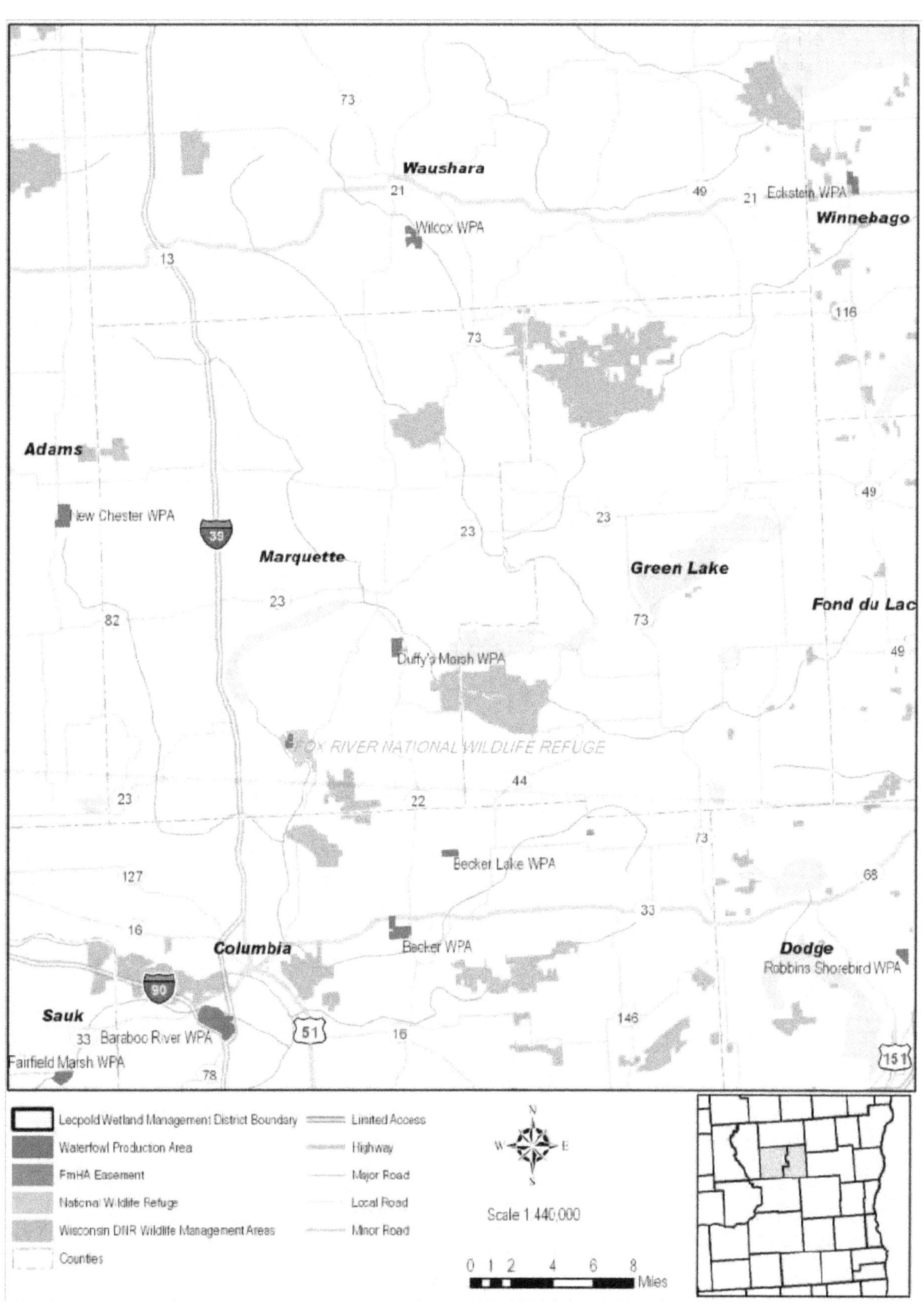

Figure 18: Fond du Lac County, Leopold Wetland Management District

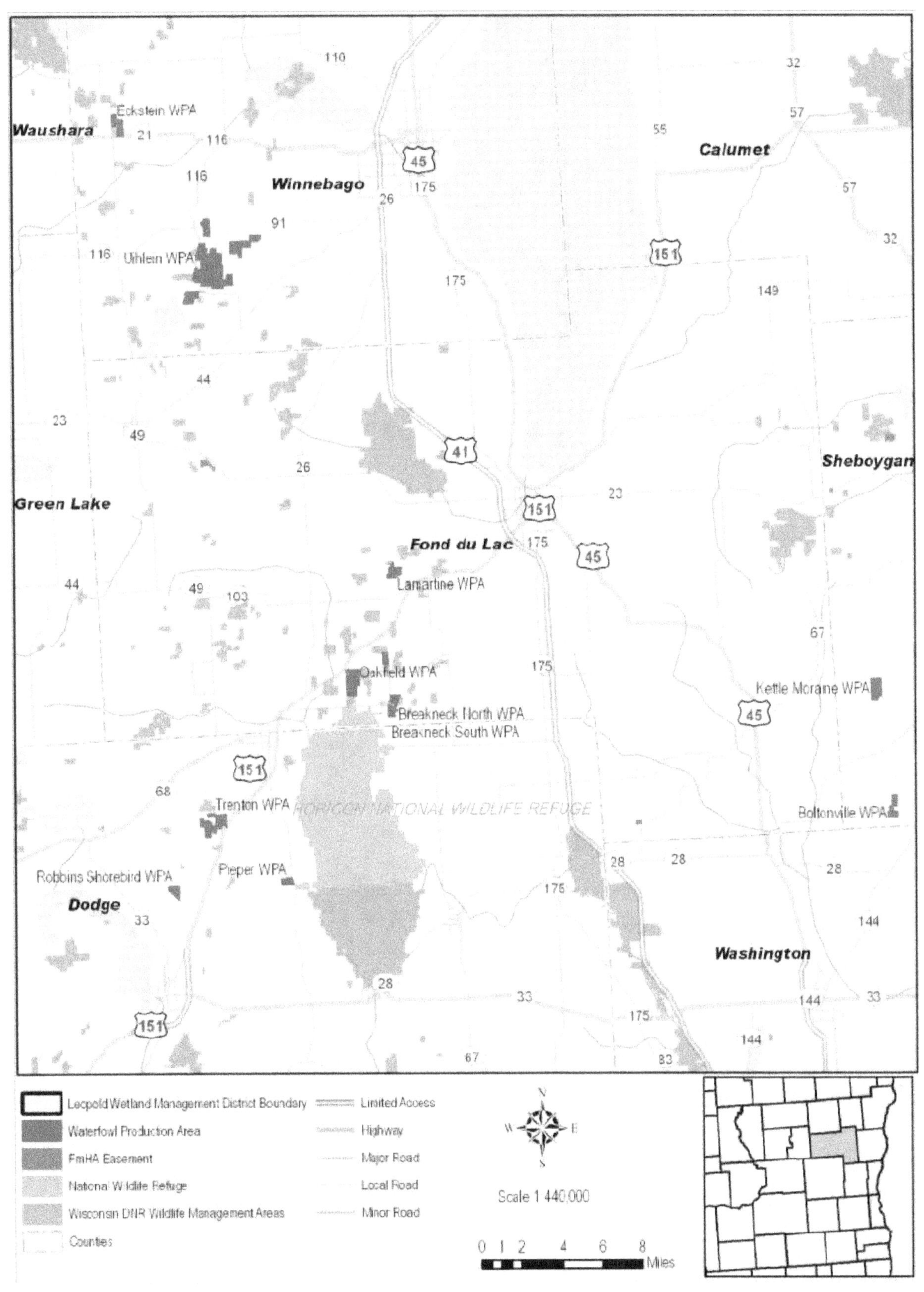

Figure 19: Sheboygan County, Leopold Wetland Management District

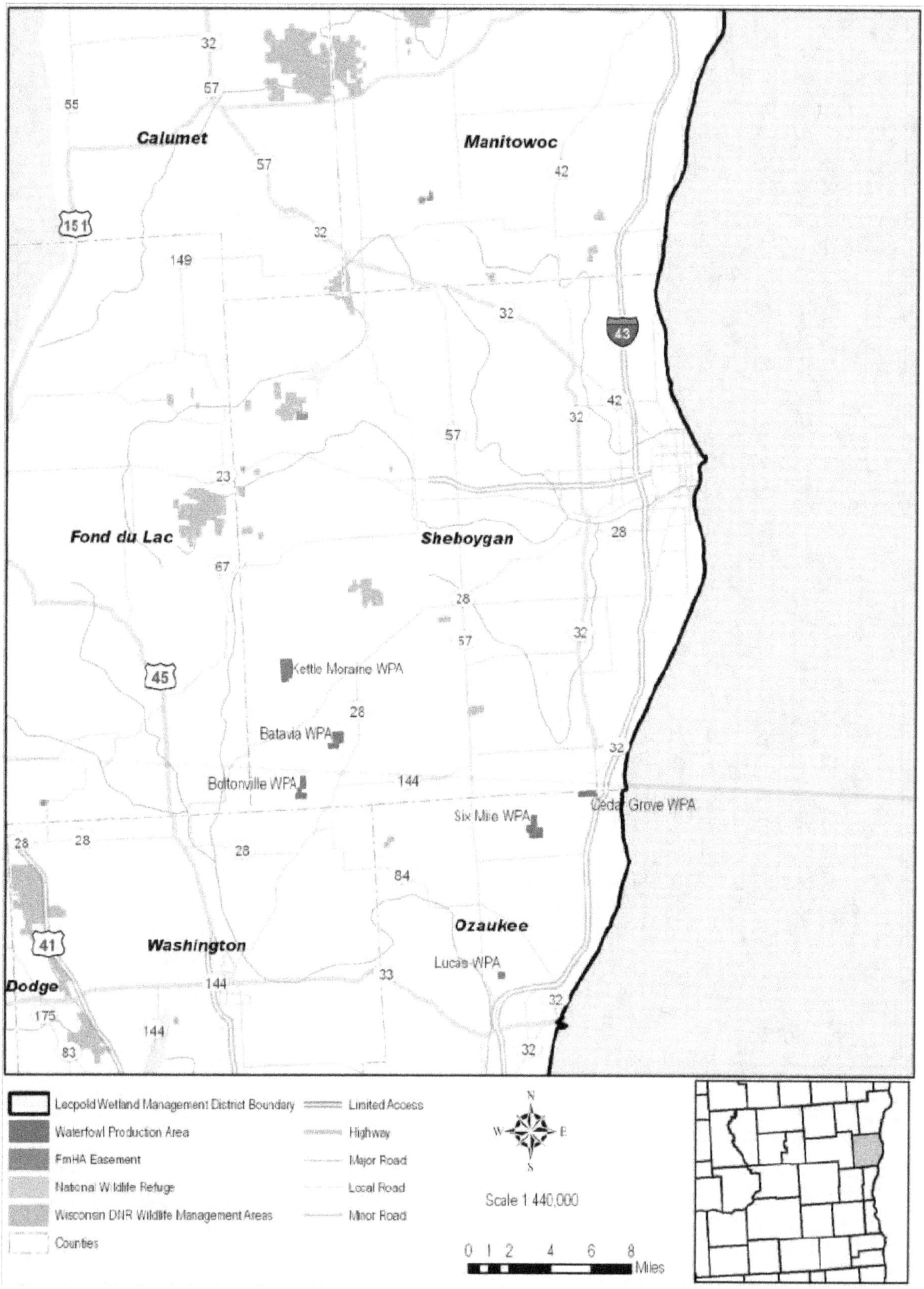

Figure 20: Sauk County, Leopold Wetland Management District

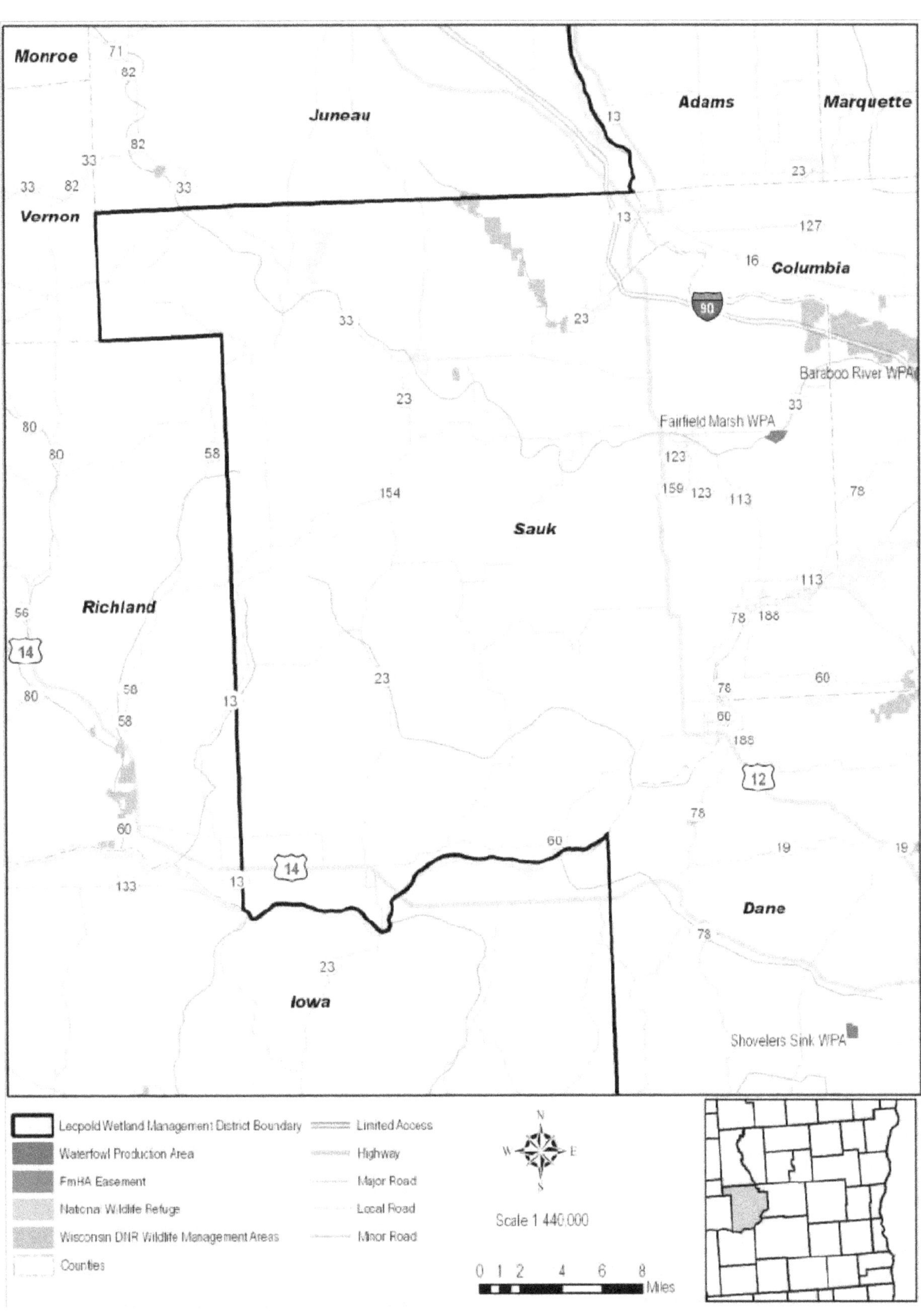

Figure 21: Columbia County, Leopold Wetland Management District

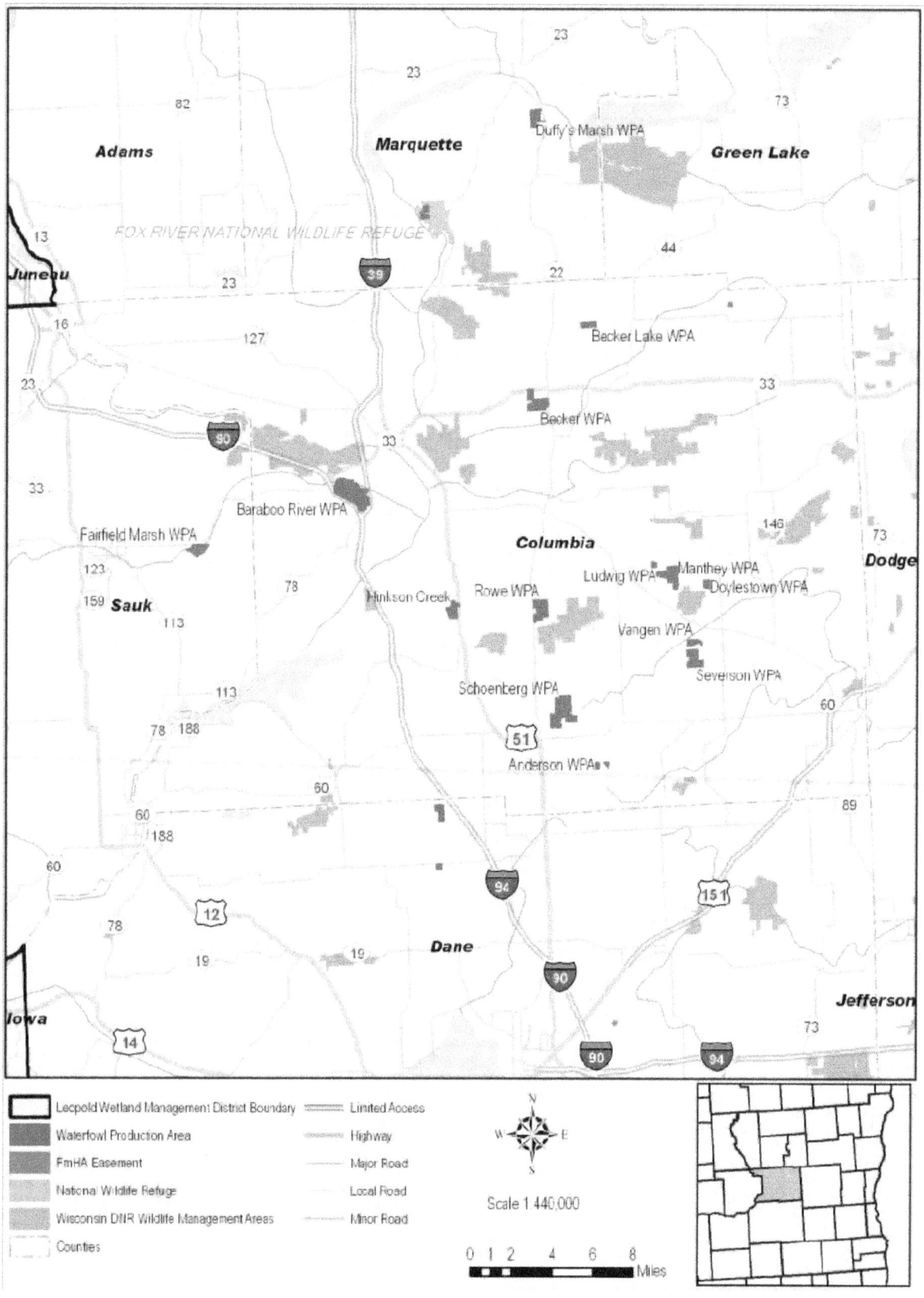

Figure 22: Dodge County, Leopold Wetland Management District

Green Lake
Fond du Lac
Lamartine WPA
Oakfield WPA
Breakneck North WPA
Breakneck South WPA
Trenton WPA
HORICON NATIONAL WILDLIFE REFUGE
Pieper WPA
Robbins Shorebird WPA
Columbia
Dodge
Washington
Dane
Jefferson
Waukesha

Leopold Wetland Management District Boundary
Waterfowl Production Area
FmHA Easement
National Wildlife Refuge
Wisconsin DNR Wildlife Management Areas
Counties
Limited Access
Highway
Major Road
Local Road
Minor Road

N
W
E
S

Scale 1:440,000

0 1 2 4 6 8 Miles

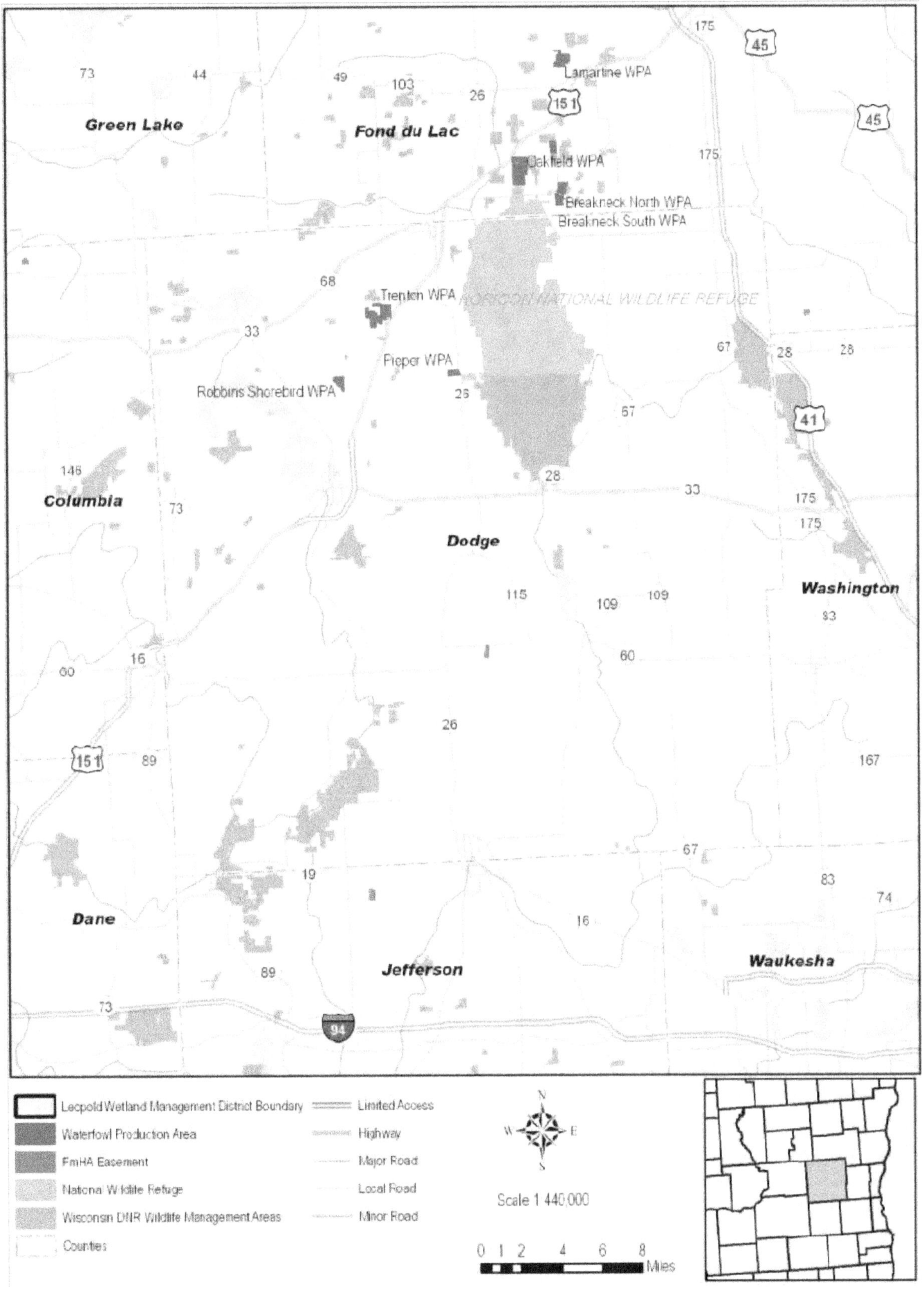

Figure 23: Washington and Ozaukee Counties, Leopold Wetland Management District

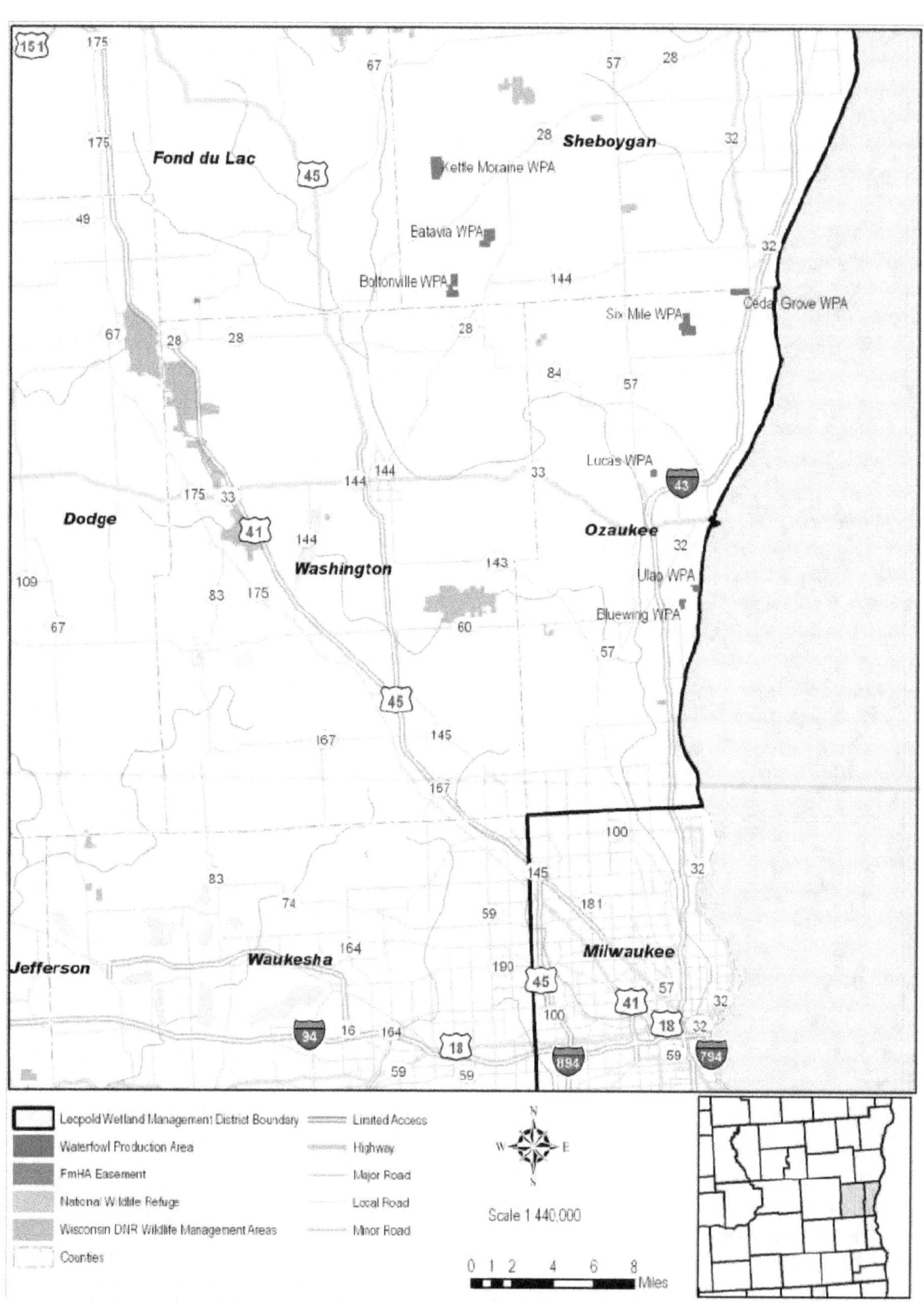

Figure 24: Dane County, Leopold Wetland Management District

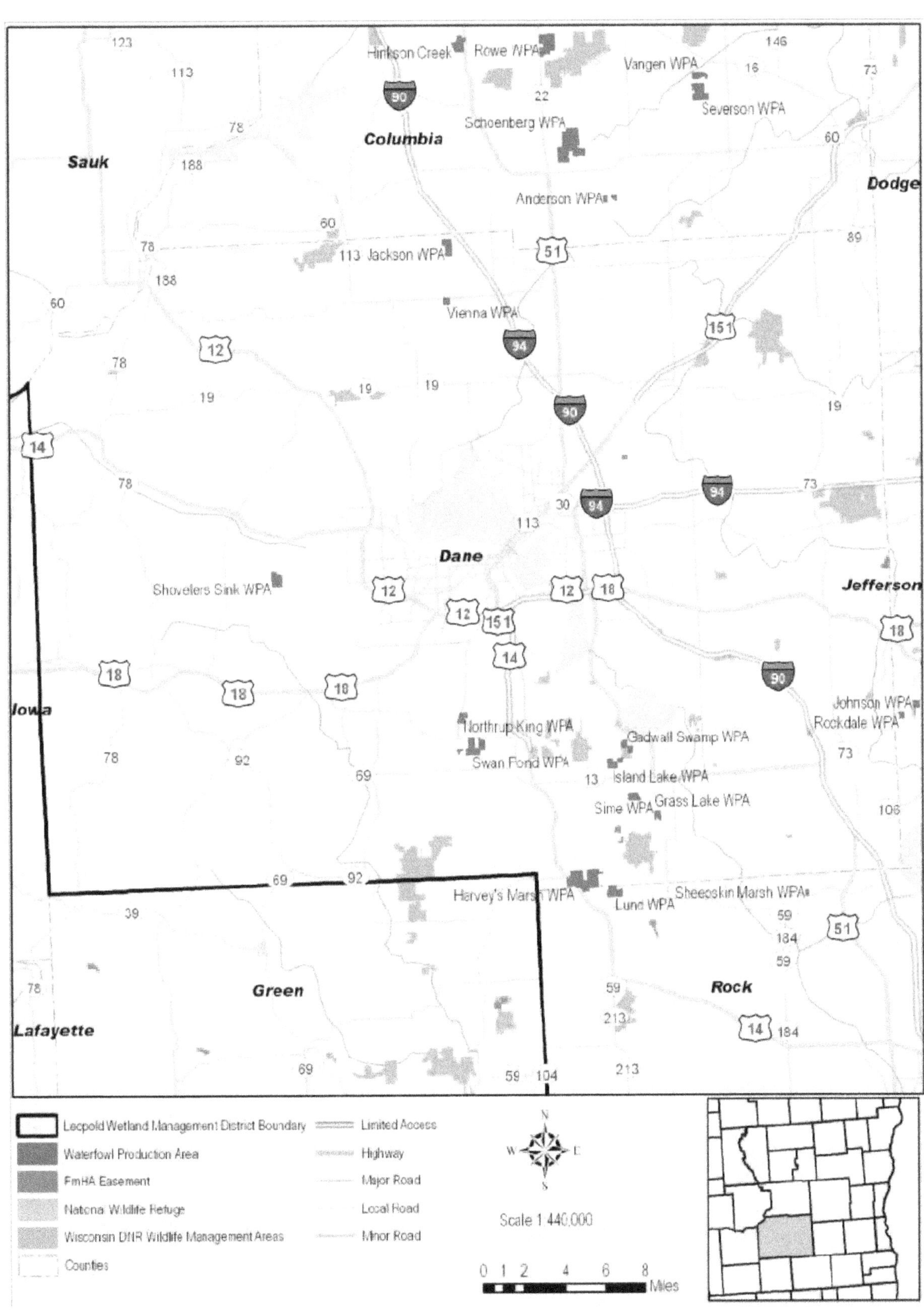

Figure 25: Jefferson County, Leopold Wetland Management District

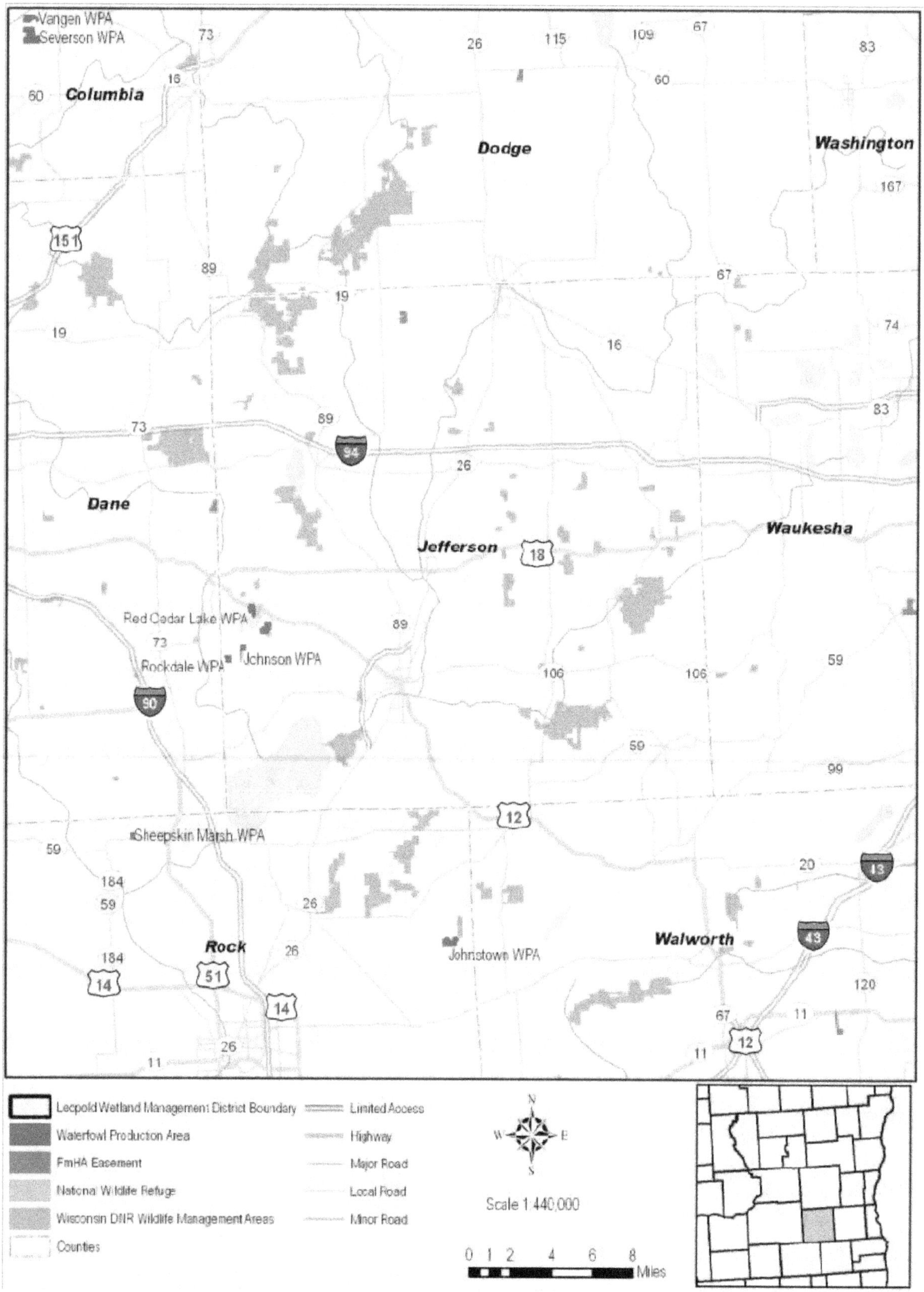

Figure 26: Waukesha County, Leopold Wetland Management District

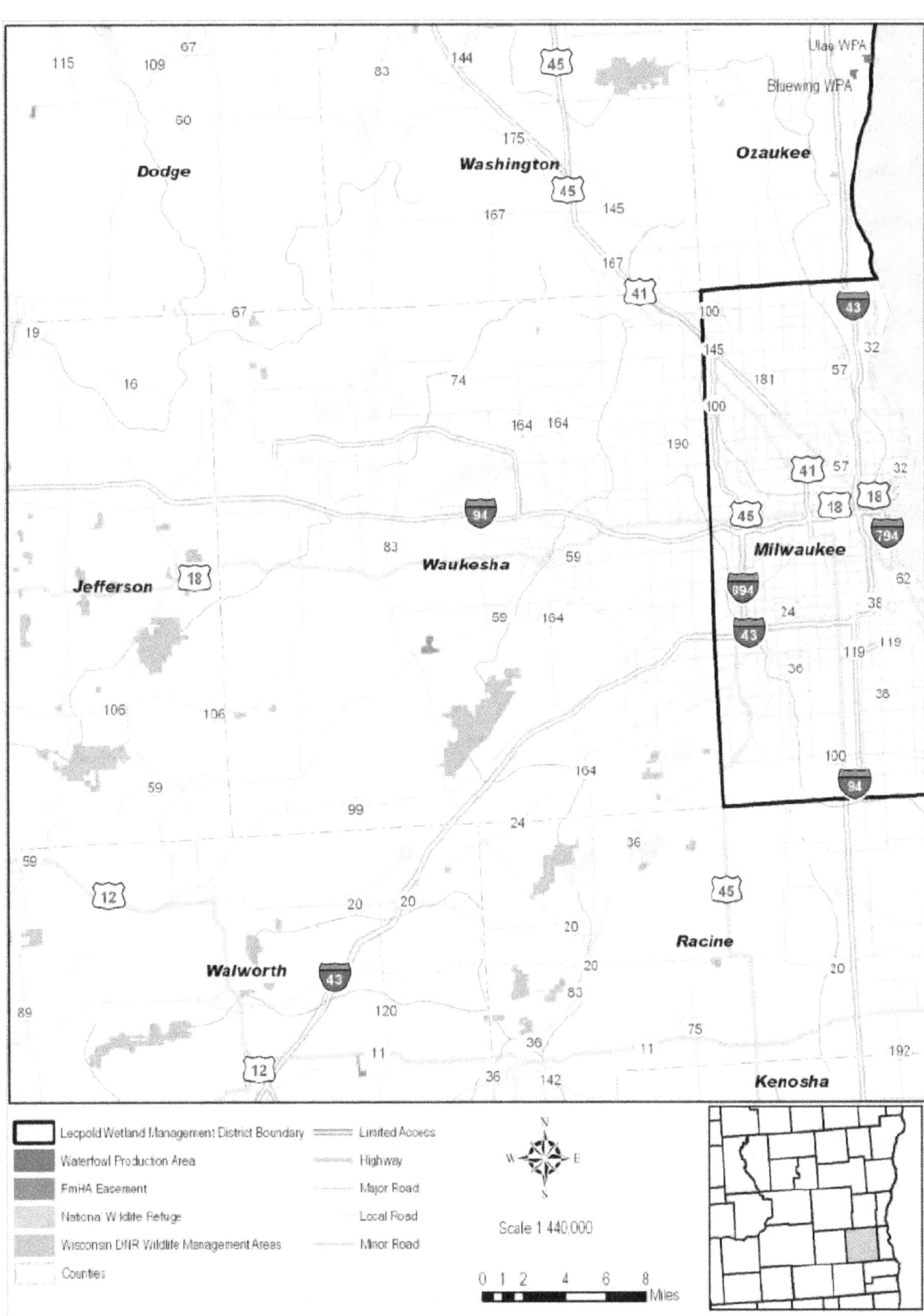

Figure 27: Rock County, Leopold Wetland Management District

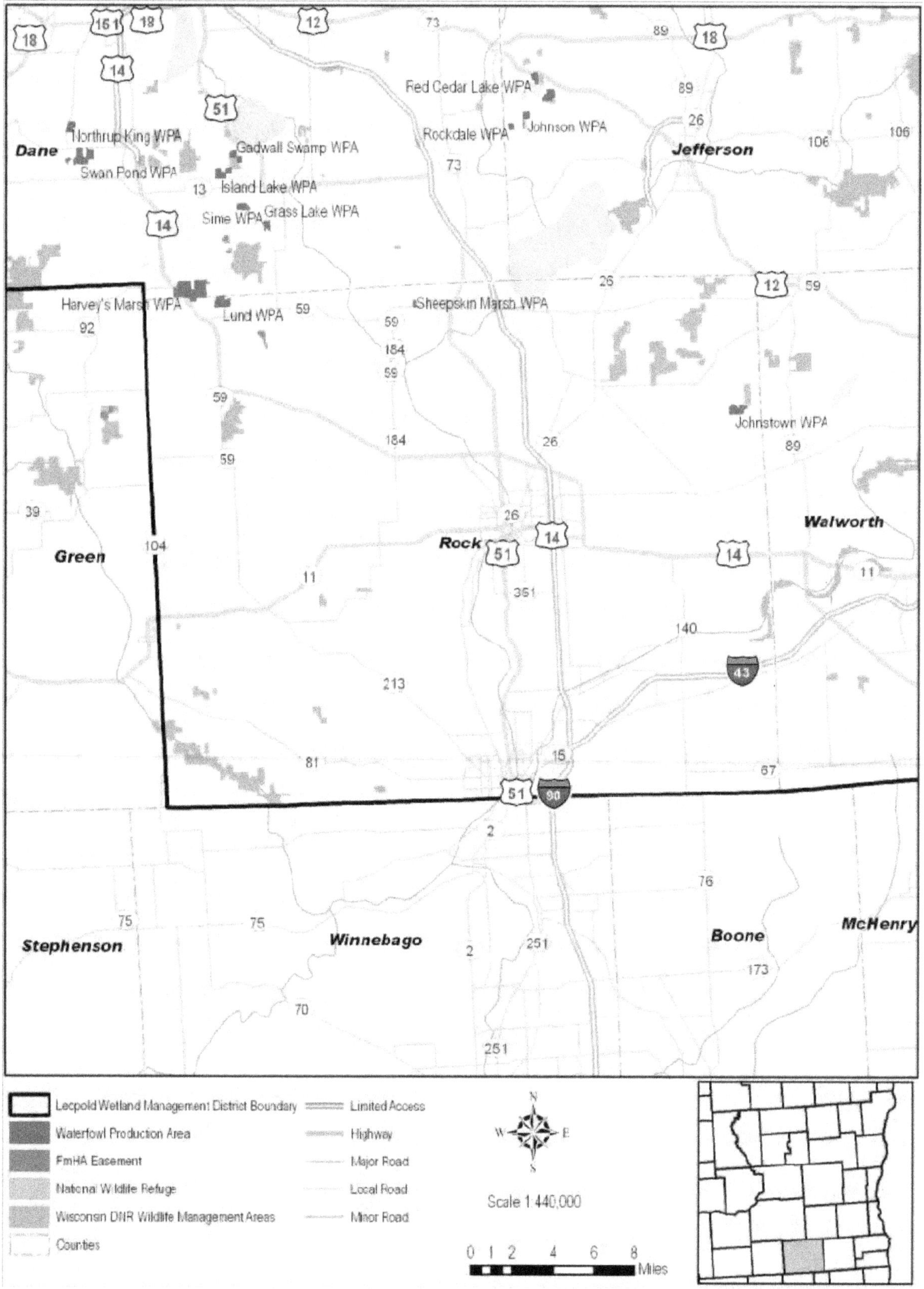

Figure 28: Walworth County, Leopold Wetland Management District

Jefferson
Waukesha
Racine
Walworth
Rock
Kenosha
Winnebago
Boone
McHenry
Lake
Johnstown WPA

Leopold Wetland Management District Boundary
Waterfowl Production Area
FmHA Easement
National Wildlife Refuge
Wisconsin DNR Wildlife Management Areas
Counties
Limited Access
Highway
Major Road
Local Road
Minor Road

Scale 1:440,000

0 1 2 4 6 8 Miles

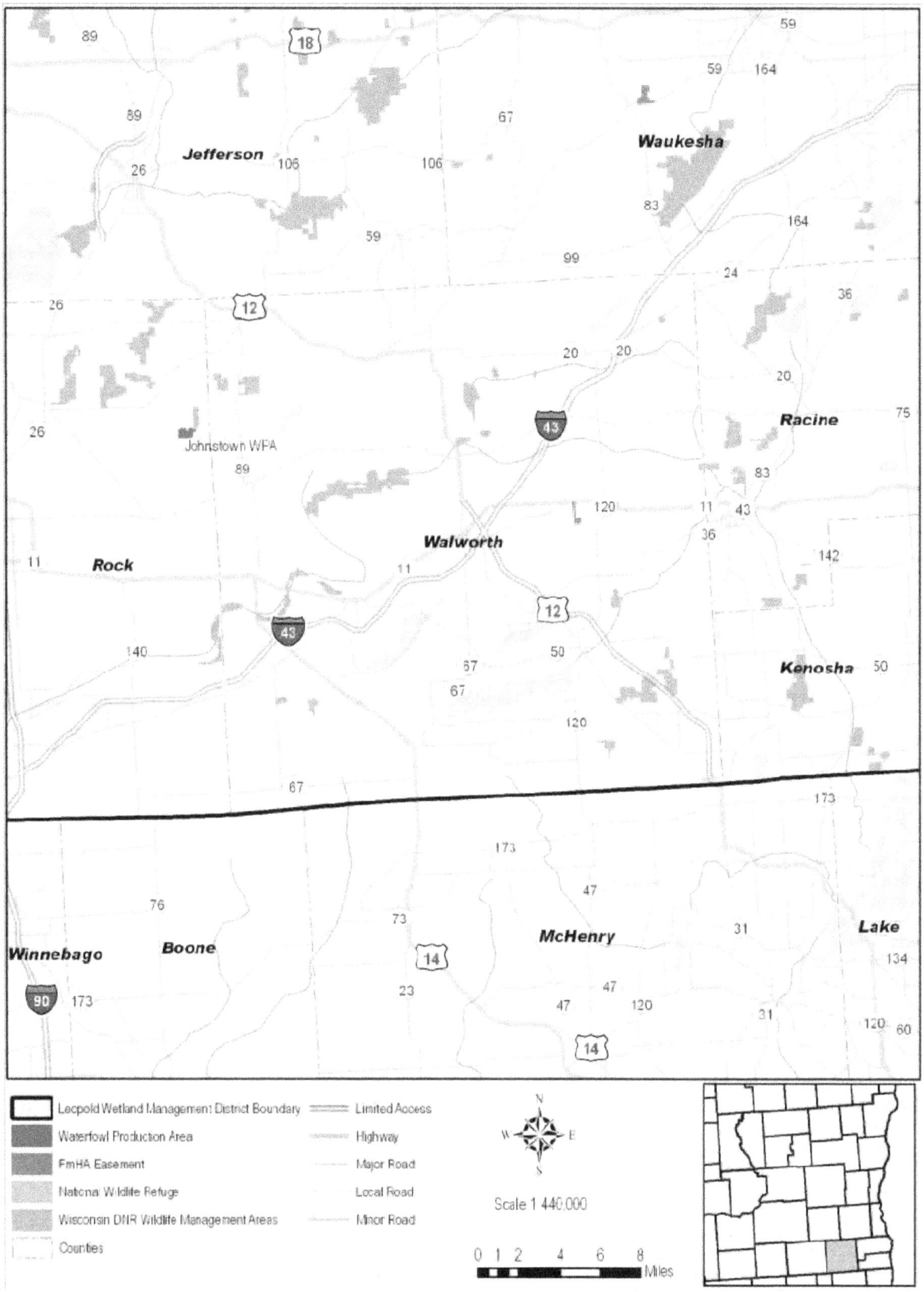

Figure 29: Racine and Kenosha Counties, Leopold Wetland Management District

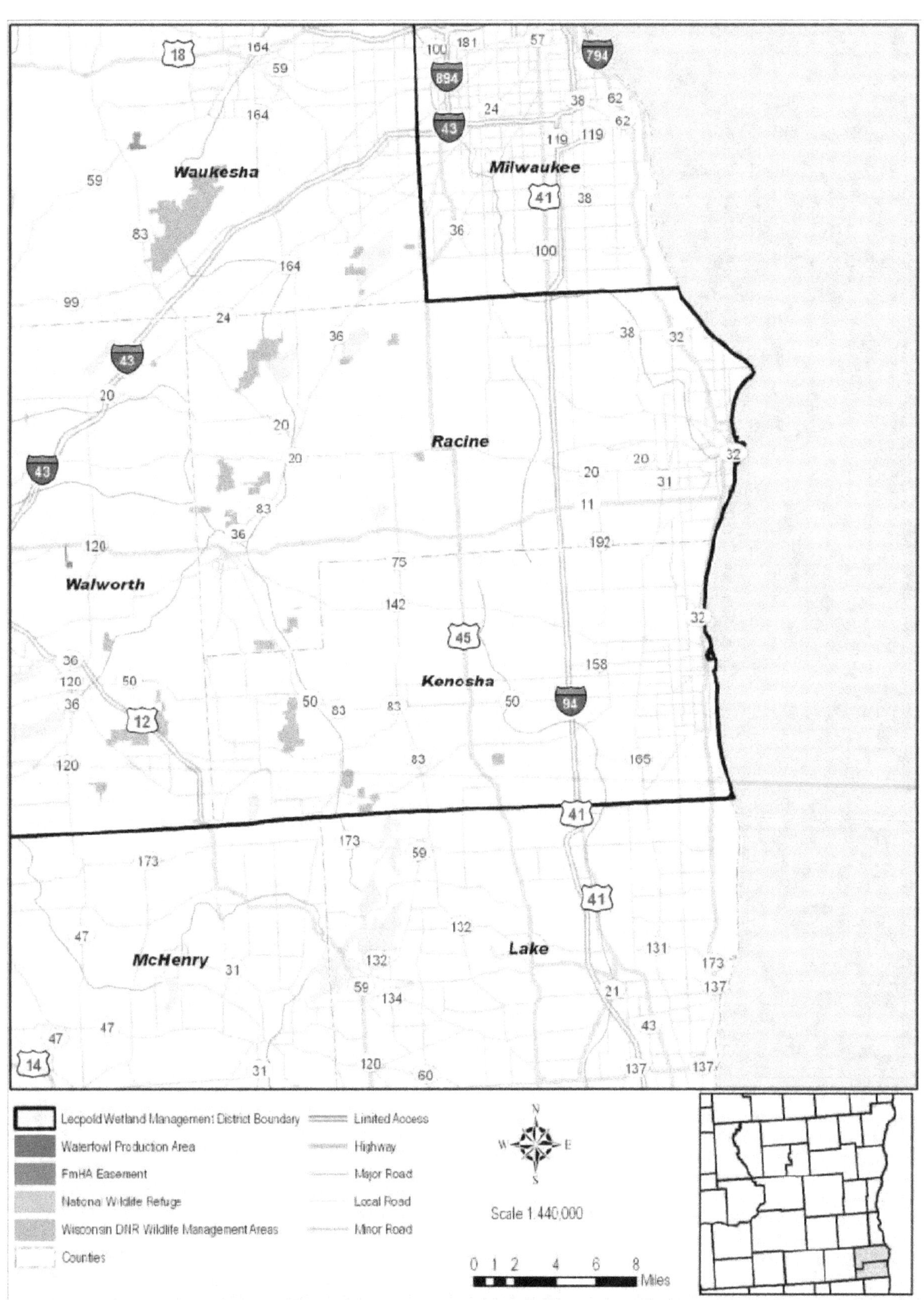

Chapter 4: Management Direction

Introduction

Goals and Objectives

This chapter presents the goals, objectives and strategies that will guide management and administration of the District over the next 15 years. This management direction represents the plan for the District and mirrors Alternative 4 in the Environmental Assessment that was prepared as part of the planning process and was included in the Draft CCP as Appendix A.

The District has four goals:

1. Preserve, restore, and enhance the ecological diversity of wetlands, grasslands, and native flora of District lands to support the conservation of breeding habitat for waterfowl, grassland birds, and other wildlife.
2. Preserve, restore, and enhance the diversity and abundance of migratory birds and other native wildlife with emphasis on waterfowl, grassland and wetland-dependent birds.
3. A broad cross section of the public enjoys and appreciates District lands.
4. Protect the integrity of biological resources within the District and the cultural resources and health and safety of visitors and Service staff on WPAs.

The goals are general statements of what the District wants to accomplish. The objectives under each goal are specific statements of what will be accomplished to help achieve the goal. Strategies listed under each objective specify the activities that will be pursued to realize an objective. The strategies may be refined or amended as specific tasks are completed or new research and information come to light. Some strategies are linked to the duties of an employee position, which indicates that the strategy will be accomplished with the help of a new staff position. When a time in number of years is noted in an objective or strategy, it refers to the number of years from approval of this CCP. If no time is given, the objective is to be accomplished within the 15 years of the life of the plan.

Prairie habitat on Leopold WMD. USFWS photo.

Goal 1: Habitat

Preserve, restore, and enhance the ecological diversity of wetlands, grasslands, and native flora of District lands to support the conservation of breeding habitat for waterfowl, grassland birds, and other wildlife.

Objective 1.1: Grasslands

Restore 200 acres of native grassland and remove 1 mile of fence row annually, on average. Within 15 years, 70 percent of the District's grassland acres will be under optimal management.

Rationale: The District currently manages 4,875 acres of grasslands including 3,395 acres of seeded warm-season grasses, 48 acres of native prairie, 1,432 acres of cool season grasses including brome and Kentucky blue grass and approximately 300 acres of cropland in the process of conversion to native prairie. Grasslands benefit numerous species of wildlife in the District. Large tracts of grasslands provide important nest sites for Mallards and Blue-winged Teal, the two most common species of upland nesting waterfowl in the District. In addition to waterfowl, grasslands provide important habitat for many other species of migratory birds. The populations of many of these species of grassland-dependent birds are decreasing due to several factors. Loss of grasslands for nesting habitat is one of those reasons. The Western Meadowlark used to be one of the most common birds in Wisconsin but since the mid-1960s its numbers have declined by 90 percent. Many of Wisconsin's other 40 species of grassland-dependent birds have declined as well. Historically, these species were found in southern and western Wisconsin in this prairie grassland/wetland dominated landscape. Many of these grassland species of birds, such as Bobolink, Grasshopper Sparrow and Western Meadowlark, are Fish and Wildlife Service Regional Species of Concern.

The planting of native grasses and forbs is designed to provide structural (height-density) and species diversity to benefit breeding grassland-dependent birds. Removal of trees and woody vegetation also makes the grassland patches more attractive to grassland nesting birds. An increase in block size also provides better habitat for many species of grassland-dependent birds. Numerous studies have shown that trees and shrubs should be removed from within and around grassland patches to decrease nest predation and brood parasitism. Patches for restoration of grassland habitat should also be as large as possible to decrease contact with edge predators.

Several techniques are used to transition fields from cropland and exotic cool-season grasses to native species with the underlying realization that we cannot recreate a pure native plant species stand. Due to many outside influences such as past farming history, agricultural chemical use, erosion, invasive species and landscape level influences by humans, we will have to live with a certain number of invasive or exotic species in the grasslands we manage in the District. Total elimination of these species is not practical.

Depending on site conditions, transition techniques for converting cool-season fields include 3-year cropping rotation and various combinations of tree removal, chemical treatment, prescribed fire, cover crops and overseeding. Factors such as the availability of farmers to crop areas, soil types, erosion potential and existing species on the site are considered in deciding how best to restore and manage the site. Optimal management conditions will be reached when prescribed fire is the primary tool used to manage and maintain the grassland.

Strategies:

1. Seed agricultural fields on new acquisitions to local ecotype native prairie grasses and forbs within 3 years of acquisition. Evaluate cool season grass fields on new acquisitions within 2 years to determine long-term grassland management needs.
2. Continue the native prairie seed nursery.
3. Add two new local ecotype grass species and five new local ecotype forb species to the nursery planting mix within 10 years of plan approval.
4. Identify unbroken remnant native prairie on WPAs within 3 years and manage these sites to maintain the genetic diversity. The wildlife biologist position will be responsible for identification and inventory of these sites.
5. Maintain cooperative grazing, haying and mowing on 150 acres of grassland habitat.
6. Using prescribed fire, burn 1,200 acres of grassland annually to maintain quality grassland habitat.
7. Remove 15 miles of fencerows within 15 years to maximize unbroken blocks of grassland cover. The seasonal tractor operator will play an important role in removing fencerows.

8. Remove pine plantations and trees from grasslands on WPAs and work with adjacent landowners. Work with neighboring private landowners to remove trees on and adjacent to common property lines.

9. Work with neighbors to establish native grassland buffers around WPAs and remove common fence rows. The wildlife refuge specialist and private lands biologist positions will be responsible for contacting and working with neighbors.

10. Through chemical application, mechanical treatments, or mowing, treat areas infested with herbaceous and woody invasive species.

11. Target tree removal, native prairie planting and land acquisition, to create grassland blocks of at least 80 acres.

Objective 1.2: Wetlands

Within 15 years, restore 75 percent of the District's historical wetland acres, manage water levels on 1,000 acres (principally Uihlein WPA), and maintain seasonal basins in an early successional state through active management.

Rationale: The District currently has 5,265 acres of wetland. These wetlands provide important habitat for a variety of species including Mallards, Blue-winged Teal, Wood Ducks and many other species of migratory waterfowl. In addition, numerous species of shorebirds and other waterbirds use these areas for breeding and migration.

Drained wetlands on WPAs will be restored when feasible. In an effort to increase the number of wetlands surrounding WPAs, an attempt will be made to restore co-owned basins. Complexes of wetlands across the landscape provide feeding and loafing areas for waterfowl pairs. Restoration and protection of these basins in proximity to large tracts of grassland on WPAs is very important.

Basins with water control structures will be managed to cycle these basins through the phases of the wetland cycle (dry/hemi-marsh/open water) to provide a variety of habitat conditions. Where several wetlands on a single WPA have water management capabilities these basins will be managed to provide different stages of the wetland cycle. Manipulation of water levels on basins with water control structures can also increase invertebrate populations following re-flooding. Invertebrates are a crucial food source for waterfowl and other wetland-dependent species. Existing natural basins on the WPAs are not manipulated since naturally occurring drought and wet years provide natural cycling of vegetation and nutrients. Other spring-fed wetland basins and lakes on the District have good stands of submergent vegetation and manipulation may result in the spread of aquatic invasive species such as hybrid cattail or phragmities throughout the basin. Active manipulation of basins will generally occur on basins with water control structures or basins affected by invasive species.

Temporary and seasonal wetlands within the District are crucial for attracting breeding waterfowl pairs to the landscape, however many of these wetlands have become choked with invasive reed canary grass or cattail. In addition, these wetlands were easily drained and filled so active restoration and management is now needed to provide temporary shallow open water on the landscape. Many of these wetlands were located in croplands before Fish and Wildlife Service acquisition, so they were subject to high rates of sedimentation. Active manipulation of these basins may be necessary to restore some of the wetland functions. In addition to providing invertebrate food sources for hen waterfowl during egg laying, these basins are extremely important breeding habitat for amphibians. Active manipulation of the wetlands may include a variety of techniques including mowing, grazing, prescribed fire or mechanical manipulation through disking or scraping. Various techniques will be used to manipulate the basins and an attempt will be made to determine the most cost effective technique to manage these basins and simulate the natural disturbances that make them extremely productive and valuable for many species of wildlife.

The results of a broken tile on a Leopold WMD conservation easement. USFWS photo.

Strategies:

1. Maintain levees and water control structures.
2. Manipulate water levels through natural flow and pumping.
3. Complete an inventory of seasonal basins on WPAs and easements.
4. Use water management and prescribed fire to manage cattail dominated basins.
5. Monitor vegetative, invertebrate, and wildlife response to active management of seasonal basins and determine the most effective technique. The wildlife biologist will design and implement the monitoring for this project.
6. Work with neighbors to restore co-owned wetland basins.

Objective 1.3: Oak Savanna

Within 15 years, inventory 90 percent of forest habitat to locate remnant oak savanna and restore 75 percent of identified potential savanna.

Rationale: Unlike the Prairie Pothole Region where trees were a minor part of the historical landscape the natural vegetation within the Wetland Management Districts of Wisconsin historically contained a mix of grassland, wetlands, woodlands, and savanna. As such these natural landscapes should be retained and restored where applicable. Oak savannas especially are one of the most endangered ecosystems in the world with less than one-tenth of 1 percent remaining. Oak savannas are a fire-dependent community dominated by an overstory of oak trees and an understory of native grasses and forbs. The understory may also contain many species of desireable native shrubs, such as hazelnut and hawthorn. In the District, numerous species of oaks, including burr, white, Hill's and black, are found in oak savannas. Without fire to control succession, these communities are overrun with aggressive tree species such as maple, ash, buckthorn, Siberian elm and box elder that thrive in the open conditions in a savanna. Eventually, as the old oak trees die, these savannas turn into forest and lose their characteristic grass/forb dominated understory. With the suppression of wildfire and human development of the landscape, oak savannas are rapidly disappearing. Restoration of oak savannas is very labor intensive and often entails dramatic changes to the landscape. The process of restoring each savanna differs based on the number and species of oak trees present, the long-term viability of burning the unit and the degree of invasion by invasive species such as buckthorn, Siberian elm and honeysuckle. Although initial restoration of savannas will involve removal of non-oak tree species and some grass/forb planting, complete restoration through repeated burning and control of brush and invasives may take 30-40 years before a more natural fire regime of burning every 8-15 years can be used.

Strategies:

1. Using prescribed fire, burn 50 acres of oak savanna annually.
2. Mechanical removal of unwanted trees on oak savanna restoration sites.
3. Plant prairie grass and forb species.
4. Monitor vegetative response to management.
5. Add oak savanna grass and forb species to nursery program to enhance species diversity within restored savannas.

Objective 1.4: Woodlands

Implement timber stand improvement on 20 percent of forest habitat.

Rationale: As previously discussed, the woodlands are a historical part of the landscape of the Wisconsin Wetland Management Districts. Currently 1,330 acres of woodlands are found on District lands. It is necessary to inventory these forested areas and determine if they should be

Wetland restoration, Leopold WMD. USFWS photo.

restored to native grassland, oak savanna or managed as woodlands. For areas that will remain as forested habitat, timber stand improvement will be used on a limited basis to maintain the long-term viability of these woodlands. Timber stand improvement includes thinning, site preparation for natural reproduction, removal of undesirable tree species and release cutting or killing of undesirable older over topping trees. Timber stand improvement can increase production of foods valued by wildlife such as acorns and nuts and increase the value of forested areas to certain species of wildlife such as Wood Ducks, deer, Wild Turkey and numerous species of migratory birds. Timber stand improvement will be a tool used in limited areas on WPAs for specific management goals.

Strategies:

1. Implement timber stand improvement on select woodlots to provide benefits to wildlife. Timber stand improvement will include thinning, site preparation for natural reproduction and release by cutting or killing undesirable older overtopping trees.

Objective 1.5: Invasive Species

Inventory 100 percent of District lands for invasive species and apply biological/mechanical/chemical control on 25 percent of District lands. The first priority for control will be on grasslands and wetlands, followed by woodlands.

Rationale: Invasive species are detrimental to native plant and animal populations. Invasive species are considered to be one of the greatest threats to the National Wildlife Refuge System, and to the Leopold Wetland Management District. The District will target control of invasive species to those that directly affect habitats used by waterfowl and grassland-dependent birds. However, many of the invasive species found in woodlots, fencerows and forest are also common early successional invaders of grassland habitat, and therefore species such as buckthorn, honeysuckle, and Siberian elm must also be controlled. Many of the same natural disturbances, such as drought, flood and wildfire, that maintain productivity of natural systems, also provide opportunities for invasive species to multiply and spread. Human activities and disturbances on the landscape such as roads, yards, over-grazed pastures, and vehicle trespass etc. also create conditions conducive to the spread of invasive species. It is very important that the District staff are able to inventory and monitor the spread of invasive species and take actions to minimize the distribution of the species or control its abundance on the landscape. We will probably never be able to eliminate these species from the landscape but targeted biological, chemical, and mechanical controls along with prescribed fire may be useful in reducing their impact on native species. Certain high-quality remnant prairies or naturally functioning wetlands may warrant a more intensive strategy to control invasive species.

Strategies:

1. Inventory and map distribution of invasive species on WPAs and associated state lands. The wildlife biologist will play an important role in completing this project in partnership with volunteers and other organizations and agencies.

2. Develop integrated pest management plan for control of the species that have the most detrimental effect on wetland and grassland habitat on the District. (Wildlife biologist).

3. Collect and distribute biocontrol agents and coordinate mechanical and chemical control activities within the District to control invasive species.

4. Develop a monitoring program with volunteers.

5. Work with adjacent landowners and the DNR to control invasive species on a landscape level, targeting blocks of wetland and grassland habitat. The wildlife refuge specialist and private lands biologist will work on this project.

Objective 1.6: Land Acquisition

Acquire 600 acres per year.

Rationale: Funds for the acquisition of WPAs in Wisconsin will always be limited. Acquisitions are an important tool that will be targeted to protect lands that produce waterfowl and maintain the long-term viability of individual WPAs or public land complexes. Acquisition and management of large blocks of permanently protected wetland/grassland habitat in conjunction with other land management agencies and organizations will provide the greatest benefit to waterfowl production within the District. A

Wood Duck. USFWS photo.

landscape level analysis in coordination with partners is needed to understand predicted waterfowl production on a District-wide scale. This analysis will provide valuable information for acquisition and management programs by the Service and its partners.

Strategies:

1. Respond to inquiries regarding land acquisition.
2. Work to acquire roundouts of existing WPAs.
3. Identify and contact landowners of key, small inholdings.
4. Acquire lands that maximize block size of grassland-wetland complexes through the acquisition of key tracts that add to existing public habitat complexes.
5. Work in partnership with Wisconsin DNR and NAWCA to achieve goals outlined for the Glacial Habitat Restoration Area, Rush Lake Winnebago System Initiative, South Central Wisconsin Prairie Pothole Habitat Initiative, Horicon Marsh Headwaters, and Southeast Coastal Habitat Initiative.
6. Continue coordinating with the Farming and Conservation Together (FACT) group for land acquisition and habitat restoration projects in the Fairfield Marsh: A Conservation Partnership.
7. Secure funding from grants and partners to assist with land acquisition efforts.
8. Investigate long-term viability of select WPAs within the District to see if they will be able to meet the conservation goals of the WPA program. If the long-term viability is threatened by urban encroachment, trade these lands for high quality lands that will meet long-term waterfowl production goals.

Goal 2: Wildlife

Preserve, restore, and enhance the diversity and abundance of migratory birds and other native wildlife with emphasis on waterfowl, grassland and wetland-dependent birds.

Objective 2.1: Waterfowl

Develop a waterfowl recruitment monitoring program within 5 years of CCP approval that will include working with partners and a university to develop a waterfowl production and survival study.

Rationale: An assessment of waterfowl production through a waterfowl recruitment monitoring program and research study would provide additional information to assist in acquisition and restoration efforts within the District. The monitoring program and research studies would attempt to determine waterfowl pair density on the landscape, nest success and brood survival. When used in combination with on-the-ground knowledge of waterfowl use, analysis of GIS information including wetland density, grassland distribution and public ownership, waterfowl recruitment data can be a very valuable tool to direct management activities. Additional information is needed to understand local waterfowl populations and factors affecting recruitment within the Leopold Wetland Management District. Numerous land use changes have occurred throughout the Upper Midwest in the last 25 years and these changes have probably affected waterfowl production and distribution.

In addition to nest density and success, other factors such as duckling survival play an important role in recruitment. The District is located on the very eastern edge of what is considered prairie pothole landscape created by glaciers. Several studies have indicated that duckling survival plays a larger role in Mallard production in the Great Lakes region than in the prairie potholes of North and South Dakota. In contrast, nest success plays a larger role in waterfowl production in the Dakotas. In addition to prairie pothole habitat, there are several known areas within the District that produce large numbers of waterfowl but do not resemble "traditional" prairie pothole habitat. In conjunction with local studies to assess waterfowl production and distribution, the recruitment data and on-the-ground knowledge of the landscape will provide valuable information for making management and acquisition decisions.

Strategies:

1. Partner with Wisconsin DNR, Great Lakes Joint Venture, and Ducks Unlimited to assess waterfowl production in Southeast Wisconsin. The wildlife biologist will take the lead on this project.
2. Partner with local university and the Service's Biological Monitoring Team to assess waterfowl production, recruitment and distribution. The wildlife biologist will take the lead with assistance from the biological technician on this project.

Objective 2.2: Federally Listed Threatened and Endangered Species

Assure that federally listed species and federally proposed species and their habitats are protected.

Rationale: At the present time two federally listed threatened or endangered species (Eastern prairie fringed orchid and Karner blue butterfly) and one species designated as a "Non-essential Experimental Population" (Whooping Crane) have been documented on District lands. Surveys for the presence of endangered species on additional WPAs will allow the District to change or modify management practices to avoid negative impacts and enhance these populations.

Wisconsin DNR electroshocking fish. USFWS photo.

Strategies:

1. Protect known occurrences of listed and proposed species.
2. Survey for presence/absence of listed and proposed species.

Objective 2.3: Regional Species of Concern

Develop baseline surveys to identify Regional Species of Concern use of District lands. Surveys will identify the presence/absence of species and abundance of select high priority species.

Rationale: Region 3's Regional Conservation Priority (RCP) list includes rare and declining species, federally listed, and recreationally important species that are of high concern in the Upper Midwest. The RCP list was developed to help prioritize management within the Region. Knowing that the species are using the habitats on the District will be an indicator of success in providing for these species, with the exception of nuisance species. The District listed 79 bird species, three mammal species, four reptiles, one fish species, and eight insect species on the Region 3 RCP list. Monitoring is a key element in determining if District management is achieving its goals of providing habitat for key wildlife species. Monitoring can be costly if high precision is sought. For this plan, a monitoring plan will be developed and a survey will be conducted to confirm species presence.

Strategies:

1. Develop monitoring plan. The biologist will complete and implement this plan with assistance from the biological technician.
2. Continue to document observed fish and wildlife species and add to District species lists.

Objective 2.4: State T&E Species and Species of Concern

Consider known populations of state listed species in management actions.

Rationale: The range of several state listed species overlaps with District lands. Surveys need to be conducted to document the presence of these spe-

Great Blue Heron. USFWS photo.

cies on District lands. Monitoring can be costly if high precision is sought. For this plan, a monitoring plan will be developed and a survey will be conducted to confirm species presence. State threatened and endangered species and Species of Greatest Conservation Need as designated in the Wisconsin Action Plan will be considered in management actions on the District.

Strategies:

1. Document the presence of state listed species and add to District species lists.

Objective 2.5: Monitoring

Assess the value of local ecotype native seed mixtures and plantings for migratory birds.

Rationale: The District needs to develop a better understanding of the value and success of our local ecotype seed plantings to migratory birds. Studies in the Dakotas have suggested that a number of grassland-dependent bird species favor areas dominated by native vegetation. Although the District uses a very diverse mix of five grass species and 30-40 forb species, an assessment of the resulting diversity and heterogeneity of the plantings will be valuable in determining if the mixes are providing quality habitat. In addition, site specific conditions and planting techniques may result in mixed stands of native plants and cool season exotic species such as brome. The conversion of many of these fields to native plant species is an experiment in finding the optimal combination of native grasses and forbs. Ongoing monitoring and assessment of these plantings is needed to refine our restoration and management process and achieve the best habitat conditions. As habitat conditions change in these fields from monotypic stands of brome to a very diverse mix of native species, the District also needs to understand changes in migratory bird populations and adjust management strategies accordingly.

Strategies:

1. Develop a partnership with a university to conduct a research study on the native seed plantings and associated migratory bird use (wildlife biologist).
2. Assess the diversity and success of native seed plantings to evaluate restoration and management techniques (wildlife biologist).

Goal 3: People

A broad cross section of the public enjoys and appreciates District lands.

Objective 3.1: Visitor Services (General)

Improve visitor services facilities and programs to raise quality of visitors' experiences.

Rationale: The District is increasingly influenced by the growth of the Madison and Milwaukee metropolitan areas. The expanding residential development challenges the District's habitat and wildlife goals. The increased population in the District also offers an opportunity to offer wildlife-dependent recreation to more people leading to a greater understanding and appreciation for the natural world and wildlife conservation. WPAs are open to compatible wildlife-dependent recreation, but the District's facilities and services are lacking. Recreation information in print and on the internet is minimal, and there are few signs offering information and identification. Upgrades to facilities and programs are needed to satisfy basic standards of service.

To evaluate improvements across the entire visitor services program and summarize progress, the District will use the evaluation standards of RAPP (Refuge Annual Performance Plan). RAPP measures act as a general indicator of how successful management is in satisfying the criteria for quality of recreation use as described in the Service Manual Chapter 605 FW1.6. Some improvements are clearly needed and inferred from the criteria in the Service manual. These improvements are identified below in the strategies and under the strategies of the wildlife-dependent activities listed in the next objectives. As the visitor services program of the District matures and more details are specified in a visitor services plan, the District will be able to move to more direct and specific measures of recreation quality. These direct measures will include a survey of visitors.

Not all WPAs are equally valuable for public access. Some have greater potential to offer quality recreation experiences. To use resources most effectively, the WPAs will be evaluated and those with the greatest potential for public use will be developed more fully. Likely WPAs to have increased attention include Uihlien, Becker, Shoveler's Sink, Schoenberg Marsh and Baraboo River. Development of public use facilities will be in addition to raising the general level of the visitor services program and some improvement at all WPAs.

Strategies:

1. Develop seven properties with parking lots, kiosks, and other compatible facilities. The Wildlife Refuge Specialist position will be responsible for developing these WPAs and coordinating long-term maintenance and management of these facilities.
2. Develop a visitor services plan based on the visitor services review completed in 2006 (wildlife refuge specialist).
3. Update the website following Regional mapping standards.
4. Improve District brochures and update the District's general brochure.
5. Update WPA maps and aerial photos.
6. Develop a work study partnership with local universities.
7. Develop and install interpretive panels on kiosks following regional standards.
8. Update boundary posting on all WPAs.
9. Install "Your Duck Stamp Dollars at Work" on all WPAs with enhanced visitor services facilities. In addition, put up these signs at other high visibility WPAs.

Objective 3.2: Hunting

Maintain a Service quality ranking of "good" and evaluate the quality of hunting visits within 15 years.

Rationale: As one of the six priority wildlife-dependent recreational uses identified in the National Wildlife Refuge System Improvement Act of 1997, hunting provides traditional recreational activities on the District with no definable adverse impacts to the biological integrity or habitat sustainability of District resources. Waterfowl production areas differ from national wildlife refuges in that they are open to hunting, fishing, and trapping by specific regulation, and open to the other wildlife-dependent recreational activities by notification in general brochures available at the District office. New and existing WPAs are thus "open until closed" versus national wildlife refuges, which are "closed until opened." Within the Leopold WMD, Blue-wing WPA in Ozaukee County and Wilcox WPA in Waushara County have been designated as closed to hunting.

In an effort to improve the quality of the hunting program, specific strategies will be implemented to meet criteria listed in the RAPP rating. The RAPP rating will give a general indication for how well the District is doing in providing quality hunting opportunities. But, to more directly and definitively evaluate the type and quality of experience as perceived by hunters, it will be necessary to get feedback from hunters. Therefore, before the end of the life of this plan, the District will survey hunters to document their experience. The survey data will be useful in evaluating the program and provide a basis for possible revisions in the program during the next cycle of planning. An increase in hunter knowledge of regulations through signage may also reduce illegal take of wildlife. Replacement of faded boundary signs and an increased emphasis on maintaining posting, parking lots and gates may also reduce trespass problems on WPAs and neighboring private lands.

Strategies:

1. See strategies under "Visitor Services (General)."
2. Develop a hunting plan.
3. Develop accessible hunting opportunities.
4. Survey hunters.

5. Install regulation signs at all WPA parking lots.
6. Replace faded and missing boundary signs on WPAs. The seasonal tractor operator will be responsible for assuring boundaries are clearly marked and posted.

Objective 3.3: Fishing

Consider the potential for recreational fishing when property is acquired and evaluate opportunities on existing waterfowl production areas if water levels increase enough to support fish.

Rationale: Although fishing is one of the six priority recreational uses identified in the National Wildlife Refuge System Improvement Act of 1997, fishing opportunities are virtually non-existant. This recreational use is secondary to the primary purpose for which the District was created and must be compatible with that purpose.

Most WPA wetlands are relatively shallow and do not support fish due to winter kill. Although several WPAs (Baraboo River, Uihlein, and Hinkson Creek) have waterways traversing or adjacent, there are higher quality fishing opportunities available on many other nearby lakes, rivers, or streams.

Strategies:

1. See strategies under "Visitor Services (General)."
2. As new acquisitions continue to be added to the WPA program, fishing opportunities will be evaluated.

Objective 3.4: Wildlife Observation and Photography

Maintain a Service quality ranking of "good" and evaluate quality of observation and photography visits within 15 years.

Rationale: Wildlife observation and photography are both priority wildlife-dependent recreational activities, which are listed in the National Wildlife Refuge System Improvement Act of 1997. These recreational uses are secondary to the primary purpose for which the District was created and must be compatible. The District has the potential to provide opportunities for wildlife observation and photography in the rapidly growing portions of the Madison and Milwaukee metropolitan areas. Some of the WPAs are scenic, but the general lack of visitor facilities and low public awareness does not promote visits by the public. The quality of a visit would be enhanced for the casual visitor by developing trail access, an observation platform, and interpretive messages. Developing visitor services amenities on the most suitable WPAs and promoting them in the local community will increase visitation and foster a connection between visitors and nature.

Strategies:

1. See strategies under "Visitor Services (General)"
2. Develop a short loop trail and overlook on at least two WPAs.
3. Develop a bird list brochure.
4. Develop a theme for interpretive materials.
5. Recruit volunteers to support observation and photography program.
6. Promote sales of duck stamps and the role of duck stamps in WPA land acquisition.

Objective 3.5: Environmental Education and Interpretation

Achieve a Service quality ranking of "good" within 5 years and evaluate quality of environmental education and interpretation visits within 15 years.

Rationale: Environmental education and interpretation are both priority wildlife-dependent recreational activities, which are listed in the National Wildlife Refuge System Improvement Act of 1997. These recreational uses are secondary to the primary purpose for which the District was created and must be compatible. Little environmental education or interpretation has occurred in the District. Interpretive themes have not been formally developed, and the District office has minimal space for interpretive information. WPA parking lots are not easily accessible for school buses, and there are no accessible trails on the District for school groups and the general public. The District's approach in the past has been to respond case-by-case to inquiries from teachers. The District staff provides interpretive programs to partners and other organizations as requested. The programs primarily consist of overviews of the District and current management practices.

District staff tie bundles of brush. USFWS photo.

Since the District will probably not have an environmental education specialist position during the life of the plan, an emphasis will be to develop educational materials and information that schools and groups can use on self-guided visits to WPAs. The value of the environmental education and interpretation program will be to increase public understanding of the WMD and its goals. This program should complement the activities of community outreach and seek to increase stewardship of WPAs and wildlife habitat.

Strategies:

1. See strategies under "Visitor Services (General)."
2. Include school bus turn-arounds among public use improvements proposed for some WPAs.
3. Seek cooperation from university programs to create environmental education materials for District programs.
4. Develop a theme for interpretive materials.
5. Upgrade interpretive materials available at headquarters.
6. Present at least five interpretive/informational programs per year.
7. Work with the Horicon NWR park ranger to complete education and interpretation projects on the WMD.
8. Develop orientation kiosks at WPAs and include interpretation.

Objective 3.6: Volunteers

Volunteers contribute 300 hours per year within 2 years of plan approval.

Rationale: Opportunities for enhancing the wildlife and visitor services programs will likely always exceed the District's budget. Therefore, all District activities will benefit from volunteer participation, and certain activities will require volunteer participation to be successful. Many of the WMD goals, such as increasing local ecotype forb and grass harvest and controlling invasive species, will require large amounts of volunteer time to complete. A coordinated and efficiently run volunteer program will be essential to achieving many District goals. The wildlife refuge specialist position will be very important in developing and coordinating the volunteer program which will be successful if there is personal contact and follow-up with the volunteers.

Strategies:

1. Recruit new volunteers to assist with resource management and visitor services.
2. Recognize and supervise volunteers as adjunct staff.
3. Coordinate volunteer activities within the resource management and visitor service programs. (Wildlife biologist and wildlife refuge specialist)
4. Follow Service guidelines for volunteer management.
5. Expand the volunteer program to include organized groups of volunteers to complete large projects such as seed harvest, seed nursery weed control and invasive species control.

Objective 3.7: Partnerships

Increase and improve partnerships over the level of the 2007 program.

Rationale: The value of a WPA is enhanced when it exists in a complex of wetlands. A WPA adjacent to other wetlands is more valuable to waterfowl than one that is isolated in an agricultural or residential landscape. And, no one organization or person can match the accomplishments of several entities working together. It is important, therefore, for the District to work with neighbors, other government agencies, and private organizations to improve the District's landscape for the benefit of migratory birds, other wildlife, and humans. Many WPAs are located immediately adjacent to or within a short distance of State Wildlife Areas or other public lands. Since the main objective of the District's habitat management program is to provide large blocks of quality wetland and grassland habitat for nesting waterfowl and other migratory birds, the Service should work with partners to assist with projects that meet this goal, regardless of ownership boundaries. Several focus areas and project areas overlap the geographic area of the District and complement the Service's goal of providing habitat for waterfowl and other grassland and wetland dependent migratory birds.

The Upper Mississippi River and Great Lakes Joint Venture Implementation Plan of 2007, as part of the North American Waterfowl Management Plan, identifies the Glacial Habitat Restoration area and south central Wisconsin Prairie Pothole Initiative, both of which include portions of the District, as high priority areas for conserving breeding waterfowl habitat. The implementation plan encourages private-public partnerships in a landscape approach to conservation. Based on the past success of the partnerships, the District will continue its participation and coordination in this program to pursue the synergistic benefits of cooperation.

Ducks Unlimited has identified a priority area in Eastern Wisconsin, which includes the District, as a focus for protecting and restoring small seasonal wetlands, re-establishing native prairie adjacent to wetlands for production habitat, and expanding existing state and federal wildlife areas. Ducks Unlimited and its partners have been active in conserving wetland and upland habitat in the past. Because of past success, the District will continue to actively work with these partners in further habitat work.

The State of Wisconsin has identified the Glacial Habitat Restoration Area (WPHRA) as a focus for the state. It is one of two HRAs in the State of Wisconsin. The GHRA was established to protect and restore 38,600 acres of grassland and 11,000 acres of wetland habitat in portions of Columbia, Dodge, Fond du Lac, and Winnebago Counties. The Wisconsin DNR and partners will use several tools, including acquisition of fee title or easements to protect important grassland and wetland habitat.

The District has been extremely active in coordinating acquisition, restoration, and management opportunities through the Lower Fox River/Green Bay Natural Resources Damage Assessment (NRDA). This NRDA is the result of levees paid by paper companies responsible for releases of PCBs into the Lower Fox River/Green bay Ecosystem and which are to be used for acquisition, restoration, and remediation.

Strategies:

1. Active implementation of the Upper Mississippi Joint Venture Plan and Ducks Unlimited Eastern Wisconsin Focus Area.
2. Active implementation of the Glacial Prairie Habitat Restoration Area in partnership with the Wisconsin DNR.
3. Work with land management organizations including the Wisconsin DNR, National Park Service, and many others to implement landscape level habitat protection and restoration.
4. Increase partnering with conservation organizations.
5. Evaluate creating a "Friends of Leopold WMD."

Objective 3.8: Community Outreach

Within 5 years identify neighbors to 40 percent of the District's WPAs and provide them with information about waterfowl management and make 5 public presentations per year to civic groups, local governments, and other organizations to develop community support and action for waterfowl management across the entire District, both on and off Service lands.

Rationale: The District considers its neighbors and visitors to be very important. The District is an asset to the community and the continued support of the community is essential for the success of the District. It is important that the District continues efforts to build and maintain open communication with neighbors to let them know the successes, challenges, and opportunities in conservation and wildlife-dependent recreation. In an ideal setting, the objective would be to achieve an appreciation of the

Aphrodite butterfly. USFWS photo.

value and need for fish and wildlife conservation among a larger percentage of the population living around the District. The success in achieving the objective would be determined through a survey of the general population. However, for an objective to be useful it must be measurable in both a conceptual and practical sense. It is not practical to propose that the District will conduct a survey of the general population anytime in the next few years, because the approvals and costs are beyond the likely resources of the District. As an alternative, the objective reflects the assumption that providing neighbors and community members with written and oral information will lead to positive conservation attitudes and action. Public understanding of the purpose of District lands, including appropriate and compatible uses, may lead to a reduction in illegal uses such as snowmobiling, dumping, littering, dog training and off-road vehicle use. Public understanding and acceptance of District purposes are also important in maintaining the long-term viability of using management practices such as grazing and prescribed fire to maintain grassland and wetland habitat.

Strategies:

1. Develop neighbors e-mail list.
2. Develop an outreach plan.
3. Work with UW Extension to develop wildlife and habitat materials for neighbors and conservation organizations on WPA management. (Wildlife refuge specialist)
4. Engage neighbors in active habitat management. (Wildlife refuge specialist)
5. Contact neighbors the day of prescribed fires.

Goal 4: Land and Visitor Protection

Protect the integrity of biological resources within the District and the cultural resources and health and safety of visitors and Service staff on WPAs.

Objective 4.1: Conservation Easements

Meet Service monitoring guidelines for FSA easements over next 15 years.

Rationale: The District is responsible for managing Farm Services Administration (FSA, formerly known as FmHA) within the 34-county District. These easements were placed on the properties when landowners defaulted on their Farmers Home Administration loans. Properties were then resold to the original landowner at a discounted price due to the easement or sold to another individual. The Service is designated as the easement manager and is responsible for habitat management on the easement and enforcement of easement provisions. These easements provide additional wetland and grassland habitat throughout the District. Several of the easements are located close to WPAs or other public lands and therefore provide complementary wildlife benefits to these lands.

The new use of the Service wetland and grassland easement program as well as partnerships with other agencies and organizations to use existing easement programs will provide long-term benefits to wildlife populations. The concept of wetland and grassland easements is to provide waterfowl habitat on a landscape scale while allowing land to remain in private ownership.

Strategies:

1. Annually inspect each FSA easement and follow up with landowner contact.
2. Send letters to new landowners informing them of existing easements on their property, along with the associated regulations.
3. Follow protocols within the Service's easement manual to handle all potential violations.

Objective 4.2: Partners for Fish and Wildlife

Restore 120 acres of wetland, grassland, and oak savanna habitat per year with emphasis on focus areas.

Rationale: Over 85 percent of the land in the Leopold WMD is in private ownership. Only by working with private landowners will the Service be able to affect migratory bird populations on a broader landscape scale. The complementary affects of restoring wetlands adjacent to WPAs or other large wetland/grassland complexes will increase the value of these grasslands by providing additional wetland habitat for waterfowl pair and feeding habitat. In addition to the on-the-ground habitat restoration, there are also significant benefits for a broader public understanding of the Service's mission and goals when private lands biologists interact with landowners. Increasing public knowledge and understanding of habitat and wildlife should also result in greater stewardship of our natural resources. The Partners for Fish and Wildlife Program will play an important role in complementing many of the other objectives and strategies in this CCP including community outreach, partnerships, identification of focus areas and landscape conservation initiatives.

Strategies:

1. Work with Wisconsin DNR, private landowners and other partners to restore important wetland, grassland, oak savanna and riparian habitat.
2. Work with USDA to facilitate available programs such as the Conservation Reserve Program (CRP), Wetlands Reserve Program (WRP) and Environmental Quality Incentives Program (EQIP) to protect valuable wildlife habitat.

Objective 4.3: Enforcement

Visitors feel safe and the resource is protected.

Rationale: The District is responsible for protecting District resources and providing a safe environment for employees and visitors. The District's law enforcement program is a critical tool in protecting trust resources, habitat, public facilities, employees, and the visiting public. To provide this essential service, the District will share regional resources and cooperate with other law enforcement authorities to meet its responsibilities.

Strategies:

1. Share regional law enforcement resources.
2. Partner with Wisconsin DNR Conservation Wardens.

Objective 4.4: Cultural Resources

Over the life of the plan, avoid and protect against disturbance of all known cultural, historic, or archeological sites.

Rationale: Cultural resources are an important facet of the country's heritage. Leopold WMD, like all national wildlife refuges and wetland management districts, remains committed to preserving archeological and historic sites against degradation, looting, and other adverse impacts.

Cultural Resources of concern for the Leopold Wetland Management District include archeological resources, historic structures, and historic cultural landscapes. The National Historic Preservation Act of 1966, as amended, is an "Act to Establish a Program of Preservation of Additional Historic Properties throughout the Nation and for other Purposes." The Act provides guidance for deciding whether cultural resources are of sufficient importance to be determined eligible for listing on the National Register of Historic Places (National

Mallard Duck nest. USFWS photo.

Register) or whether significance of integrity are strong enough to support the property to be nominated as a National Historic Landmark.

The National Historic Preservation Act of 1966, as amended, in section 110, directs Federal Agencies to make efforts to minimize harm to National Historic Landmarks in their project planning. Numerous historic properties lie within the counties of the Leopold Wetland Management District. Actions resulting from the CCP will require Section 106 Compliance, if those actions affect historic property. Section 106 of the Historic Preservation Act of 1966, as amended, is a Federal process that ensures cultural resources are taken into consideration during project planning and execution. The affected environment and environmental consequences that may result from actions proposed in the Leopold CCP will require consideration of any cultural resource areas affected by the project, e.g., those areas where ground disturbance, changes in flooding patterns, or modifications to cultural resources would occur.

The District must ensure archeological and cultural values are described, identified, and taken into consideration prior to implementing undertakings. It is also essential that new site discoveries are documented. In order to meet these responsibilities, the District intends to maintain an open dialogue with the Regional Historic Preservation Officer (RHPO) and to provide the RHPO with information about new archeological site discoveries. The District will also cooperate with Federal, state, and local agencies, American Indian tribes, and the public in managing cultural resources on the Refuge.

Strategies:

1. Conduct site-specific surveys prior to ground disturbing projects and protect known archeological, cultural and historic sites.
2. Identify and nominate to the National Register of Historic Places all historic properties including those of religious and cultural significance to Indian tribes.
3. Inform the RHPO early in project planning to ensure compliance with Section 106 of National Historic Preservation Act.
4. Contract with cultural resources firms specializing in Wisconsin to conduct Phase I surveys prior to undertakings that could adversely affect historic resources.
5. In the event of inadvertent discoveries of ancient human remains, follow instructions and procedures indicated by the RHPO.
6. Ensure archeological and cultural values are described, identified, and taken into consideration prior to implementing undertakings.
7. Inspect the condition of known cultural resources on the District and report to the RHPO changes in the conditions.
8. Integrate historic preservation with planning and management of other resources and activities.

Chapter 5: Plan Implementation

Introduction

This chapter summarizes the actions, funding, coordination, and monitoring to implement the CCP. As noted in the inside cover of this document, this plan does not constitute a commitment for staffing increases, operational and maintenance increases, or funding for future land acquisition. These decisions are at the discretion of Congress in overall appropriations, and in budget allocation decisions made at the Washington and Regional levels of the Service.

Building a dike. USFWS photo.

New and Existing Projects

This CCP outlines an ambitious course of action for the future management of the Leopold Wetland Management District. It will require considerable staff commitment as well as funding commitment to actively manage the wildlife habitats and add and improve public use facilities. The District will continually need appropriate operational and maintenance funding to implement the objectives in this plan. A full listing of unfunded District projects and operational needs can be found in Appendix H. A brief description of the highest priority District projects is listed in the following paragraphs.

Minimum Refuge Operations Needs

The project will provide funds to operate the District office including expenses for heating, air conditioning, required safety inspections, electrical expenses, and safety improvements. These funds will also allow for the upkeep of District facilities including parking lots, interpretive kiosks, interpretive trails, and water control structures. It is important to provide a quality experience for visitors who come to the District each year. The project will help pay fuel bills, electric bills and the day-to-day costs of operating a District. (First Year Cost: $108,000, recurring annual cost $108,000)

Prairie Restoration on WPAs and Easements

Quality prairie grassland on the District's WPAs is essential to meet the waterfowl production goals of the District. In addition, numerous species of migratory birds benefit from native prairie grassland. Fully 70 percent (3,425 acres) of the District grasslands are seeded warm-season grasses and forbs or remnant prairie, however only 20 percent (989 acres) is derived from Wisconsin genotype seed. The remaining grasslands are either cool season exotic grasses such as smooth brome, Kentucky bluegrass, and quackgrass, which do not provide diverse habitat for wildlife, or non-Wisconsin varieties of grasses and forbs that do not match the phenology of locally adapted native species. This project will renovate the remaining cool season and grass fields and start to convert non-locally adapted warm-season fields in the District in the next 10 years. This project will address equipment purchase, temporary staff time, chemical, seed and contracts for brush cutting and seed removal. (First Year Cost: $333,000, recurring annual cost $67,000)

Savanna Restoration

While not considered prime waterfowl habitat when compared to grassland and wetland habitats, savannas in Wisconsin were an integral part of the historic landscape. The exclusion of fire and grazing over the years have degenerated this unique habitat and allowed invasive tree and brush species to replace the historical overstory and understory vegetation structure and composition. The goal of this project will be to restore and manage remnant oak savanna ecosystems throughout the District using timber harvest, brush removal, chemical treatment, seeding, and prescribed burning. This project will address equipment purchase, temporary staff time, chemical, seed, and contracts for brush removal. (First Year Cost: $119,000, recurring annual cost $35,000)

Wetland Restoration

Fully 50 percent of the historical wetland acres in the state have been lost to drainage, agriculture, and development. Because of the potential for agricultural production, and more recently urban development, the lands that fall within the District have been particularly hard hit; losses in some counties are estimated at over 75 percent. Wetlands and associated quality grassland habitats provide pair bonding, breeding, brood rearing, and migrational habitat for several species of waterfowl, however Mallard and Blue-wing Teal are of particular concern to the District. This project is to restore and manage all types of wetlands from shallow temporary basins to deep marsh wetlands for the benefit of waterfowl and other waterbirds. This project will address equipment purchase, temporary staff time, chemical, seed, and construction contracts for wetland restorations. (First Year Cost: $370,000, recurring annual cost $81,000)

Blue-winged Teal brood. USFWS photo.

Enhance Biological Program (District Biologist & Biological Technician)

The biologist positions would enable the District to develop a biological program with an emphasis on evaluating and refining management actions to provide quality habitat for wildlife. With assistance from the biological technician, the biologist would also be responsible for coordinating data collection to monitor waterfowl use and recruitment within the District. The data collected from numerous surveys and biological programs would be very useful in making biologically based decisions within the District. Focus areas for acquisition, restoration and management would be developed and refined using this data. (First Year Cost: $287,000, recurring annual cost $74,000)

Enhance Visitor Services Program (Wildlife Refuge Specialist & Seasonal Tractor Operator)

The WPAs in 17 counties provide important recreational opportunities for Wisconsin residents. They also provide an opportunity to reconnect people with nature. The purpose of the project will be to construct and maintain entrance signs, boundary signs, wildlife observation platforms, trails, kiosks, parking lots and boundary fences on WPAs. Some WPAs will also be developed that will provide public opportunities for the Service's six priority wildlife-dependent recreational uses: hunting, fishing, wildlife observation, wildlife photography, interpretation and environmental education. (First Year Cost: $207,000, recurring annual cost $54,000)

Control of Invasive Species, Noxious Weeds and Woody Invaders

Invasive species are detrimental to plant and animal populations. In addition, grassland habitat on the District is negatively impacted by other noxious weeds and woody invaders such as box elder, Canada thistle, and spotted knapweed. The purpose of the project is to control these unwanted plant species and provide quality wetland, grassland and

Table 9: Current and Proposed Staffing Under the CCP

Current Staff- 8.2 FTEs	Proposed Additions – 3.5 FTEs
District Manager	
Wildlife Refuge Specialist	Wildlife Refuge Specialist with emphasis in public use
Wildlife Biologist	Wildlife biologist & Biological Technician
Maintenance Worker	Permanent Seasonal tractor operator
Administrative Technician	
2- Private Lands Wildlife Biologists	
Fire Management Specialist	
Lead Fire Technician (19pp)	

woodland habitat on the District. The project would be in partnership with neighboring landowners and agencies in an effort to take a landscape approach to habitat management. Funds will be used for chemical, contract plant removal and temporary staff. (First Year Cost: $136,000, recurring annual cost $45,000)

Replace Facilities (Headquarters and Maintenance Facilities)

The current headquarters and maintenance facilities are inadequate to meet the needs of the Service. The facilities are not universally accessible and are not of an adequate size to support current staffing levels. Presently, the station headquarters is a converted two-story house with little room for interpretive exhibits for visitors, and there are safety concerns. The maintenance facilities consist of two small pole barns and a two-car garage. There is no building to repair and maintain equipment year round. It is important to have adequate indoor secure storage to protect the Service's investment in equipment and supplies. These proposed facilities would include a headquarters (office) and maintenance shop to store and repair all equipment. (One Time Cost: $4.0 million)

Staffing

Implementing the vision set forth in this CCP will require changes in the organizational structure of the District. Existing staff will direct their time and energy in new directions and new staff members will be added to assist in these efforts. Table 9 presents current staffing and the increases proposed for the District in this plan. Figure 30 shows the staffing organization at Leopold WMD.

Partnership Opportunities

Partnerships are an essential element for the successful accomplishment of goals, objectives, and strategies at Leopold WMD. The objectives outlined in this CCP need the support and the partnerships of federal, state and local agencies, non-governmental organizations and individual citizens. District staff will continue to seek creative partnership opportunities to achieve the vision of the District.

We expect to continue to work with the following notable partners, while developing new partnerships:

- County Agencies
- County Land and Water Conservation Departments
- Wisconsin Department of Natural Resources
- Wisconsin Department of Agriculture, Trade, & Consumer Protection
- National Park Service
- Natural Resources Conservation Service (USDA)
- Ozaukee/Washington County Land Trust
- Towns
- Ducks Unlimited
- Wisconsin Waterfowl Association
- Pheasants Forever
- Wings over Wisconsin
- University of Wisconsin Extension
- University of Wisconsin – Stevens Point
- Portage Charter School

Figure 30: Current Staff, Leopold Wetland Management District

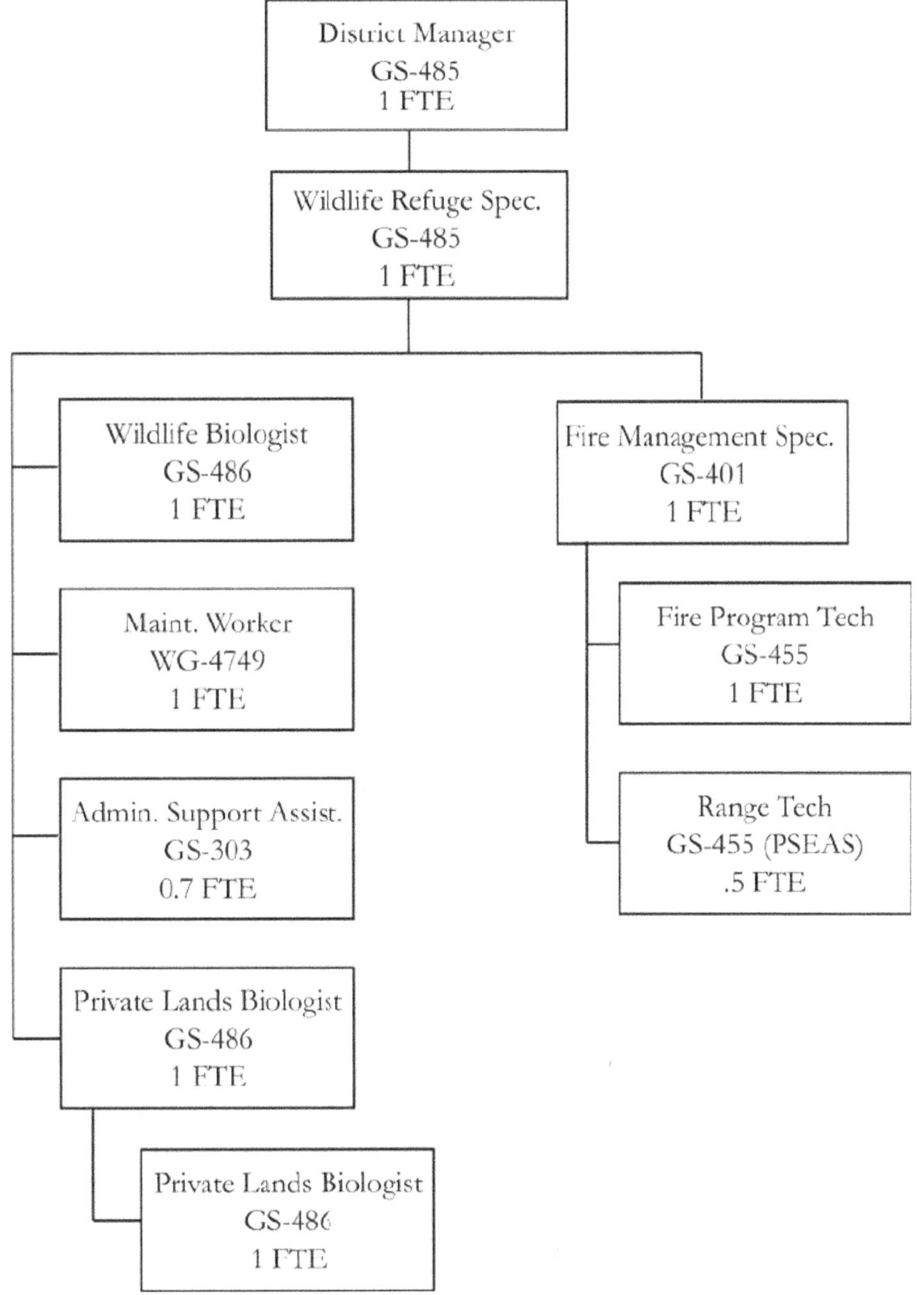

- Aldo Leopold Foundation
- Sand County Foundation
- Madison Audubon Society

Step-Down Management Plans

The CCP is a plan that provides general concepts and specific wildlife, habitat, and people related objectives. Step-down management plans provide greater detail to managers and employees who will carry out the strategies described in the CCP. The District staff will revise or develop the following step-down plans:

- Habitat Management Plan (within 5 years)
- Visitor Services Plan (within 8 years)
- Habitat and Wildlife Monitoring Plans (within 8 years)

The Fire Management Plan, approved in 2007, provides direction and establishes procedures to guide various wildland fire program activities. The Fire Management Plan covers the historical and ecological role of fire, fire management objectives, preparedness, suppression, fire management actions and responses, fire impacts, use of prescribed fire and fire management restrictions.

Monitoring and Evaluation

The direction set forth in this CCP and specifically identified strategies and projects will be monitored throughout the life of this plan. On a periodic basis, the Regional Office will assemble a station review team whose purpose will be to visit the District and evaluate current activities in light of this plan. The team will review all aspects of District management, including direction, accomplishments and funding. The goals and objectives presented in this CCP will provide the baseline for evaluation of this field station.

Monarch butterfly. USFWS photo.

Plan Review and Revision

The CCP is meant to provide guidance to District managers and staff over the next 15 years. However, the CCP is also a dynamic and flexible document and several of the strategies contained in this plan are subject to uncontrollable events of nature. Likewise, many of the strategies are dependent upon Service funding for staff and projects. Because of all these factors, the recommendations in the CCP will be reviewed periodically and, if necessary, revised to meet new circumstances. If any revisions are major, the review and revision will include the public.

Appendix A: Finding of No Significant Impact

Finding of No Significant Impact

Environmental Assessment and Comprehensive Conservation Plan for Leopold Wetland Management District, Wisconsin

An Environmental Assessment (EA) has been prepared to identify management strategies to meet the conservation goals of the Leopold Wetland Management District (WMD). The EA examined the environmental consequences that each management alternative could have on the quality of the physical, biological, and human environment, as required by the National Environmental Policy Act of 1969 (NEPA). The EA evaluated four alternatives for the future management of the Refuge.

The alternative selected for implementation is *Alternative 4*. The preferred alternative for Leopold WMD increases the acreage subject to habitat management activities, increases monitoring of habitat and wildlife, and expands and improves the quality of visitor services.

For reasons presented above and below, and based on an evaluation of the information contained in the Environmental Assessment, we have determined that the action of adopting Alternative 4 as the management alternative for the District is not a major federal action which would significantly affect the quality of the human environment, within the meaning of Section 102 (2) (c) of the National Environmental Policy Act of 1969.

Additional Reasons:

1. Future management actions will have a neutral or positive impact on the local economy.
2. This action will not have an adverse impact on threatened or endangered species.

Supporting References:

Environmental Assessment
Comprehensive Conservation Plan

Regional Director   Date 9/29/08

Charles M. Wooley
Acting Regional Director

Appendix B: Glossary

Glossary

Adaptive Management

A systematic process for continually improving management policies and practices by learning from the outcomes of operational programs.

Alternative

A set of objectives and strategies needed to achieve refuge goals and the desired future condition.

Biological Diversity

The variety of life forms and its processes, including the variety of living organisms, the genetic differences among them, and the communities and ecosystems in which they occur.

Biological Integrity

Biotic composition, structure, and functioning at genetic, organism, and community levels comparable with historic conditions, including the natural biological processes that shape genomes, organisms, and communities.

Compatible Use

A wildlife-dependent recreational use, or any other use on a refuge that will not materially interfere with or detract from the fulfillment of the mission of the Service or the purposes of the refuge.

Comprehensive Conservation Plan

A document that describes the desired future conditions of the refuge, and specifies management actions to achieve refuge goals and the mission of the National Wildlife Refuge System.

Conservation Easement

A popular method of land conservation used by private individuals, land trusts and governments. Conservation easements involve the acquisition of specific land rights for the purpose of achieving defined habitat objectives.

Cultural Resources

"Those parts of the physical environment -- natural and built -- that have cultural value to some kind of sociocultural group ... [and] those non-material human social institutions...." Cultural resources include historic sites, archeological sites and associated artifacts, sacred sites, traditional cultural properties, cultural items (human remains, funerary objects, sacred objects, and objects of cultural patrimony), and buildings and structures.

Ecosystem

A dynamic and interrelated complex of plant and animal communities and their associated non-living environment.

Ecotype

A subspecies or race of a species which has adapted specifically to cope with a particular set of environmental conditions.

Endangered Species

Any species of plant or animal defined through the Endangered Species Act as being in danger of extinction throughout all or a significant portion of its range, and published in the Federal Register.

Environmental Assessment

A systematic analysis to determine if proposed actions would result in a significant effect on the quality of the environment.

Goals

Descriptive statements of desired future conditions.

Habitat Fragmentation

The discontinuity in the spatial distribution of resources and conditions present in an area at a given scale that affects occupancy, reproduction, or survival in a particular species. [Citation:

Franklin, Alan B., Barry R. Noon, and T. Luke George. 2002. What Is Habitat Fragmentation? Studies in Avian Biology No. 25:20-29.]

High Quality Recreation

Wildlife-dependent recreational programs that meet criteria defined in Section 1.6 of 605 FW 1.

Invasive Species

Invasive species are alien species whose introduction causes or is likely to cause economic or environmental harm or harm to human health. Executive Order 13112 requires the District to monitor, prevent, and control the presence of invasive species.

Issue

Any unsettled matter that requires a management decision. For example, a resource management problem, concern, a threat to natural resources, a conflict in uses, or in the presence of an undesirable resource condition.

National Wildlife Refuge System

All lands, waters, and interests therein administered by the U.S. Fish and Wildlife Service as wildlife refuges, wildlife ranges, wildlife management areas, waterfowl production areas, and other areas for the protection and conservation of fish, wildlife and plant resources.

Objectives

A concise statement of what we want to achieve. The statement is specific, measurable, achievable, results oriented, and time-fixed.

Preferred Alternative

The Service's selected alternative identified in the environmental assessment and fully developed in the Comprehensive Conservation Plan.

Prescribed Fire

Prescribed fire is any fire ignited to meet specific objectives. Before lighting the fire, a written prescribed fire plan must be approved and National Environmental Policy Act requirements must be followed.

Recruitment

A term used by biologists to describe the rate at which breeding hens produce young for the fall population.

Scoping

A process for determining the scope of issues to be addressed by a comprehensive conservation plan and for identifying the significant issues. Involved in the scoping process are federal, state and local agencies; private organizations; and individuals.

Species

A distinctive kind of plant or animal having distinguishable characteristics, and that can interbreed and produce young. A category of biological classification.

Strategies

A general approach or specific actions to achieve objectives.

Threatened Species

Those plant or animal species likely to become endangered species throughout all of or a significant portion of their range within the foreseeable future. A plant or animal identified and defined in accordance with the 1973 Endangered Species Act and published in the Federal Register.

Undertaking:

"A project, activity, or program funded in whole or in part under the direct or indirect jurisdiction of a Federal agency, including those carried out by or on behalf of a Federal agency; those carried out with Federal financial assistance; those requiring a Federal permit, license or approval...," i.e., all Federal actions.

Vegetation

Plants in general, or the sum total of the plant life in an area.

Vegetation Type

A category of land based on potential or existing dominant plant species of a particular area.

Waterfowl Production Area

Waterfowl production area means any wetland or pothole area acquired pursuant to section 4(c) of the amended Migratory Bird Hunting Stamp Act (72 Stat. 487; 16 U.S.C. 718d(c)), owned or controlled by the United States and administered by the U.S. Fish and Wildlife Service as a part of the National Wildlife Refuge System. (50CFR25.12--Sec. 25.12)

Watershed

The entire land area that collects and drains water into a stream or stream system.

Wetland

Areas such as lakes, marshes, and streams that are inundated by surface or ground water for a long enough period of time each year to support, and that do support under natural conditions, plants and animals that require saturated or seasonally saturated soils.

Wetland Management District

An administrative unit of the U.S. Fish and Wildlife Service charged with acquiring, overseeing and managing waterfowl production areas and easements within a specified group of counties.

Wildlife-dependent Recreational Use

A use of refuge that involves hunting, fishing, wildlife observation and photography, or environmental education and interpretation, as identified in the National Wildlife Refuge System Improvement Act of 1997.

Wilderness

A wilderness, in contrast with those areas where man and his own works dominate the landscape, is hereby recognized as an area where the earth and its community of life are untrammeled by man, where man himself is a visitor who does not remain. An area of wilderness is further defined to mean in this chapter an area of undeveloped Federal land retaining its primeval character and influence, without permanent improvements or human habitation, which is protected and managed so as to preserve its natural conditions and which (1) generally appears to have been affected primarily by the forces of nature, with the imprint of man's work substantially unnoticeable; (2) has outstanding opportunities for solitude or a primitive and unconfined type of recreation; (3) has at least five thousand acres of land or is of sufficient size as to make practicable its preservation and use in an unimpaired condition; and (4) may also contain ecological, geological, or other features of scientific, educational, scenic, or historical value. (Public Law 88-577)

Appendix C: Species Lists

Species That Potentially Occur on Leopold WMD

This bird list was compiled by the Horicon Marsh Bird Club and contains species that have been recorded on Horicon Marsh. This list is our best approximation of the species expected to occur on the District.

List of Potential Bird Species on Leopold WMD[1]

Species	Nesting on the Refuge	Probable Abundance by Season A: Abundant, should find on every trip C: Common, should find 75% of trips U: Uncommon, present but in lesser numbers R: Rare, infrequent or few identifications H: Accidental, not expected at this location			
		Spring	Summer	Fall	Winter
Loons					
Common Loon		R	R	H	
Grebes					
Pied-billed Grebe	✓	C	C	C	R
Horned Grebe		R		R	
Red-necked Grebe	✓	R	R	R	
Eared Grebe		R	R	R	
Pelicans					
American White Pelican	✓	C	C	C	
Cormorants					
Double-crested Cormorant	✓	C	C	C	R
Bitterns, Herons					
American Bittern	✓	U	U	U	R
Least Bittern	✓	U	U	U	
Great Blue Heron	✓	A	A	A	R
Great Egret	✓	C	C	C	
Snowy Egret		R	R	R	
Little Blue Heron		R	R	R	
Cattle Egret		R	R	R	
Green Heron	✓	U	U	U	
Black-crowned Night-Heron	✓	C	C	C	R
American Vultures					
Turkey Vulture	✓	U	U	R	
Swans, Geese and Ducks					
Gr. White-fronted Goose		R		R	R

List of Potential Bird Species on Leopold WMD[1] (Continued)

Species	Nesting on the Refuge	Probable Abundance by Season A: Abundant, should find on every trip C: Common, should find 75% of trips U: Uncommon, present but in lesser numbers R: Rare, infrequent or few identifications H: Accidental, not expected at this location			
		Spring	Summer	Fall	Winter
Snow Goose		U		U	U
Ross's Goose		R		R	
Canada Goose	✓	A	A	A	U
Cackling Goose		U		U	R
Mute Swan		R	R	R	R
Trumpeter Swan		R	R	R	R
Tundra Swan		U	U	U	R
Wood Duck	✓	C	C	C	R
Gadwall	✓	U	U	U	R
American Wigeon	✓	C	U	C	R
American Black Duck		U	U	U	R
Mallard	✓	A	A	A	R
Blue-winged Teal	✓	C	C	C	
Northern Shoveler	✓	C	U	C	R
Northern Pintail		U	U	U	R
Green-winged Teal	✓	C	C	A	R
Canvasback		U	R	U	R
Redhead	✓	C	C	C	R
Ring-necked Duck		C	U	C	R
Greater Scaup		R		R	R
Lesser Scaup		C	U	C	R
Bufflehead		U	U	U	R
Common Goldeneye		C	U	C	R
Hooded Merganser	✓	U	U	U	R
Common Merganser		U	R	U	R
Red-breasted Merganser		R		R	R
Ruddy Duck	✓	A	C	A	R
Eagles, Hawks and Allies					
Osprey		U	U	U	
Bald Eagle	✓	U	U	U	R
Northern Harrier	✓	C	C	C	U
Sharp-shinned Hawk	✓	U	R	U	U
Cooper's Hawk	✓	U	U	U	U

List of Potential Bird Species on Leopold WMD[1] (Continued)

Species	Nesting on the Refuge	Probable Abundance by Season A: Abundant, should find on every trip C: Common, should find 75% of trips U: Uncommon, present but in lesser numbers R: Rare, infrequent or few identifications H: Accidental, not expected at this location			
		Spring	Summer	Fall	Winter
Northern Goshawk		R	H	R	R
Red-shouldered Hawk		R	R	R	R
Broad-winged Hawk		U		U	
Red-tailed Hawk	✓	C	C	C	C
Rough-legged Hawk		U		U	U
Falcons					
American Kestrel	✓	C	C	C	C
Merlin		R		R	R
Peregrine Falcon		R	R	R	
Partridges, Grouse					
Gray Partridge	✓	U	U	U	U
Ring-necked Pheasant	✓	C	C	C	C
Wild Turkey	✓	U	U	U	U
Rails, Gallinules, Coots					
Yellow Rail		R	R	R	
King Rail	✓	U	U	U	
Virginia Rail	✓	C	C	C	R
Sora	✓	C	C	C	
Common Moorhen		C	C	C	
American Coot	✓	A	A	A	R
Cranes					
Whooping Crane		H	H	H	
Sandhill Crane	✓	C	C	C	H
Plovers					
Black-bellied Plover		U		U	
American Golden-Plover		U		U	
Semipalmated Plover		C		C	
Killdeer	✓	A	A	A	R
Stilts, Avocets					
Black-necked Stilt	✓	R	R	R	
American Avocet		R	R	R	
Sandpipers, Phalaropes, and Allies					
Greater Yellowlegs		C	U	C	
Lesser Yellowlegs		C	U	C	

List of Potential Bird Species on Leopold WMD[1] (Continued)

Species	Nesting on the Refuge	Probable Abundance by Season			
		A: Abundant, should find on every trip C: Common, should find 75% of trips U: Uncommon, present but in lesser numbers R: Rare, infrequent or few identifications H: Accidental, not expected at this location			
		Spring	Summer	Fall	Winter
Solitary Sandpiper		C	U	C	
Willet		R	R	R	
Spotted Sandpiper	✓	U	U	U	
Hudsonian Godwit		R	R	R	
Marbled Godwit		R	R	R	
Ruddy Turnstone		R	R	R	
Red Knot		R	R	R	
Sanderling		R	R	R	
Semipalmated Sandpiper		C	U	C	
Least Sandpiper		C	U	C	
White-rumped Sandpiper		U	U	U	
Baird's Sandpiper		U	U	U	
Pectoral Sandpiper		C	U	C	
Dunlin		C	U	C	
Stilt Sandpiper		U	U	U	
Buff-breasted Sandpiper		R	R	R	
Short-billed Dowitcher		C	U	C	
Long-billed Dowitcher		U	U	C	
Wilson's Snipe	✓	C	U	C	R
American Woodcock	✓	U	U	U	
Wilson's Phalarope	✓	U	U	U	
Red-necked Phalarope		R	U	R	
Gulls, and Terns					
Bonaparte's Gull		U		U	
Ring-billed Gull		A	U	A	R
Herring Gull		U	R	U	R
Caspian Tern		R	R	R	
Common Tern		R	R	R	
Forster's Tern	✓	C	C	U	
Black Tern	✓	C	C	U	
Pigeons, Doves					
Rock Pigeon	✓	C	C	C	C
Mourning Dove	✓	A	A	A	A

List of Potential Bird Species on Leopold WMD[1] (Continued)

Species	Nesting on the Refuge	Probable Abundance by Season (A: Abundant, should find on every trip; C: Common, should find 75% of trips; U: Uncommon, present but in lesser numbers; R: Rare, infrequent or few identifications; H: Accidental, not expected at this location)			
		Spring	Summer	Fall	Winter
Cuckoos					
Black-billed Cuckoo	✓	R	R	R	
Yellow-billed Cuckoo	✓	R	R	R	
Owls					
Eastern Screech-Owl	✓	U	U	U	U
Great Horned Owl	✓	C	C	C	C
Snowy Owl		R		R	R
Barred Owl		C	C	C	C
Long-eared Owl		R	R	R	R
Short-eared Owl		U	U	U	U
Goatsuckers					
Common Nighthawk	✓	U	U	U	
Whip-poor-will		H	H	H	
Swifts					
Chimney Swift	✓	C	C	C	
Hummingbirds					
Ruby-throated	✓	U	U	U	
Kingfishers					
Belted Kingfisher	✓	C	C	C	R
Woodpeckers					
Red-headed	✓	R	R	R	R
Red-bellied	✓	C	C	C	C
Yellow-bellied Sapsucker		C		U	R
Downy	✓	C	C	C	C
Hairy	✓	C		C	C
Northern Flicker	✓	C	C	C	R
Flycatchers					
Olive-sided Flycatcher		U		U	
Eastern Wood-Pewee	✓	C	C	C	
Yellow-bellied Flycatcher		U		U	
Acadian Flycatcher	✓	R	R	R	
Alder Flycatcher		R		R	
Willow Flycatcher	✓	C	C	C	

List of Potential Bird Species on Leopold WMD[1] (Continued)

Species	Nesting on the Refuge	Probable Abundance by Season A: Abundant, should find on every trip C: Common, should find 75% of trips U: Uncommon, present but in lesser numbers R: Rare, infrequent or few identifications H: Accidental, not expected at this location			
		Spring	Summer	Fall	Winter
Least Flycatcher	✓	C	C	C	
Eastern Phoebe	✓	C	C	C	
Great Crested Flycatcher	✓	C	C	C	
Eastern Kingbird	✓	C	C	C	
Shrikes					
Northern Shrike		R		R	U
Vireos					
Yellow-throated Vireo	✓	U	U	U	
Blue-headed Vireo		U		U	
Warbling Vireo	✓	C	C	C	
Philadelphia Vireo		U	R	U	
Red-eyed Vireo	✓	C	C	C	
Jays, Crows					
Blue Jay	✓	A	A	A	A
American Crow	✓	A	A	A	A
Larks					
Horned Lark	✓	U	U	U	U
Swallows					
Purple Martin	✓	C	C	C	
Tree Swallow	✓	A	A	A	
N. Rough-winged Swallow	✓	U	U	U	
Bank Swallow	✓	U	U	U	
Cliff Swallow	✓	U	U	U	
Barn Swallow	✓	C	C	C	
Titmice					
Black-capped Chickadee	✓	A	A	A	A
Nuthatches					
Red-breasted		U	U	U	U
White-breasted	✓	C	C	C	C
Creepers					
Brown Creeper	✓	U	U	U	U
Wrens					
Carolina Wren		H			H

List of Potential Bird Species on Leopold WMD[1] (Continued)

Species	Nesting on the Refuge	Probable Abundance by Season			
		A: Abundant, should find on every trip C: Common, should find 75% of trips U: Uncommon, present but in lesser numbers R: Rare, infrequent or few identifications H: Accidental, not expected at this location			
		Spring	Summer	Fall	Winter
House Wren	✓	A	A	A	
Winter Wren		U		U	R
Sedge Wren	✓	C	C	C	
Marsh Wren	✓	A	A	A	R
Kinglets					
Golden-crowned		C		C	R
Ruby-crowned		C		C	R
Gnatcatchers					
Blue-gray	✓	C	U	C	
Thrushes					
Eastern Bluebird	✓	C	C	C	R
Veery	✓	U	U	U	
Gray-cheeked Thrush		U		U	
Swainson's Thrush		U		U	
Hermit Thrush		C		C	
Wood Thrush	✓	U	U	U	
American Robin	✓	A	A	A	R
Mockingbirds, Thrashers					
Gray Catbird	✓	A	A	U	
Northern Mockingbird		R	R	R	
Brown Thrasher	✓	U	U	U	R
Starlings					
European Starling	✓	A	A	A	C
Pipits					
American Pipit		R		R	
Waxwings					
Cedar Waxwing	✓	U	C	C	R
Warblers					
Blue-winged		U	R	U	
Golden-winged	✓	U	R	U	
Tennessee		U	R	U	
Orange-crowned		U		U	
Nashville		U	R	U	

List of Potential Bird Species on Leopold WMD[1] (Continued)

Species	Nesting on the Refuge	Probable Abundance by Season			
		A: Abundant, should find on every trip C: Common, should find 75% of trips U: Uncommon, present but in lesser numbers R: Rare, infrequent or few identifications H: Accidental, not expected at this location			
		Spring	Summer	Fall	Winter
Northern Parula		U	R	U	
Yellow	✓	A	A	C	
Chestnut-sided	✓	U	U	U	
Magnolia		U	R	U	
Cape May		U		U	
Black-throated Blue		R		R	
Yellow-rumped		A		A	
Black-throated Green		U	R	U	
Blackburnian		U	R	U	
Pine		U	R	U	
Palm		C	R	C	
Bay-breasted		U	R	U	
Blackpoll		U	R	U	
Cerulean		R	R	R	
Black-and-white		U	R	U	
American Redstart	✓	C	U	C	
Prothonotary	✓	R	R	R	
Ovenbird	✓	U	U	U	
Northern Waterthrush	✓	U	R	U	
Connecticut		R	R	R	
Mourning	✓	R	R	R	
Common Yellowthroat	✓	A	A	C	
Hooded		H	H	H	
Wilson's		U	R	U	
Yellow-breasted Chat		H	H	H	
Canada		R	R	R	
Tanagers					
Summer Tanager		R	R		
Scarlet Tanager	✓	U	U	U	
Sparrows					
Eastern Towhee	✓	R	R	R	
American Tree Sparrow		C		C	A
Chipping Sparrow	✓	C	C	U	

List of Potential Bird Species on Leopold WMD[1] (Continued)

Species	Nesting on the Refuge	Probable Abundance by Season			
		A: Abundant, should find on every trip C: Common, should find 75% of trips U: Uncommon, present but in lesser numbers R: Rare, infrequent or few identifications H: Accidental, not expected at this location			
		Spring	Summer	Fall	Winter
Clay-colored Sparrow	✓	R	R	R	
Field Sparrow	✓	U	U	U	R
Vesper Sparrow	✓	U	U	U	
Savannah Sparrow	✓	C	C	C	
Grasshopper Sparrow	✓	R	R	R	
Henslow's Sparrow	✓	R	R	R	H
Fox Sparrow		U		U	R
Song Sparrow	✓	A	A	A	U
Lincoln's Sparrow		U		U	
Swamp Sparrow	✓	A	A	A	R
White-throated Sparrow		C	R	C	R
White-crowned Sparrow		U	R	U	H
Dark-eyed Junco		A		C	A
Lapland Longspur		R	H	R	R
Snow Bunting		U		U	U
Cardinal and Allies					
Northern Cardinal	✓	A	A	A	A
Rose-breasted Grosbeak	✓	C	C	C	
Indigo Bunting	✓	C	C	C	
Dickcissel	✓	R	R	R	
Blackbirds					
Bobolink	✓	C	C	U	
Red-winged Blackbird	✓	A	A	A	U
Eastern Meadowlark	✓	C	C	C	R
Western Meadowlark	✓	R	R	R	H
Yellow-headed Blackbird	✓	C	C	C	R
Rusty Blackbird		C	U	C	R
Brewer's Blackbird		C	R	C	R
Common Grackle	✓	A	A	A	U
Brown-headed Cowbird	✓	C	C	C	U
Orchard Oriole	✓	R	R	R	
Baltimore Oriole	✓	C	C	C	

List of Potential Bird Species on Leopold WMD[1] (Continued)

Species	Nesting on the Refuge	Probable Abundance by Season A: Abundant, should find on every trip C: Common, should find 75% of trips U: Uncommon, present but in lesser numbers R: Rare, infrequent or few identifications H: Accidental, not expected at this location			
		Spring	Summer	Fall	Winter
Finches					
Purple Finch		R		R	U
House Finch	✓	A	A	A	A
Common Redpoll					R
Pine Siskin		R		R	U
American Goldfinch	✓	A	A	A	C
Old World Sparrows					
House Sparrow	✓	A	A	A	A

1. Bird list courtesy of the Horicon Marsh Bird Club

List of Common Wisconsin Mammals[1]

Common Name	Scientific Name
Virginia Opossum	*Didelphis virginiana*
Northern Short-tailed Shrew	*Blarina brevicauda*
Least Shrew	*Cryptotis parva*
Arctic Shrew	*Sorex arcticus*
Masked Shrew	*Sorex cinereus*
Pygmy Shrew	*Sorex hoyi*
Water Shrew	*Sorex palustris*
Star-nosed Mole	*Condylura cristata*
Eastern Mole	*Scalopus aquaticus*
Big Brown Bat	*Eptesicus fuscus*
Silver-haired Bat	*Lasionycteris noctivagans*
Red Bat	*Lasiurus borealis*
Hoary Bat	*Lasiurus cinereus*
Little Brown Bat	*Myotis lucifugus*
Northern Myotis	*Myotis septentrionalis*
Indiana Bat	*Myotis sodalis*
Eastern Pipistrelle	*Pipistrellus subflavus*
Coyote	*Canis latrans*
Gray Wolf	*Canis lupus*
Gray Fox	*Urocyon cinereoargenteus*
Red Fox	*Vulpes vulpes*
Black Bear	*Ursus americanus*
Common Raccoon	*Procyon lotor*
Northern River Otter	*Lontra canadensis*
American Marten	*Martes americana*
Fisher	*Martes pennanti*
Ermine	*Mustela erminea*
Long-tailed Weasel	*Mustela frenata*
Least Weasel	*Mustela nivalis*
American Mink	*Mustela vison*
American Badger	*Taxidea taxus*
Striped Skunk	*Mephitis mephitis*
Eastern Spotted Skunk	*Spilogale putorius*
Canada Lynx	*Lynx canadensis*
Bobcat	*Lynx rufus*
Northern Flying Squirrel	*Glaucomys sabrinus*
Southern Flying Squirrel	*Glaucomys volans*

List of Common Wisconsin Mammals[1] (Continued)

Common Name	Scientific Name
Woodchuck	*Marmota monax*
Eastern Gray Squirrel	*Sciurus carolinensis*
Eastern Fox Squirrel	*Sciurus niger*
Franklin's Ground Squirrel	*Spermophilus franklinii*
Thirteen-lined Ground Squirrel	*Spermophilus tridecemlineatus*
Least Chipmunk	*Tamias minimus*
Eastern Chipmunk	*Tamias striatus*
Red Squirrel	*Tamiasciurus hudsonicus*
Plains Pocket Gopher	*Geomys bursarius*
American Beaver	*Castor canadensis*
Southern Red-backed Vole	*Clethrionomys gapperi*
Prairie Vole	*Microtus ochrogaster*
Meadow Vole	*Microtus pennsylvanicus*
Woodland Vole	*Microtus pinetorum*
House Mouse	*Mus musculus*
Muskrat	*Ondatra zibethicus*
White-footed Mouse	*Peromyscus leucopus*
Deer Mouse	*Peromyscus maniculatus*
Norway Rat	*Rattus norvegicus*
Western Harvest Mouse	*Reithrodontomys megalotis*
Southern Bog Lemming	*Synaptomys cooperi*
Woodland Jumping Mouse	*Napaeozapus insignis*
Meadow Jumping Mouse	*Zapus hudsonius*
Common Porcupine	*Erethizon dorsatum*
Elk	*Cervus elaphus*
White-tailed Deer	*Odocoileus virginianus*
Snowshoe Hare	*Lepus americanus*
White-tailed Jackrabbit	*Lepus townsendii*
Eastern Cottontail	*Sylvilagus floridanus*

1. *Adapted from Wisconsin DNR: http://dnr.wi.gov/org/es/science/publications/VertChklist/Mammalslist.html*

List of Wisconsin Amphibians[1]

Common Name	Scientific Name
Central Newt	*Notophthalmus viridescens louisianensis*
Common Mudpuppy	*Necturus maculosus maculosus*
Blue-spotted Salamander	*Ambystoma laterale*
Spotted Salamander	*Ambystoma maculatum*
Eastern Tiger Salamander	*Ambystoma tigrinum tigrinum*
Four-toed Salamander	*Hemidactylium scutatum*
Eastern Red-backed Salamander	*Plethodon cinereus*
Eastern American Toad	*Bufo americanus americanus*
Blanchard's Cricket Frog	*Acris crepitans blanchardi*
Northern Spring Peeper	*Pseudacris crucifer crucifer*
Chorus Frog	*Pseudacris triseriata*
Cope's Gray Treefrog	*Hyla chrysoscelis*
Gray Treefrog	*Hyla versicolor*
American Bullfrog	*Rana catesbeiana*
Northern Green Frog	*Rana clamitans melanota*
Pickerel Frog	*Rana palustris*
Northern Leopard Frog	*Rana pipiens*
Mink Frog	*Rana septentrionalis*
Wood Frog	*Rana sylvatica*

1. *Adapted from Wisconsin DNR: http://dnr.wi.gov/org/es/science/publications/VertChklist/Amphlist.html*

List of Wisconsin Reptiles[1]

Common Name	Scientific Name
Stinkpot	*Sternotherus odoratus*
Eastern Snapping Turtle	*Chelydra serpentina serpentina*
Painted Turtle	*Chrysemys picta*
Wood Turtle	*Clemmys insculpta*
Blanding's Turtle	*Emydoidea blandingii*
Northern Map Turtle	*Graptemys geographica*
Ouachita Map Turtle	*Graptemys ouachitensis*
False Map Turtle	*Graptemys pseudogeographica*
Ornate Box Turtle	*Terrapene ornata ornata*
Smooth Softshell Turtle	*Apalone mutica*
Spiny Softshell Turtle	*Apalone spinifera*
Six-lined Racerunner	*Cnemidophorus sexlineatus*
Common Five-lined Skink	*Eumeces fasciatus*
Northern Prairie Skink	*Eumeces septentrionalis septentrionalis*
Western Slender Glass Lizard	*Ophisaurus attenuatus attenuatus*
Eastern Racer	*Coluber constrictor*
Ring-necked Snake	*Diadophis punctatus*
Black Ratsnake	*Elaphe obsoleta obsoleta*
Western Foxsnake	*Elaphe vulpina*
Eastern Hog-nosed Snake	*Heterodon platirhinos*
Eastern Milksnake	*Lampropeltis triangulum triangulum*
Northern Watersnake	*Nerodia sipedon sipedon*
Smooth Greensnake	*Opheodrys vernalis*
Bullsnake	*Pituophis catenifer*
Queen Snake	*Regina septemvittata*
Dekay's Brownsnake	*Storeria dekayi*
Northern Red-bellied Snake	*Storeria occipitomaculata occipitomacu-*
Butler's Gartersnake	*Thamnophis butleri*
Western Ribbonsnake	*Thamnophis proximus*
Plains Gartersnake	*Thamnophis radix*
Northern Ribbonsnake	*Thamnophis sauritus septentrionalis*
Common Gartersnake	*Thamnophis sirtalis*
Timber Rattlesnake	*Crotalus horridus*
Eastern Massasauga	*Sistrurus catenatus catenatus*

1. *Adapted from Wisconsin DNR: http://dnr.wi.gov/org/es/science/publications/VertChklist/Reptileslist.html*

List of Plants That Potentially Occur on Leopold Wetland Management District

Scientific Name	Common Name
Agrostis alba	Red top
Agrostis stolonifera var. palustris	Creeping bent
Agropyron repens	Quackgrass
Andropogon gerardii	Big bluestem
Andropogon scoparius	Little bluestem
Bouteloua curtipendula	Side-oats grama
Bouteloua gracilis	Blue grama
Bouteloua hirsute	Hairy grama
Bromus inermis	Smooth brome grass
Calamagrostis canadensis	Bluejoint
Calamovilfa longifolia	Sand reedgrass
Deschampsia caespitosa	Tufted hairgrass
Elymus Canadensis	Canada wild rye
Elymus hystrix	Bottlebrush grass
Elymus virginicus	Virginia wild-rye
Eragrostis spp.	Lovegrass
Hordeum jubatum	Foxtail barley
Koeleria macrantha	Junegrass
Leersia oryzoides	Rice cutgrass
Muhlenbergia cuspidate	Plains muhly
Muhlenbergia richardsonis	Mat muhly
Panicularia pallida	Pale Manna-grass
Panicum virgatum	Switchgrass
Phalaris arundinacea	Reed canary grass
Phleum pretense	Timothy
Phragmites australis	Plume grass
Phragmites communis	Flag grass
Poa arida	Plains bluegrass/bunch speargrass
Poa pratensis	Kentucky bluegrass
Sorghastrum nutans	Indiangrass
Spartina pectinata	Prairie cordgrass

List of Plants That Potentially Occur on Leopold Wetland Management District (Continued)

Scientific Name	Common Name
Sporobolus heterolepis	Prairie dropseed
Stipa comata	Needle and Thread
Stipa spartea	Porcupine grass
Aquatic Monocots	
Carex atherodes	Slough sedge
Ceratophyllum demersum	Coontail
Juncus spp.	Rushes
Lemna spp.	Duckweeds
Myriophyllum spp.	Milfoils
Nelumbo lutea	American lotus
Nymphaea spp.	White water lily
Potamogeton spp.	Pondweeds
Ranunculus spp.	Aquatic buttercup
Sagittaria latifolia	Arrowhead/Duck potato
Schoenoplectus acutus	Hardstem bulrush
Schoenoplectus tabernaemontani	Softstem bulrush
Sparganium spp.	Bur-reed
Typha angustifolia	Narrow-leaved cattail
Typha latifolia	Broad-leaved cattail
Utricularia vulgaris	Greater Bladderwort
Vallisneria spp.	Wild celery
Zizania aquatica	Wild rice
Trees and Shrubs	
Acer negundo	Box elder
Acer saccharinum	Silver maple
Amelanchier arborea	Serviceberry
Amorpha canescens	Lead plant
Amorpha fruticosa	False indigo
Betula nigra	River birch
Betula pumila	Bog birch
Carya ovata	Shagbark hickory

List of Plants That Potentially Occur on Leopold Wetland Management District (Continued)

Scientific Name	Common Name
Cephalanthus occidentalis	Buttonbrush
Cornus racemosa	Grey dogwood
Cornus stolonifera	Red-osier dogwood
Corylus Americana	American hazelnut
Crataegus pruinosa	Frosted hawthorn
Elaeagnus angustifolia	Russian olive
Fraxinus pennsylvanica	Green ash
Juglans niger	Black walnut
Picea mariana	Black spruce
Populus deltoids	Cottonwood
Populus tremuloides	Trembling aspen
Prunus Americana	Wild plum
Prunus virginiana	Chokecherry
Quercus coccinea	Scarlet oak
Quercus ellipsoidalis	Northern pin oak
Quercus macrocarpa	Bur Oak
Quercus rubra	Northern red oak
Rhus glabra	Smooth sumac
Ribes americanum	Currant
Rosa spp.	Wild rose
Rubus spp.	Raspberry
Salix amygdaloides	Peach-leaved willow
Salix exigua	Sandbar willow
Salix nigra	Black willow
Symphoricarpos occidentalis	Snowberry
Tilia Americana	American basswood
Ulmus Americana	American elm
Ulmus pumila	Siberian elm
Zanthoxylum americanum	Common prickly-ash
Vines	
Vitus riparia	Riverbank grape

List of Plants That Potentially Occur on Leopold Wetland Management District (Continued)

Scientific Name	Common Name
Forbs	
Achillea millefolium	Yarrow
Allium canadense	Wild garlic
Allium cernuum	Nodding wild onion
Allium stellatum	Prairie onion
Allium tricoccum	Wild leek
Ambrosia artemisiifolia	Common ragweed
Anemone Canadensis	Meadow anemone
Anemone cylindrical	Thimbleweed
Apocynum cannabinum	Indian hemp
Aquilegia Canadensis	Columbine
Aralia nudicaulis	Wild sarsaparilla
Artemisia campestris	Wormwood
Artemisia frigida	Field wormwood
Artemisia ludoviciana	White sage
Asclepias amplexicaulis	Clasping milkweed
Asclepias syriaca	Common milkweed
Asclepias verticillata	Whorled milkweed
Aster ericoides	Heath/White aster
Aster lanceolatus (simplex)	Panicled aster
Aster oblongifolius	Aromatic aster
Aster sericeus	Silky aster
Bidens spp.	Beggarticks
Botrychium campestre	Prairie moonwort
Brassica nigra	Mustard
Caltha palustris	Marsh marigold
Cardamine bulbosa	Spring cress
Castilleja coccinea	Indian paintbrush
Chrysopsis villosa	Hairy golden aster
Clematis virginiana	Virgin's-bower
Cicuta maculate	Water hemlock

List of Plants That Potentially Occur on Leopold Wetland Management District (Continued)

Scientific Name	Common Name
Cirsium arvense	Canada thistle
Cirsium spp.	Native thistle spp.
Convolvulus arvensis	Field bindweed
Corydalis aurea	Golden corydalis
Cuscuta gronovii	Common dodder
Cypripedium candidum	White lady's slipper
Dalea candida	White prairie clover
Dalea purpureum	Purple prairie clover
Dalea villosa	Silky prairie clover
Delphinium carolinianum	Prairie larkspur
Echinacea pallida	Pale purple coneflower
Equisetum hyemale	Scouring rush
Equisetum laevigatum	Smooth horsetail
Erigeron strigosus	Daisy fleabane
Eupatorium maculatum	Spotted joe pye weed
Eupatorium perfoliatum/altissimum	Common/Tall boneset
Euphorbia podperae	Leafy spurge
Galium concinnum	Shining bedstraw
Gaura coccinea	Scarlet gaura
Gaura longiflora	Large-flowered gaura
Gentiana andrewsii	Bottle gentian
Gentiana puberulenta	Downy gentian
Geum triflorum	Prairie smoke
Glechoma hederacea	Ground ivy
Glycycrrhiza lepidota	Wild licorice
Grindelia squarrosa	Gumweed
Helianthus grosseserratus	Saw-toothed sunflower
Helianthus pauciflorus	Prairie sunflower
Hepatica acutiloba	Sharp-lobed hepatica
Heuchera richardsonii	Prairie alum-root
Houstonia longifolia	Long-leaved bluets

List of Plants That Potentially Occur on Leopold Wetland Management District (Continued)

Scientific Name	Common Name
Hydrophyllum virginianum	Virginia waterleaf
Hypoxis hirsute	Yellow star grass
Lactuca canadensis	Wild lettuce
Lepidium virginicum	Wild pepper-grass
Liatris aspera	Rough blazing star
Liatris punctata	Dotted blazing star
Lilium philadelphicum	Prairie lily Hoary puccoon
Lithospermum canescens	Fringed puccoon
Lithospermum incisum	Pale spiked lobelia
Lobelia spicata	Cut-leaved Water-Horehound
Lycopus americanus	Western Water-Horehound
Lycopus asper	Black medic
Medicago lupulina	*Alfalfa*
Medicago sativa	*Yellow sweet-clover*
Melilotus officinalis	*White sweet-clover*
Melilotus alba	*Wild mint*
Mentha arvensis	*Wild pepper-grass*
Monarda fistulosa	*Wild bergamot*
Myosurus minimus	*Tiny mouse's-tail*
Ranunculaceae (Crowfoot Family)	
Oenothera biennis	Evening primrose
Onosmodium bejariense	False gromwell
Oxalis spp.	Wood-sorrel
Pedicularis lanceolata	Swamp lousewort
Pedicularis Canadensis	Wood betony
Pediomelum argophyllum	Silverleaf scurf-pea
Pediomelum esculentum	Prairie turnip (breadroot)
Penstemon grandiflorus	Large-flowered beard tongue
Penstemon pallidus	Pale beard tongue
Phlox pilosa	Prairie phlox
Polygonum pensylvanicum	Pinkweed

List of Plants That Potentially Occur on Leopold Wetland Management District (Continued)

Scientific Name	Common Name
Polygonum punctatum	Dotted smartweed
Polygonum tenue	Slim knotweed
Portulaca oleracea	Purslane
Potentilla arguta	Prairie/Tall cinquefoil
Prenanthes alba	White lettuce
Prenanthes racemosa	Rattlesnake root
Fabaceae (Bean family)	
Pulsatilla patens	Pasque flower
Ranunculus spp.	Buttercup
Ratibida pinnata	Yellow coneflower
Rhus radicans	Poison ivy
Rudbeckia hirta	Black-eyed Susan
Rumex crispus	Curly dock
Rumex altissimus	Pale dock
Sanguinaria Canadensis	Bloodroot
Sium suave	Water-parsnip
Silphium perfoliatum	Cup plant
Silphium terebinthinaceum	Prairie dock
Smilax herbacea	Carrion flower
Solanum nigrum	Black nightshade
Solidago Canadensis	Canada goldenrod
Solidago gigantean	Late goldenrod
Solidago juncea	Early goldenrod
Solidago nemoralis	Old-field goldenrod
Solidago ridellii	Riddell's goldenrod
Solidago rigida	Stiff goldenrod
Sonchus arvensis	Field sow-thistle
Sonchus asper	Spiny-leaved sow-thistle
Stachys palustris	Hedge-nettle
Sisyrinchium campestre	Prairie blue-eyed grass
Talinum teretifolium	Prairie fame flower

List of Plants That Potentially Occur on Leopold Wetland Management District (Continued)

Scientific Name	Common Name
Thalictrum dasycarpum	(Purple) Meadow rue
Tradescantia ohiensis	Common spiderwort
Tragopogon dubius	Meadow goat's beard
Trifolium pretense	Red clover
Urtica dioica	Stinging nettle
Verbascum spp.	Mullein
Verbena hastate	Blue vervain
Verbena stricta	Hoary vervain
Veronia fasiculata	Common ironweed
Veronica peregrina	Purslane speedwell
Scrophulariaceae (Figwort Family)	
Vicia americana	American vetch
Viola canadensis	Canadian white violet
Viola pedata	Bird's-foot violet
Viola pubescens	Downy yellow violet
Viola sororia	Hairy wood violet
Woodsia oregano	Oregon woodsia
Zigadenus elegans	White camass
Zizia aurea	Golden Alexander
Cactus	
Opuntia fragilis	Prickly Pear/Pencil cactus
Opuntia humifsusa	Eastern prickly-pear cactus
Ferns	
Athyrium filix-femina	Common lady fern
Cystopteris fragilis	Bladder fern
Woodsia ilvensis	Rusty woodsia fern
Mosses	
Lycopodium spp.	

Appendix D: Regional Conservation Priority Species

Species of Regional Conservation Priority

Birds

Species	USFWS				Wisconsin DNR		
	Fed T&E	Region 3 SCP	BCR 23	BCR 12	Wis. T&E	Wis. SCP	Wis. MHGB
Henslow's Sparrow		✓	✓		T	✓	✓
Yellow Rail (1)		✓		✓	T	✓	✓
Piping Plover	E	✓		✓	E	✓	
Kirtlands Warbler	E	✓		✓		✓	
Cerulean Warbler		✓	✓		T	✓	
Barn Owl		✓			E	✓	✓
Loggerhead Shrike		✓			E	✓	✓
Bell's Vireo		✓			T	✓	✓
Golden-winged Warbler		✓	✓	✓		✓	
Bobolink		✓	✓			✓	✓
Le Conte's Sparrow (2)		✓		✓		✓	✓
Nelson's Sharp-tailed Sparrow (3)		✓		✓		✓	✓
Bald Eagle	T	✓				✓	
Whooping Crane – Eastern	T	✓				✓	
Common Tern		✓			E	✓	
Forester' Tern		✓			E	✓	
Trumpeter Swan		✓			E	✓	
Peregrine Falcon		✓			E	✓	
Worm-eating Warbler		✓			E	✓	
Red-shouldered Hawk		✓			T	✓	
Kentucky Warbler		✓			T	✓	
Acadian Flycatcher		✓			T	✓	
Black-billed Cuckoo		✓	✓			✓	
Red-headed Woodpecker		✓	✓			✓	
Wood Thrush		✓		✓		✓	
Connecticut Warbler		✓		✓		✓	
Canada Warbler		✓		✓		✓	

Birds (Continued)

Species	USFWS				Wisconsin DNR		
	Fed T&E	Region 3 SCP	BCR 23	BCR 12	Wis. T&E	Wis. SCP	Wis. MHGB
Blue-winged Teal		✓				✓	✓
Northern Harrier		✓				✓	✓
Upland Sandpiper		✓				✓	✓
Wilson's Phalarope		✓				✓	✓
Short-eared Owl		✓				✓	✓
Dickcissel		✓				✓	✓
Eastern Meadowlark		✓				✓	✓
Western Meadowlark		✓				✓	✓
Field Sparrow		✓				✓	✓
Grasshopper Sparrow		✓				✓	✓
Sedge Wren		✓	✓	✓			
Greater Prairie Chicken (4)					T	✓	✓
Bewick's Wren		✓			E		
American Bittern		✓				✓	
American Black Duck		✓				✓	
Canvasback		✓				✓	
Lesser Scaup		✓				✓	
Northern Goshawk		✓				✓	
King Rail		✓				✓	
Whimbrel		✓				✓	
Hudsonian Godwit		✓				✓	
Marbled Godwit		✓				✓	
Buff-breasted Sandpiper		✓				✓	
Short-billed Dowitcher		✓				✓	
American Woodcock		✓				✓	
Black Tern		✓				✓	
Whip-poor-will		✓				✓	
Olive-sided Flycatcher		✓				✓	
Blue-winged Warbler		✓				✓	
Prothonotary Warbler		✓				✓	
Louisiana Waterthrush		✓				✓	
Rusty Blackbird		✓				✓	

Birds (Continued)

Species	USFWS				Wisconsin DNR		
	Fed T&E	Region 3 SCP	BCR 23	BCR 12	Wis. T&E	Wis. SCP	Wis. MHGB
Caspian Tern					E		
Yellow-throated Warbler					E		
Snowy Egret					E		
Red-necked Grebe					E		
Hooded Warbler					T		
Great Egret					T		
Osprey					T		
Yellow-crowned Night-Heron					T		
Veery				✓		✓	
Sharp-tailed Grouse						✓	✓
Vesper Sparrow						✓	✓
Stilt Sandpiper		✓					
Common Loon		✓					
Least Tern		✓					
Long-eared Owl		✓					
Double-crested Cormorant		✓					
Chuck-will's-widow		✓					
Northern Flicker		✓					
Cape May Warbler		✓					
Black-throated Blue Warbler		✓					
Prairie Warbler		✓					
Orchard Oriole		✓					
Mallard		✓					
Northern Pintail		✓					
Black Rail		✓					
Common Moorhen		✓					
Greater Yellowlegs		✓					
Least Bittern		✓					
Black-crowned Night-Heron		✓					
Snow Goose		✓					
Canada Goose – Resident		✓					
Canada Goose – Migrant		✓					

Birds (Continued)

Species	USFWS				Wisconsin DNR		
	Fed T&E	Region 3 SCP	BCR 23	BCR 12	Wis. T&E	Wis. SCP	Wis. MHGB
Wood Duck		✓					
Yellow-billed Cuckoo						✓	
Black-backed Woodpecker						✓	
Brown Thrasher*						✓	
Willow Flycatcher						✓	
Least Flycatcher						✓	
Horned Grebe						✓	
Redhead						✓	
Northern Bobwhite*						✓	
American Golden Plover						✓	
Solitary Sandpiper						✓	
Lark Sparrow						✓	
Red Crossbill						✓	
Dunlin						✓	
Rose-breasted Grosbeak				✓			
Savanna Sparrow*							✓
Clay-colored Sparrow*							✓
Brewer's Blackbird* (5)							✓

* Grassland species ranked on 12 criteria and identified by Sample and Mossman (1997) as having high management concern but not listed in USFWS Region 3 as Species of Management Concern or Resource Conservation Priority Species or Wisconsin Special Concern lists.

Numbers associated with a species indicate that the species occurs within that local area within the District. District staff will consider these species when conducting activities within the areas identified.

1. Rush Lake Area
2. Winnebago/Marquette
3. Rush Lake
4. NE Adams County
5. Shrub areas

Mammals

Species	USFWS		Wisconsin DNR	
	Federal T&E	Region 3 SCP	Wis. T&E	Wis. SCP
Gray Wolf	E	✓	T	✓
Canada Lynx	T	✓		
American Martin			E	✓
Water Shrew				✓
Silver-haired Bat				✓
Northern Long-eared Bat				✓
Eastern Red Bat				✓
Hoary Bat				✓
Franklin's Ground Squirrel				✓
Northern Flying Squirrel				✓
Prairie Vole				✓
Woodland Vole				✓
Woodland Jumping Mouse				✓
Moose				✓
White-tailed Jackrabbit				✓
Gray Bat		✓		
Indiana Bat		✓		

Crustaceans

	USFWS		Wisconsin	
Species	Federal T&E	Region 3 SCP	Wisconsin T&E	Wisconsin SCP[1]
Illinois Cave Amphipod	E	✓		
Rusty Crayfish				

1. *See the attached list from Wisconsin's Srategy for Wildlife Species of Greatest Conservation Need*

Fish

Species	USFWS		Wisconsin DNR	
	Federal T&E	Region 3 SCP	Wis. T&E	Wis. SCP
Crystal Darter		✓	E	✓
Skipjack Herring			E	✓
Gravel Chub			E	✓
Bluntnose Darter			E	✓
Starhead Topminnow			E	✓
Goldeye			E	✓
Striped Shiner			E	✓
Black Redhorse			E	✓
Pallid Shiner			E	✓
Slender Madtom			E	✓
Blue Sucker		✓	T	✓
Paddlefish		✓	T	✓
Black Buffalo			T	✓
Longear Sunfiish			T	✓
Redfin Shiner			T	✓
Speckled Chub			T	✓
River Redhorse			T	✓
Greater Redhorse			T	✓
Pugnose Shiner			T	✓
Ozark Minnow			T	✓
Gilt Darter			T	✓
Lake Sturgeon		✓		✓
Kiyi		✓		✓
Shortjawed Cisco		✓		✓
American Eel				✓
Redside Dace				✓
Western Sand Darter				✓
Lake Chubsucker				✓
Banded Killfish				✓

Fish (Continued)

Species	USFWS		Wisconsin DNR	
	Federal T&E	Region 3 SCP	Wis. T&E	Wis. SCP
Least Darter				✓
Lake Trout		✓		
Brook Trout		✓		
Coho Salmon		✓		
Chinook Salmon		✓		
Lake Whitefish		✓		
Rainbow Trout		✓		
Pallid Sturgeon		✓		
Shovelnose Sturgeon		✓		
Walleye		✓		
Yellow Perch		✓		
Plains Minnow		✓		
Western Silvery Minnow		✓		
Muskelunge		✓		
Fathead Chub		✓		
Sea Lamprey		✓		
Eurasian Ruffy		✓		
Round Goby		✓		
Big-head Carp		✓		
Grass Carp		✓		

Insects

Species	Federal		Wisconsin	
	Federal T&E	Region 3 SCP	Wisconsin T&E	Wisconsin SCP[1]
Hine's Emerald Dragonfly	E	✓	E	
Karner Blue Butterfly	E	✓	E	
American Burying Beetle	E	✓	E	
Hungerford's Crawling Water Beetle	E	✓		
Mitchel's Satyr Butterfly	E	✓		
Powesheik Skipper		✓	E	
Pecatonica River Mayfly			E	
Red-tailed Prairie Leafhopper			E	
Flat-headed Mayfly			E	
Swamp Metalmark			E	
Northern Blue Butterfly			E	
Extra-striped Snaketail Dragonfly			E	
Saint Croix Snaketail Dragonfly			E	
Silphium Borer Moth			E	
Phlox Moth			E	
Warpaint Emerald Dragonfly			E	
Regal Fritillary			E	
Knobels Riffle Beetle			E	
Lake Huron Locust			E	
Spatterdock Darner Dragonfly			T	
Frosted Elfin			T	
Prairie Leafhopper			T	
Pygmy Snaketail Dragonfly			T	
Ottoe Skipper		✓		
Wabash Belted Skimmer		✓		

1. *See the attached list from Wisconsin's Srategy for Wildlife Species of Greatest Conservation Need*

Reptiles and Amphibians

Species	USFWS		Wisconsin DNR	
	Federal T&E	Region 3 SCP	Wisconsin T&E	Wisconsin SCP
Massasauga Rattlesnake	C	✓	E	✓
Blanchard's Cricket Frog			E	✓
Slender Glass Lizard			E	✓
Queen Snake			E	✓
Ornate Box Turtle			E	✓
Western Ribbon Snake			E	✓
Northern Ribbon Snake			E	✓
Wood Turtle			T	✓
Blanding's Turtle			T	✓
Butler's Garter Snake			T	✓
Timber Rattlesnake		✓		✓
Four-toed Salamander				✓
Mudpuppy				✓
Boreal Chorus Frog				✓
Pickerel Frog				✓
Mink Frog				✓
Midland Smooth Softshell Turtle				✓
Northern Prairie Skink				✓
Prairie Race Runner				✓
Yellow-bellied Racer				✓
Prairie Ring-neck Snake				✓
Black Rat Snake				✓
Bullsnake				✓

Snails

Species	USFWS		Wisconsin DNR	
	Federal T&E	Region 3 SCP[1]	Wis. T&E	Wis. SCP[2]
Midwest Pleistocene Vertigo		✓	E	
Occult Vertigo		✓	E	
Wing Snaggletooth			T	
Cherrystone Drop			T	
Fridgid Ambersnail		✓		
Iowa Pleistocene Vertigo		✓		
Briarton Pleistocene vertigo		✓		
Vertigo bollesiana		✓		
Vertigo cristata		✓		
Vertigo paradoxa		✓		

1. *Region 3 Species of Conservation Priority are documented for the Upper Mississippi River/*

2. *See the attached list from Wisconsin's Srategy for Wildlife Species of Greatest Conservation Need*

Plants

Species	Federal T&E	Region 3 SCP[1]	Wisconsin T&E
Leafy Prairie Clover	E	✓	
Minnesota Trout Lily	E	✓	
Michigan Mokey-flower	E	✓	
Small Whorled Pogonia	T	✓	
Western Prairie Fringed Orchid	T	✓	
American hart's-tongue fern	T	✓	
Dwarf Lake Iris	T	✓	E
Eastern Prairie Fringed Orchid	T	✓	E
Fassett's Locoweed	T	✓	E
Northern Wild Monkshood	T	✓	E
Pitcher's Thistle	T	✓	E
Prairie Bush-clover	T	✓	E
Mead's Milkweed	T	✓	
Decurrent False Aster	T	✓	
Leedy's Roseroot	T	✓	
Hall's Bulrush		✓	
Pale False Foxglove		✓	
Carolina Anemone			E
Hudson Bay Anemone			E
Lake Cress			E
Purple Milkweed			E
Green Spleenwort			E
Alpine Milk Vetch			E
Prairie Plum			E
Coopers Milk Vetch			E
Prairie Moonwort			E
Moonwort			E
Goblin Fern			E
Floating Marsh Marigold			E
Wild Hyacinth			E

Plants (Continued)

Species	Federal T&E	Region 3 SCP[1]	Wisconsin T&E
Crow-spur Sedge			E
Smooth-sheathed Sedge			E
Hop-like Sedge			E
Intermediate Sedge			E
Schweinitz's Sedge			E
Brook Grass			E
Stoneroot			E
Hemlock-parsley			E
Beak Grass			E
Lanceolate Whitlow-cress			E
Neat Spike-rush			E
Wolf Spike-rush			E
Angle-stemmed Spikerush			E
Harbinger-of-Spring			E
Chestnut Sedge			E
Umbrella Sedge			E
Northern Commandra			E
Pale False Foxglove			E
Bog Rush			E
Dotted Blazing Star			E
Auricled Twayblade			E
Fly Honeysuckle			E
Smith Melic Grass			E
Large-leaved Sandwort			E
Mat Muhly			E
Louisiana Broomrape			E
Small-flowered Grass-of-Parnassus			E
Smooth Phlox			E
Butterwort			E
Heart-leaved Plantain			E
Western Jacob's Ladder			E

Plants (Continued)

Species	Federal T&E	Region 3 SCP[1]	Wisconsin T&E
Pink Milkwort			E
Spotted Pondweed			E
Rough White Lettuce			E
Great White Lettuce			E
Pine-drops			E
Small Shinleaf			E
Small Yellow Water Crowfoot			E
Lapland Buttercup			E
Lapland Rosebay			E
Wild Petunia			E
Sand Dune Willow			E
Satiny Willow			E
Hall's Bulrush			E
Netted Nut-rush			E
Small Skullcap			E
Selago-like Spikemoss			E
Fire Pink			E
Blue-stemmed Goldenrod			E
Lake Huron Tansy			E
Hairy Meadow Parsnip			E
Foamflower			E
Purple False Oats			E
Dwarf Bilberry			E
Mountain Cranberry			E
Squashberry			E
Sand Violet			E
Muskroot			T
Round Stemmed False Foxglove			T
Yellow Giant Hyssop			T
Small Round-leaved Orchis			T
Prairie Indian Plaintain			T

Plants (Continued)

Species	Federal T&E	Region 3 SCP[1]	Wisconsin T&E
Dwarf Milkweed			T
Wooly Milkweed			T
Prairie Milkweed			T
Pinnatifid Spleenwort			T
Forked Aster			T
Kitten Tails			T
Sand Reed			T
Large Water Starwort			T
Calypso Orchid			T
Carey's Sedge			T
Beautiful Sedge			T
Coast Sedge			T
Handsome Sedge			T
Garbers Sedge			T
Lenticular Sedge			T
Michaux's Sedge			T
Drooping Sedge			T
Prairie Thistle			T
Rams-head Ladys-slipper			T
White Ladys-slipper			T
English Sundew			T
Linear-leaved Sundew			T
Pale Purple Coneflower			T
Beaked Spike Rush			T
Thickspike Wheatgrass			T
Western Fescue			T
Blue Ash			T
Yellowish Gentian			T
Cliff Cudweed			T
Round Fruited St. John's Wort			T
Slender Bush Clover			T

Plants (Continued)

Species	Federal T&E	Region 3 SCP[1]	Wisconsin T&E
Bladderpod			T
Broad-leaved Twayblade			T
Brittle Prickly Pear			T
Clustered Broomrape			T
Marsh Grass-of-Parnassus			T
Wild Quinine			T
Sweet Coltsfoot			T
Tubercled Orchid			T
Bog Bluegrass			T
Braun's Holly Fern			T
Prairie-parsley			T
Algal-leaved Pondweed			T
Sheathed Pondweed Seaside Crowfoot			T
Bald Rush			T
Hawthorn-leaved Gooseberry			T
Flat-leaved Willow			T
Tussock Bulrush			T
Plains Ragwort			T
Snowy Campion			T
Dune Goldenrod			T
Clustered Bur Reed			T
False Asphodel			T
Snow Trillium			T
Spike Trisetum			T
Marsh Valerian			T
Tall Grass Prairie and/or the Great Lakes Ecosystems but may or may not occur in Wisconsin.			
*** - See the attached list from Wisconsin's Srategy for Wildlife Species of Greatest Conservation Need			

1. *Region 3 Species of Conservation Priority are documented for the Upper Mississippi River/*

Appendix E: Compliance Requirements

Compliance Requirements

Rivers and Harbor Act (1899) (33 U.S.C. 403)

Section 10 of this Act requires the authorization by the U.S. Army Corps of Engineers prior to any work in, on, over, or under a navigable water of the United States.

Antiquities Act of 1906. 16 U.S.C. 431 et seq.

Authorizes the scientific investigation of antiquities on Federal land and provides penalties for unauthorized removal of objects taken or collected without a permit.

Migratory Bird Treaty Act, 16 U.S.C. 703 et seq.

Designates the protection of migratory birds as a Federal responsibility. This Act enables the setting of seasons, and other regulations including the closing of areas, Federal or non Federal, to the hunting of migratory birds.

Migratory Bird Conservation Act, 16 U.S.C. 715 et seq.

Establishes procedures for acquisition by purchase, rental, or gift of areas approved by the Migratory Bird Conservation Commission.

Fish and Wildlife Coordination Act 16 U.S.C. 661 et seq. (1934)

Requires that the Fish and Wildlife Service and State fish and wildlife agencies be consulted whenever water is to be impounded, diverted or modified under a Federal permit or license. The Service and State agency recommend measures to prevent the loss of biological resources, or to mitigate or compensate for the damage. The project proponent must take biological resource values into account and adopt justifiable protection measures to obtain maximum overall project benefits. A 1958 amendment added provisions to recognize the vital contribution of wildlife resources to the Nation and to require equal consideration and coordination of wildlife conservation with other water resources development programs. It also authorized the Secretary of Interior to provide public fishing areas and accept donations of lands and funds.

Migratory Bird Hunting Stamp Act. Also known as the Duck Stamp Act, 16 U.S.C. 718 et seq. (1934)

Requires every waterfowl hunter 16 years of age or older to carry a stamp and earmarks proceeds of the Duck Stamps to buy or lease waterfowl habitat. A 1958 amendment authorizes the acquisition of small wetland and pothole areas to be designated as 'Waterfowl Production Areas,' which may be acquired without the limitations and requirements of the Migratory Bird Conservation Act.

Historic Sites, Buildings and Antiquities Act. Also known as the Historic Sites Act of 1935, 16 U.S.C. 461 et seq.

Declares it a national policy to preserve historic sites and objects of national significance, including those located on refuges. Provides procedures for designation, acquisition, administration, and protection of such sites.

Refuge Revenue Sharing Act,16 U.S.C. 715s (1935)

Requires revenue sharing provisions to all fee-title ownerships that are administered solely or primarily by the Secretary through the Service.

Transfer of Certain Real Property for Wildlife Conservation Purposes Act, 16 U.S.C. 667b-667d (1948)

Provides that upon a determination by the Administrator of the General Services Administration, real property no longer needed by a Federal agency can be transferred without reimbursement to the Secretary of Interior if the land has particular value for migratory birds, or to a State agency for other wildlife conservation purposes.

Federal Records Act of 1950, 44 U.S.C. 31

Directs the preservation of evidence of the government's organization, functions, policies, decisions, operations, and activities, as well as basic historical and other information.

Fish and Wildlife Act of 1956, 16 U.S.C. 742a et seq.

Established a comprehensive national fish and wildlife policy and broadened the authority for acquisition and development of refuges.

Refuge Recreation Act, 16 U.S.C. 460k et seq. (1962)

Allows the use of refuges for recreation when such uses are compatible with the refuge's primary purposes and when sufficient funds are available to manage the uses.

Wilderness Act of 1964, 16 U.S.C. 1131 et seq.

Directed the Secretary of Interior, within 10 years, to review every roadless area of 5,000 or more acres and every roadless island (regardless of size) within National Wildlife Refuge and National Park Systems and to recommend to the President the suitability of each such area or island for inclusion in the National Wilderness Preservation System, with final decisions made by Congress. The Secretary of Agriculture was directed to study and recommend suitable areas in the National Forest System.

Land and Water Conservation Fund Act of 1965, 16 U.S.C. 460 et seq.

Uses the receipts from the sale of surplus Federal land, outer continental shelf oil and gas sales, and other sources for land acquisition under several authorities.

National Wildlife Refuge System Administration Act of 1966, 16 U.S.C. 668dd, 668ee

Defines the National Wildlife Refuge System and authorizes the Secretary to permit any use of a refuge provided such use is compatible with the major purposes for which the refuge was established. The Refuge Improvement Act clearly defines a unifying mission for the Refuge System; establishes the legitimacy and appropriateness of the six priority public uses (hunting, fishing, wildlife observation and photography, or environmental education and interpretation); establishes a formal process for determining compatibility; established the responsibilities of the Secretary of Interior for managing and protecting the System; and requires a Comprehensive Conservation Plan for each refuge by the year 2012. This Act amended portions of the Refuge Recreation Act and National Wildlife Refuge System Administration Act of 1966.

National Historic Preservation Act, 16 U.S.C. 470 et seq. (1966)

Establishes as policy that the Federal Government is to provide leadership in the preservation of the nation's prehistoric and historic resources. Section 106 requires Federal agencies to consider impacts their undertakings could have on historic properties; Section 110 requires Federal agencies to manage historic properties, e.g., to document historic properties prior to destruction or damage; Section 101 requires Federal agencies to consider Indian tribal values in historic preservation programs, and requires each Federal agency to establish a program leading to inventory of all historic properties on its land.

Architectural Barriers Act of 1968, 42 U.S.C. 4151 et seq.

Requires federally owned, leased, or funded buildings and facilities to be accessible to persons with disabilities.

National Environmental Policy Act of 1969, 42 U.S.C. 4321 et seq.

Requires the disclosure of the environmental impacts of any major Federal action significantly affecting the quality of the human environment.

Uniform Relocation Assistance and Real Property Acquisition Policies Act of 1970, 42 U.S.C. 4601 et seq.

Provides for uniform and equitable treatment of persons who sell their homes, businesses, or farms to the Service. The Act requires that any purchase offer be no less than the fair market value of the property.

Endangered Species Act of 1973, 16 U.S.C. 1531 et seq.

Requires all Federal agencies to carry out programs for the conservation of endangered and threatened species.

Rehabilitation Act of 1973, 29 U.S.C. 701 et seq.

Requires programmatic accessibility in addition to physical accessibility for all facilities and programs funded by the Federal government to ensure that anybody can participate in any program.

Archaeological and Historic Preservation Act 16 U.S.C.469-469c

Directs the preservation of historic and archaeological data in Federal construction projects.

Clean Water Act of 1977, 33 U.S.C. 1251

Requires consultation with the Corps of Engineers (404 permits) for major wetland modifications.

Surface Mining Control and Reclamation Act of 1977, 30 U.S.C. 1201 et seq.

Regulates surface mining activities and reclamation of coal-mined lands. Further regulates the coal industry by designating certain areas as unsuitable for coal mining operations.

Executive Order 11988 (1977)

Each Federal agency shall provide leadership and take action to reduce the risk of flood loss and minimize the impact of floods on human safety, and preserve the natural and beneficial values served by the floodplains.

Executive Order 11990

Executive Order 11990 directs Federal agencies to (1) minimize destruction, loss, or degradation of wetlands and (2) preserve and enhance the natural and beneficial values of wetlands when a practical alternative exists.

Executive Order 12372 (Intergovernmental Review of Federal Programs)

Directs the Service to send copies of the Environmental Assessment to State Planning Agencies for review.

American Indian Religious Freedom Act, 42 U.S.C. 1996, 1996a (1976)

Directs agencies to consult with native traditional religious leaders to determine appropriate policy changes necessary to protect and preserve American Indian religious cultural rights and practices.

Fish and Wildlife Improvement Act of 1978, 16 U.S.C. 742a

Improves the administration of fish and wildlife programs and amends several earlier laws including the Refuge Recreation Act, the National Wildlife Refuge System Administration Act, and the Fish and Wildlife Act of 1956. It authorizes the Secretary to accept gifts and bequests of real and personal property on behalf of the United States. It also authorizes the use of volunteers on Service projects and appropriations to carry out a volunteer program.

Archaeological Resources Protection Act of 1979, 16 U.S.C. 470aa et seq.

Protects materials of archaeological interest from unauthorized removal or destruction and requires Federal managers to develop plans and schedules to locate archaeological resources.

Farmland Protection Policy Act, Public Law 97-98, 7 U.S.C. 4201 (1981)

Minimizes the extent to which Federal programs contribute to the unnecessary and irreversible conversion of farmland to nonagricultural uses.

Emergency Wetlands Resources Act of 1986, 16 U.S.C. 3901 et seq.

Promotes the conservation of migratory waterfowl and offsets or prevents the serious loss of wetlands by the acquisition of wetlands and other essential habitats.

Federal Noxious Weed Act of 1974, 7 U.S.C. 2801 et seq.

Requires the use of integrated management systems to control or contain undesirable plant species, and an interdisciplinary approach with the cooperation of other Federal and State agencies.

Native American Graves Protection and Repatriation Act, 25 U.S.C. 3001 et seq. (1990)

Requires Federal agencies and museums to inventory, determine ownership of, and repatriate cultural items under their control or possession.

Americans with Disabilities Act of 1990, 42 U.S.C. 12101 et seq.

Prohibits discrimination in public accommodations and services.

Executive Order 12898 (1994)

Establishes environmental justice as a Federal government priority and directs all Federal agencies to make environmental justice part of their mission. Environmental justice calls for fair distribution of environmental hazards.

Executive Order 12996 Management and General Public Use of the National Wildlife Refuge System (1996)

Defines the mission, purpose, and priority public uses of the National Wildlife Refuge System. It also presents four principles to guide management of the System.

Executive Order 13007 Indian Sacred Sites (1996)

Directs Federal land management agencies to accommodate access to and ceremonial use of Indian sacred sites by Indian religious practitioners, avoid adversely affecting the physical integrity of such sacred sites, and where appropriate, maintain the confidentiality of sacred sites.

National Wildlife Refuge System Improvement Act of 1997, 16 U.S.C. 668dd

Considered the "Organic Act of the National Wildlife Refuge System. Defines the mission of the System, designates priority wildlife-dependent public uses, and calls for comprehensive refuge planning. Section 6 requires the Service to make a determination of compatibility of existing, new and changing uses of Refuge land; and Section 7 requires the Service to identify and describe the archaeological and cultural values of the refuge.

National Wildlife Refuge System Volunteer and Community Partnership Enhancement Act of 1998, 16 U.S.C. 742a

Amends the Fish and Wildlife Act of 1956 to promote volunteer programs and community partnerships for the benefit of national wildlife refuges, and for other purposes.

National Trails System Act, 16 U.S.C. 1241 et seq. (1968)

Assigns responsibility to the Secretary of Interior and thus the Service to protect the historic and recreational values of congressionally designated National Historic Trail sites.

Treasury and General Government Appropriations Act, Pub. L. 106-554, §1(a)(3), Dec. 21, 2000, 114 Stat. 2763, 2763A–125

In December 2002, Congress required federal agencies to publish their own guidelines for ensuring and maximizing the quality, objectivity, utility, and integrity of information that they disseminate to the public (44 U.S.C. 3502). The amended language is included in Section 515(a). The Office of Budget and Management (OMB) directed agencies to develop their own guidelines to address the requirements of the law. The Department of the Interior instructed bureaus to prepare separate guidelines on how they would apply the Act. The U.S. Fish and Wildlife Service has developed "Information Quality Guidelines" to address the law.

Cultural Resources and Historic Preservation

The National Wildlife Refuge System Improvement Act of 1997, Section 6, requires the Service to make a determination of compatibility of existing, new and changing uses of Refuge land; and Section 7 requires the Service to identify and describe the archaeological and cultural values of the refuge.

The National Historic Preservation Act (NHPA), Section 106, requires Federal agencies to consider impacts their undertakings could have on historic properties; Section 110 requires Federal agencies to manage historic properties, e.g., to document historic properties prior to destruction or damage; Section 101 requires Federal agencies consider Indian tribal values in historic preservation programs, and requires each Federal agency to establish a program leading to inventory of all historic properties on its land.

The Archaeological Resources Protection Act of 1979 (ARPA) prohibits unauthorized disturbance of archeological resources on Federal and Indian land; and other matters. Section 10 requires establishing "a program to increase public awareness" of archeological resources. Section 14 requires plans to survey lands and a schedule for surveying lands with "the most scientifically valuable archaeological resources." This Act requires protection of all archeological sites more than 100 years old (not just sites meeting the criteria for the National Register) on Federal land, and requires archeological investigations on Federal land be performed in the public interest by qualified persons.

The Native American Graves Protection and Repatriation Act of 1990 (NAGPRA) imposes serious delays on a project when human remains or other cultural items are encountered in the absence of a plan.

The American Indian Religious Freedom Act (AIRFA) iterates the right of Native Americans to free exercise of traditional religions and use of sacred places.

EO 13007, Indian Sacred Sites (1996), directs Federal agencies to accommodate access to and ceremonial use, to avoid adverse effects and avoid blocking access, and to enter into early consultation.

Appendix F: Compatibility Determinations

In accordance with the Refuge Improvement Act of 1997, no uses for which the Service has authority to regulate may be allowed on a unit of the Refuge System unless it is determined to be compatible. A compatible use is a use that, in the sound professional judgment of the refuge or wetland management district manager, will not materially interfere with or detract from the fulfillment of the National Wildlife Refuge System mission or the purposes of the national wildlife refuge or wetland management district. Managers must complete a written compatibility determination for each use, or collection of like-uses, that is signed by the manager and the Regional Chief of Refuges in the respective Service region. Draft compatibility determinations applicable to uses described in this CCP were published with the Draft CCP and EA and received 30 days of public review.

Signed compatibility determinations are on file at Leopold Wetland Management District for the following activities:

- Collection of Edible Wild Plant Foods for Personal Use
- Cooperative Farming
- One-time Recognition Dedication Cermemonies on Waterfowl Production Areas
- Disability Access to Waterfowl Production Areas
- Use of WPAs for Fire Department Training: Burning Structures
- Interpretation and Environmental Education
- Recreational Fishing
- Establishing Food Plots for Resident Wildlife
- Controlled Grazing on Waterfowl Production Areas and Conservation Easements
- Haying
- Hunting Resident Game and Furbearers
- Installation of Bird Nest Boxes or Structures by Individuals or Organized Groups
- Wildlife Observation and Photography (Including the Means of Access such as Hiking, Snowshoeing, Cross-country Skiing and Canoeing
- Research by a Third Party
- Placement of New, Small Parking Areas on Waterfowl Production Areas
- Short-term Upland Disturbance for Highway or Other Public Interest Projects with No ROW Expansion and Full Restoration
- Wood Cutting/Timber Harvest
- Trapping of Furbearers
- Placement of Wetland Accesses/Ramps in Support of Priority Public Use

Compatibility determinations were recently approved and are available for review for Wood Cutting/Timber Harvest on Becker WPA, a Weather Station on Becker WPA, Construction and Use of Boardwalk and Viewing Platform on Ulao Waterfowl Production Area, and Tesoro Pipeline Right-Of-Way.

Appendix G: Literature Cited

Literature Cited

Cowardin, L. M., V. Carter, F. C. Golet, and E. T. LaRoe. 1979. Classification of wetlands and deepwater habitats of the United States. U.S. Fish and Wildlife Service FWS/OBS-79/31. Washington. D.C.

Curtis, John T. 1959. The vegetation of wisconsin, an ordination of plant communities. University of Wisconsin Press.

Dahl, T.E. 1990. Wetland losses in the United States: 1780-1980. U.S. Department of the Interior. Fish and Wildlife Service. Washington D.C.

Dai, X., Boutton, T. W., Hailemichael, M., Ansley, R. J., Jessup, K. E. 2006. Soil Carbon and Nitrogen Storage in Response to Fire in a Temperate Mixed-Grass Savanna. J Environ Qual. 35: 1620-1628.

Egan-Bruhy, Kathryn C. 2003. Comprehensive Conservation Plan, Archaeological and Historic Resources, Leopold and St. Croix Wetland Management District, Wisconsin. Commonwealth Cultural Resources Group, Inc., Jackson, Michigan

Ensor, K. and S. Smith. 1994. Herbicide concentrations in select waterfowl production area wetlands in west central Minnesota, 1993. Report to the U.S. Fish and Wildlife Service. Office of Environmental Contaminants. Federal Building, Fort Snelling, Twin Cities

Freemark, K. and M. Csizy. 1993. Effect of different habitats vs. agricultural practices on breeding birds. Pages 284-285 (abstract) in Agricultural Research to Protect Water Quality: Proceeding of the Conference. Feb. 21-24, 1993. Minneapolis, MN Soil and Water Conservation Society

Grue, C.E., L. R. DeWeese, P. Mineau, G.A. Swanson, J.R. Foster and P. M. Arnold, J. Huckins, P. J. Sheechan and W. K. Marshall, A. P. Ludden. 1986. Potential impacts of agricultural chemicals on waterfowl and other wildlife inhabiting prairie wetlands: an evaluation of research needs and approaches. Trans. 51st N. A. Wildl. And Nat. Res. Conf. 357-383

Kantrud, H.A., J.B. Millar, and A.G. van der Valk. 1989. Vegetation of wetlands of the prairie pothole region. p. 132-187. *In* A.G. van der Valk (ed.) Northern Prairie Wetlands. Iowa State University Press, Ames, IA, USA

National Assessment Synthesis Team, *Climate Change Impacts on the United States: The Potential Consequences of Climate Variability and Change*, U.S. Global Change Research Program, Washington DC, 2000. www.usgcrp.gov

Radeloff, Volker C. et al. 2006. Housing growth 1940-2030 in the U.S. Midwest. Forest Ecology and Management, University of Wisconsin - Madison. (http://www.silvis.forest.wisc.edu/projects/HousingGrowth.asp)

Sample, David W., and Michael J. Mossman. 1997. Managing habitat for grassland birds - a guide for Wisconsin. Wisconsin Department of Natural Resources, Madison, WI, PUBL-SS-925-97. 154 pp. Jamestown, ND: Northern Prairie Wildlife Research Center Online. http://www.npwrc.usgs.gov/resource/birds/wiscbird/index.htm (Version 03JUN2002).

Schroeder, Richard L., Wayne J. King, and John E.Cornely. 1998. Selecting Habitat Management Strategies on Refuges. Information and TechnologyReport USGS/BRD/ITR—1998-003. 16pp.

Tiner, R.W., Jr. 1984. Wetlands of the United States: current status and recent trends. National Wetlands Inventory, U.S. Department of the Interior, Fish and Wildlife Service, Washington, D.C.

Tome, M. W., C. Grue, L. R. DeWeese. 1991. Ethyl parathion in wetlands following aerial application to sunflowers in North Dakota. Wildl. Soc. Bull. 19:450-457.

U.S. Department of Energy, Office of Fossil Energy and Office of Science. 1999. Carbon sequestration research and development. http://www.fossil.energy.gov/programs/sequestration/publications/1999/rdreport

U.S. Fish and Wildlife Service. 1993. Birds of Horicon National Wildlife Refuge, Wisconsin. U.S. Fish and Wildlife Service. Unpaginated.

U.S. Fish and Wildlife Service. 2002. Finding Solutions to Habitat Loss. International Migratory Bird Day Information. (http://birds.fws.gov/imbd.htm

Van Horn, Kent, and Kim Benton. 2007. Wisconsin waterfowl strategic plan 2008-2018. Wisconsin Department of Natural Resources. 56 pages.

Weller, M. W. 1982. Freshwater Marshes: University of Minnesota Press, Minneapolis, MN.

Wisconsin Agricultural Statistics Service, Wisconsin. 2004. Agricultural Statistics. From www.nass.usda.gov/wi/rlsetoc.htm.)

Wisconsin Department of Natural Resources. 1995. Wisconsin's biodiversity as a management issue. Wisconsin Department of Natural Resources, Madison, WI. 240 pages.

Wisconsin Department of Natural Resources. 2005 Wisconsin Wildlife Action Plan. 4 pp. (http://www.teaming.com/summary_reports/Wisconsin.pdf)

Wisconsin Department of Natural Resources. 2005. Wisconsin's Strategy for Wildlife Species of Greatest Conservation Need. Madison, WI.

Appendix H: Refuge Operating Needs System and Maintenance Management System

Refuge Operating Needs System

Unfunded District Projects and Operational Needs, Leopold WMD

Project Number	Project Title	Cost Estimate (Thousands)
99008	Expand Biological Program	$127
99005	Expand Public Use and Education Program.	$146
99003	Expand Biological Program	$160
98017	Increase Equipment and Facilities Maintenance	$61
00002	Improve Meeting District Goals and Objectives.	$197
04001	Provide Public Safety, Security, and Resource Protection	$148
00014	Provide Law Enforcement Equipment	80
98002	Restoration of grassland habitats.	$103
00001	Increase habitat management productivity.	$102
98019	Restore wetland habitats on district lands.	$81
99010	Restore grassland habitats	$333
00006	Increase management capability with a GIS	$22
98001	Restore and maintain grassland habitats	$67
99006	Improve land management activities.	$130
98009	Control invasive woody vegetation.	$292
99011	Minimum Refuge Operations Needs	$108
00005	Enhanced wetland easement enforcement program.	$27
00009	Ensure Comprehensive Conservation Planning is Science Based and Involves the Public	$250
06001	Improved Water Management Capabilities	$370

Example of Leopold WMD Deferred Maintenance and Construction Projects

Project Description	Cost	Work Order Type
Leopold WPA Parking Lot Improvements	$80,000.00	CI
Construct Maintenance Facilities	$940,000.00	CI
Construct water management facilities on WPAs.	$512,000.00	CI
Office Co-Location Administration Building Construction	$4,380,000.00	CI
WPA Parking Lot and Trail Head Improvements	$225,000.00	CI
Construct Visitor Contact Points on Baraboo River WPA	$50,000.00	CI
Construct Visitor Information Facilities	$150,000.00	CI
WCS Wilcox General Rehab	$7,757.00	DM
Parking Public Rte 907 General Rehab	$3,166.00	DM
Levee Wilcox General Rehab	$2,194.00	DM
Parking Public Rte 914 General Rehab	$12,000.00	DM
Parking Public Rte 920 General Rehab	$3,831.00	DM
Parking Public Rte 915 General Rehab	$4,034.00	DM
Parking Public Rte 916 Schoenberg Marsh - Harvey Road	$5,140.00	DM
Parking Public Rte 947 General Rehab	$3,246.00	DM
Building Equipment Storage General Rehab	$9,960.00	DM
Road Public Rte 202 Harvey's Marsh WPA West	$19,811.00	DM
Parking Public Rte 936 General Rehab	$12,433.00	DM
Restore Eroded Levee on Harveys Marsh WPA	$16,646.14	DM
Harveys Marsh WPA Dike Erosion Repair	$17,000.00	DM
Harveys Marsh WPA Dike Erosion Repair	$17,000.00	DM
Harvey's Marsh WPA WCS Replacement	$29,000.00	DM
Levee Shoveler Sink General Rehab	$9,289.37	DM
Parking Public Rte 941 Shoveler Sink - County S	$5,776.00	DM
Levee Trenton Aalsma Tract General Rehab	$1,182.00	DM
Trenton WPA Dike General Rehab	$1,863.00	DM
Trenton WPA WCS Replacement	$46,000.00	DM
Levee Trenton WPA DU2 General Rehab	$26,468.00	DM
Replace Water Control Structure on Trenton WPA	$15,000.00	DM
Levee Blue Wing General Replacement	$11,131.00	DM

Appendix I: List of Preparers

List of Preparers

District Staff

Steve Lenz, District Manager

Bruce Luebke, Wildlife Refuge Specialist

Jim Lutes, Wildlife Biologist

Regional Office Staff

John Schomaker, Refuge Planner

Gabriel DeAlessio, Biologist-GIS

John Dobrovolny, Regional Historic Preservation Officer

Jane Hodgins, Technical Writer/Editor

Appendix J: Response to Comments Received on the Draft Comprehensive Conservation Plan

Response to Comments Received on the Draft Comprehensive Conservation Plan

During the comment period for the Draft CCP, we received a comment letter from the Wisconsin Department of Natural Resources (pages 164-165) and an email comment from the National Park Service, Midwest Regional Office, Cultural Resources Management (pages 166-167).

Response to Wisconsin DNR

We appreciate the Department's support of our management goals. We will continue to work, as noted in Chapter 5, with the Department and other conservation organizations within our shared conservation mission. We respond below to each of the bulleted points of the Department's letter.

First bullet – The Service WMD offices integrate Joint Venture documents into their planning and implementation of habitat management and restoration activities as discussed under "Migratory Bird Conservation Initiatives" in Chapter 3 of the CCP. Acquisition funding and available properties vary each year, so it is difficult to set specific wetland protection goals by wetland habitat type and acreage in support of the Joint Venture.

The Service considers waterfowl, grassland birds, species of concern, threatened and endangered species, and other trust species in making habitat management decisions. To be more explicit, the rationale under Objective 2.4 has been modified to add the State's Species of Greatest Conservation Need in its management considerations. Other species are also considered in management decisions but the priority is trust species.

Second bullet – We agree that increased coordination to achieve common goals will be beneficial to all parties involved and lead to a landscape approach to conservation issues. Our support of coordinated efforts is acknowledged in our discussion of existing and future partnerships.

Third bullet – We, too, see the value in the coordination of data collection, which would provide better data. This is another example of benefits gained through partnerships.

Fourth bullet – The Service will continue to work with the Wisconsin DNR to address CWD concerns or management implications on WPAs.

Fifth bullet – Public uses on WPAs are evaluated for their compatibility with the purpose of the WPA. At the present time, the CCP proposes public use improvements such as trails, boardwalks, and observation platforms on only a limited number of WPAs. The majority of the WPAs will continue to be managed with few public use modifications. When compatible, hunting along with the other big six uses (fishing, wildlife observation, environmental education, interpretation, photography) are encouraged on WPAs. The Service also recognizes that promotion of the value of WPAs to all members of the public is an important part of reconnecting people with nature and supporting the intent of the National Wildlife Refuge Improvement Act of 1997.

Sixth bullet – Your continued support for trapping opportunities is noted.

Seventh bullet – Until complete invasive species inventories are conducted on each WPA it is difficult to determine the specific levels of control and the appropriate priority species. Priority for invasives control is stated in terms of attempting to control or limit invasive species in priority wetland and grassland habitat, because these are the most important habitat types for federal trust species.

Response to National Park Service

We have added a paragraph in the CCP and EA that better describes the extent of historic places within the District and edited sentences in both documents to more accurately report the relationship of waterfowl production areas and historic places.

State of Wisconsin \ DEPARTMENT OF NATURAL RESOURCES

Jim Doyle, Governor
Matthew J. Frank, Secretary

101 S. Webster St.
Box 7921
Madison, Wisconsin 53707-7921
Telephone 608-266-2621
FAX 608-267-3579
TTY Access via relay - 711

August 22, 2008

Leopold Wetland Management District
Attention: CCP Comment
W10040 Cascade Mountain Road
Portage, WI 53901

St. Croix Wetland Management District
Attention: CCP Comment
1764 95th Street
New Richmond, WI 54017

Subject: Leopold and St. Croix WMD Comprehensive Conservation Plan

Dear Mr. Lenz and Mr. McConnell:

Thank you for the opportunity to comment on the Leopold Wetland Management District (WMD) and St. Croix WMD Comprehensive Conservation Plans (CCP). As these plans note, the two WMD's share issues and a joint planning process was used to develop the individual CCP's. Because of these shared issues, the following comments are made regarding both CCP's, unless otherwise noted.

The Wisconsin Department of Natural Resources (Department) supports the primary management goals listed in Chapter 4 of each plan. We encourage the U.S. Fish and Wildlife Service (Service) to work hand-in-hand with the Department and other conservation land groups to help maintain the integrity of the area's natural resources and in keeping with the legislative mandates within the National Wildlife Refuge System Improvement Act of 1997. In light of the shared mission we have to protect and promote natural resources, the Department and Service can benefit by working together on mutual goals.

More specifically:

- The Department is committed to the "all-bird" habitat goals and objectives of the recently revised Upper Mississippi River and Great Lakes Region Joint Venture (UMRGLRJV). We suggest that each CCP would be strengthened by a more prominent support of the UMRGLRJV goals and objectives by wetland habitat type and acreage. As the Service was heavily involved with the revision of the UMRGLRJV, it stands to reason that Service programs would integrate this important habitat initiative within their planning documents and habitat activities.

  Likewise, habitat work undertaken by the Service, both wetland and upland, should consider benefits to a variety of species, especially those focal species designated in the UMRGLRJV Implementation Plan or as Species of Greatest Conservation Need as designated in the Wisconsin Action Plan.

dnr.wi.gov
wisconsin.gov

- Department and Service field staff and regional and state program administrators should meet on a regular basis to coordinate mutually beneficial activities and increase the awareness of each agency's initiatives, concerns, and ideas. Other habitat partners should be included in these meetings as appropriate.

- We support increased resource inventory and research, as the plan states, especially if data is collected by consistent and statistically valid means. Please work with the Department to facilitate, where appropriate, the cooperative collection of this mutually beneficial information to manage wildlife habitat.

- We are pleased that deer hunting continues to be allowed. In light of both the impact excessive deer can have on native species and ongoing concerns about chronic wasting disease (CWD) in Wisconsin, hunting offers a tool to control deer populations. As CWD management in Wisconsin evolves, the Department would seek USFWS cooperation in both research and management activities where applicable on Service properties.

- Modifications meant to improve visitor services on federal lands such as wildlife observation stations, parking lots, trails, or boardwalks should be evaluated as to their effect on key wildlife habitat and the ability of people to participate in other compatible uses, especially hunting. Physical modifications to federal properties should not negatively impact valuable wildlife habitat. Likewise, such modifications should, at a minimum, have a neutral affect on the ability of hunters to use the land or, preferably, should improve hunting opportunities.

- We are pleased that trapping is a compatible use at federal lands within each WMD. Besides providing a valuable resource harvested by Wisconsin trappers, trapping can benefit the production of grassland nesting bird species by the removal of predators.

- The control of non-native invasive species is an ongoing concern for habitat managers. Rather than stating a percentage of invasives to be controlled as is currently shown in the draft CCP's, it may be beneficial to consider a layered approach that takes into account the degree to which invasive species may be controlled, the relative impact presented by certain invasive species, and the quality of the property at which an invasive species may appear.

Again, thank you for the opportunity to comment on each CCP. The Department looks forward to working with the Service within these important areas in Wisconsin.

Sincerely,

Ricky Lien
Wetland Habitat Specialist
Bureau of Wildlife Management

cc: Tom Hauge – WM/6
Bill Vander Zouwen – WM/6
Eric Lobner – Fitchburg
Tami Ryan – Milwaukee
Jeff Pritzl – Green Bay
Kris Belling – Eau Claire
Mike Zeckmeister – Antigo

Rebecca_Kumar@nps.gov
08/21/2008 11:57 AM

To: r3planning@fws.gov
cc: don_stevens@nps.gov, Michele_Curran@nps.gov
Subject: Leopold WMD Comment

August 21, 2008

Leopold Wetland Management District
Attention: CCP Comment
W10040 Cascade Mountain Road
Portage, Wisconsin 59301

Re: Leopold Wetland Management District, Comprehensive Conservation Plan and Environmental Assessment

To Whom It May Concern:

This email is being sent in response to the draft Leopold Wetland Management District Comprehensive Conservation Plan and Environmental Assessment. In reviewing the management plan and environment assessment, it has been observed that neither plan mentions the previously documented National Historic Landmark (NHL) properties that are located within the proposed boundary. Cultural Resources are only identified as Early American Properties that have archeological components. The National Park Service, Midwest Regional Office, Cultural Resources Management, is requesting that these historic properties be included in the study. The Wisconsin State Historic Preservation Office located in Madison, Wisconsin is a valuable resource to contact regarding the names and locations of National Register of Historic Places properties also located within the boundary. The list below gives the name and county of the 21 National Historic Landmarks located within the proposed boundary. Please be sure to address these valuable resources to our nation's history in the Conservation Plan and Environmental Assessment.

Fond du Lac County: Little White School HouseNHL

Manitowoc County: USS COBIA NHL

Marquette County: Fountain Lake Farm NHL

Sauk County: Ringling Brothers Circus Winter Headquarters NHL, Van Hise Rock NHL, Aldo Leopold Shack and Farm - new NHL proposal currently on review in Washington

Columbia County: Farmers and Merchants Union Bank NHL

Dane County: First Unitarian Meeting Society NHL, Harold Bradley House NHL, Herbert and Katherine 1st House NHL, Herbert and Katherine 2nd House NHL, Robert M. Lafollette House NHL, University of Wisconsin Science Hall NHL, University of Wisconsin Armory and Gymnasium NHL, University of Wisconsin North Hall NHL, University of Wisconsin Dairy Barn NHL, Wisconsin State Capitol NHL

Waukesha County: Ten Chimneys NHL

Racine County: Herbert Johnson House NHL, Administration Building and Research Tower SC Johnson Company NHL

Rock County: Milton House NHL

Sincerely,

/s/

Rebecca Kumar

~ ~

Rebecca Kumar
Historian

National Park Service
Midwest Regional Office
601 Riverfront Drive
Omaha, NE 68102

PH: 402-661-1932

~ ~

Live today for tomorrow it will all be history.
Proverb

www.ingramcontent.com/pod-product-compliance
Lightning Source LLC
Chambersburg PA
CBHW081211280526
45787CB00006B/2384
* 9 7 8 1 5 0 5 7 2 2 1 4 7 *